A MATTER OF CONSCIENCE

ESSAYS ON THE WORLD WAR II
HEART MOUNTAIN DRAFT RESISTANCE
MOVEMENT

A Matter of Conscience

Essays on the World War II Heart Mountain Draft Resistance Movement

Edited and Contributions by Mike Mackey

A Western History Publications Book
Western History Publications
P. O. Box 291
Powell, Wyoming 82435

Printed by
Mountain States Lithographing
Casper, Wyoming

Cover Design by Tina Fagan

Cover photo courtesy of the George Nozawa Collection
Back cover quotes
Yosh Kuromiya, from William Hohri's
Resistance
Jack Tono, from John Tateishi's
And Justice for All

ISBN 0-9661556-6-1

Table of Contents

Dedication

This book is dedicated to the Heart Mountain
resisters of conscience.

Acknowledgments

The conference and teacher training workshop which resulted in the publication of this book was organized by the Heart Mountain Wyoming Foundation. The conference, "Protest and Resistance: An American Tradition," was made possible by a generous grant from the Furumoto Research Foundation, and the tireless efforts of HMWF Board members, particularly Pat Wolfe and Carolyn Takeshita. The Board would also like to thank Mickey Takeshita, Lois Ramirez, George Brooks III, LaDonna Zall, The Wyoming Council for the Humanities, the University of Wyoming Department of American Studies, Laramie County Community College, and all of those who worked so hard in the presentation phase of the conference. Lastly, the Board would like to thank former Heart Mountain resister Takashi Hoshizaki. Tak's tireless efforts in every aspect of this project are what have made it a success.

The editor would like to thank all of those who worked so hard to rework their presentations into the articles which appear in this book. I would also like to thank Takashi Fujitani and Roger Daniels who did not participate in the conference, yet agreed to contribute to this publication. As always I must thank Winifred Wasden for her copy editing work, Laurie Mackey for her indexing work, and Arthur Hansen and Roger Daniels for their suggestions. This publication was made possible by the generosity and farsightedness of the California Civil Liberties Public Education Project. Lastly, and most importantly, I must acknowledge the Heart Mountain draft resisters who took an unpopular stand in defense of the their constitutional rights.

Preface

A recent conference and teacher training workshop treating the Heart Mountain draft resistance movement, sited in Cheyenne, Wyoming, in June of 2001, was made possible, in large part, by a California Civil Liberties Public Education Project (CCLPEP) grant. The collection of essays comprising this published anthology is solely owing to CCLPEP's largess. The draft resistance movement at Heart Mountain and other War Relocation Authority (WRA) camps represent an important chapter in Japanese American history in general, and in the World War II eviction and detention experience of people of Japanese ancestry in particular. Even though this subject remains today as a very divisive one within the Japanese American community, the CCLPEP realized its signal importance and supported the conference and workshop leading to the publication of this book. This action conforms with the CCLPEP's commitment to presenting the American public with a well-rounded education as regards the Japanese American wartime situation.

A number of nationally recognized scholars contributed to the workshop and this publication. I would ask that critics and reviewers keep in mind that scholars, whose expertise may lie in other areas, were willing to come forward and contribute articles on subjects requested by the conference organizers. Although I feel that this publication makes a significant contribution to the scholarship in this area, I ask everyone who reads this book to keep in mind that this was a *Public Education* project, and the work by all contributors is greatly appreciated.

The organization of the Cheyenne conference/workshop required some contributors to make two, three, and sometimes four different presentations. Accordingly, I asked those individuals to reorganize and combine their presentations into single essays. Even though this was a taxing and time-consuming task, the contributors came through with "flying-colors."

There were several suggestions as to how this anthology should be organized, all of which had their good points. However, in the end I tried to present these essays in a manner acceptable to the conference/workshop organizers, and since this is a *public education* project, in such a way as to make this topic more easily understood by the student and general reader. I hope that I have succeeded in that goal. Naturally, I accept full responsibility for any criticisms of this publication's contents and organization.

Many readers of this anthology likely will feel that, at the time the resisters took their stand, their treatment by the United States government, the majority of the Nisei generation, and the general public was wrong. However, as Roger Daniels judiciously observes in his introduction, one must

iv

reflect back upon and evaluate what was going on in the world, the United States, and the Japanese American community in the early 1940's. Assessing the stand taken by the Japanese American draft resisters in the post-1960's—a time after the Civil Rights movement led by Dr. Martin Luther King Jr., the *Free Speech* movement at Berkeley, the anti Vietnam War protests, the *American Indian Movement*, the *Women's Rights* movement had gained popularity and acceptance—neither gives one a full understanding of the risks the resisters were taking, nor explains the attitudes of American society and the Japanese American community toward draft resistance in the 1940's. As the noted historian, Frederick Jackson Turner, wrote in 1891, "Each age tries to form its own conception of the past. Each age writes the history of the past anew with reference to the conditions uppermost in its own time."

The first section of the anthology deals with background information designed to give the reader a better understanding of the circumstances that led up to the Heart Mountain draft resistance movement. Gail Nomura was asked by conference/workshop organizers to place the World War II Japanese American experience within the larger context of prewar anti-Asian developments within the United States. As some of the resisters themselves have pointed out, it was not only relocation, but a long history of anti-Japanese attitudes and legislation (both state and federal) that contributed to their stand against conscription. The next essay, by Takashi Fujitani, was not presented at the Cheyenne conference, but rather is one that I solicited at the suggestion of Arthur Hansen, my colleague and friend. The Nisei have often been labeled as "The Quiet Americans," but Fujitani challenges the perception of the Japanese as a people who have always gone along with the status-quo and seldom, if ever, resisted their leaders. The third essay in this section looks at the general attitude and attendant agenda of the Japanese American Citizens League (JACL), arguably the resisters' harshest critic, through the eyes of author William Hohri.

Part II of the anthology looks at the resisters themselves. The first essay by Frank Emi, one of the last surviving leaders of the Heart Mountain Fair Play Committee, describes his personal experiences as a moving spirit in the resistance movement. The second contribution to this section is an essay about the experiences of Jack Tono, one of the few resisters who went out and began searching (in the National Archives in Washington D.C., Denver Colorado, and state and university archives in Cheyenne and Laramie, Wyoming,) for answers concerning his imprisonment as a resister. The third essay in this section presents the personal thoughts and feelings of one Heart Mountain draft resister, Yosh Kuromiya, about his wartime posture and his resulting penitentiary imprisonment and eventual exoneration. Finally, historian Arthur Hansen, who gave three or four addresses at the Cheyenne conference/workshop, was asked to bring those presentations together in a single essay and to include some of his recent research regarding dissident

Japanese American newspaperman James Omura, who was arrested and later tried in a federal court along with the Heart Mountain FPC leadership for editorially supporting their organized stand against the draft.

The next section of the anthology, Part III, looks at the legal aspects of the conviction and incarceration of the Heart Mountain draft resisters. In the first essay, William Hohri raises some legal and moral questions regarding the defense of the resisters and whether they should have been sent to prison. In the concluding contribution, Eric Muller, author of the critically acclaimed, *Free to Die for Their Country*, uses his legal expertise to review the resisters' case and the constitutional questions which the resisters themselves were trying to raise.

In the anthology's final section, Amy Iwasaki Mass assesses the psychological effects of relocation. George Tsukuda offers a psychological evaluation of the resister's backgrounds in comparison to those Nisei who did not resist the draft. Tsukuda raises the question of whether or not the family environment of the resisters contributed to the more free-thinking and non-compliant attitude characterizing some of them. Lawson Inada, the eminent Sansei poet, authored the collection's Afterword. Based upon his personal experiences as a college professor and former internee, Inada discusses the importance of teaching this subject and offers suggestions to teachers as to how they might profitably go about it.

As stated previously, the focus of the Cheyenne conference/workshop was *public education*; it is hoped that this publication will serve as an educational tool for all of those interested in learning more about the World War II, Japanese American draft resistance movement.

Mike Mackey
Powell, Wyoming
March, 2002

About the Authors

Roger Daniels is the Charles Phelps Taft Professor of History at the University of Cincinnati. He began studying the Japanese American experience in the 1950s. Among his books are *Concentration Camps USA* (1971), the nine-volume document collection, *America's Concentration Camps* (1989), and *Prisoners Without Trial* (1993). From 1981 through 1983 he served as a consultant to the Commission on the Wartime Relocation and Internment of Civilians.

Frank Emi is one of the last surviving leaders of the Heart Mountain Fair Play Committee. Even though he was ineligible for the draft as a result of his marital status, he felt that it was important to fight for his constitutional rights, and those of his fellow internees.

Takashi Fujitani is Associate Professor of History at the University of California at San Diego. He is the author of *Tenno no pejento* [The Emperor's Pageants] (1994) and *Splendid Monarchy: Power and Pageantry in Modern Japan* (1996). He is the co-editor of *Japanese Civilization in the Modern World: Nation-State and Empire* (2000) and *Perilous Memories: The Asia-Pacific War(s)* (2001).

Arthur Hansen is Professor of History and Asian American Studies, and Director of the Center for Oral and Public History at California State University, Fullerton. He is Vice-President/President-Elect of the Oral History Association. Hansen is also a consultant within the Japanese American National Museum's curatorial unit and heads up JANM's publication and life history programs. His current publishing plans include editing the memoirs of the late Nisei activist James Matsumoto Omura and compiling an anthology of his own articles and oral histories about World War II Nikkei resistance activity.

William M. Hohri received his B.A. from the University of Chicago in 1949. He chaired the National Council for Japanese American Redress from 1979 through 1989. Hohri is the author of *Repairing America: An Account of the Movement for Japanese-American Redress* (1988), and *Resistance: Challenging America's Wartime Internment of Japanese-Americans* (2001).

Lawson Fusao Inada is currently a member of the Department of English faculty at Southern Oregon University where he teaches writing and poetry. His essays, fiction, and poetry have been published in numerous anthologies. Professor Inada's most recent book is *Only What We Could Carry: The Japanese American Internment Experience* (2000).

Yosh Kuromiya was born in Sierra Madre, California in 1923. In 1944, during his internment at Heart Mountain, Wyoming, Kuromiya joined with others in protesting the government's policy of drafting internees from America's ten concentration camps. Although his stand landed him in a federal penitentiary, Kuromiya knows in his heart that he made the right choice. Yosh Kuromiya retired in 1995 after working many years as a landscape architect.

Mike Mackey is an independent historian living in Powell, Wyoming. He has published numerous books and articles dealing with the Japanese American experience. He has also served as guest editor for such scholarly journals as *Peace & Change*, and *Journal of the West*.

Amy Iwasaki Mass received her D. S. W. from the University of California, Los Angeles. She held a post-doctoral fellowship at the Asian American Studies Center at U.C.L.A. and has taught at Whittier College and the University of California, Berkeley. She has published numerous articles and essays which have appeared in scholarly journals and several anthologies.

Eric Muller is a professor of law at the University of North Carolina, Chapel Hill, where he teaches criminal and constitutional law. From 1994 to 1998, he was an assistant professor at the University of Wyoming College of Law. It was while teaching at Wyoming that he first heard about the Heart Mountain draft resistance movement. Muller's most recent book is *Free to Die for Their Country: The Story of the Japanese American Draft Resisters in World War II* (2001).

Gail Nomura is a noted researcher and educator in the field of Asian American Studies. She has co-edited two anthologies, *Frontiers of Asian American Studies*, and *Bearing Dreams, Shaping Visions: Asian Pacific American Perspectives*, and is the author of numerous chapters and articles on this subject. She is currently working with Louis Fiset and Shirley Hune on an anthology dealing with Japanese Americans and Japanese Canadians in the Pacific Northwest.

George Tsukuda holds a Ph.D. in psychology. He is currently completing work on a project funded by the California Civil Liberties Public Education Project.

Introduction

Heart Mountain - After Sixty Years

by Roger Daniels

This volume commemorates an inglorious event in the American past, a past that happened six decades ago in what seems a different world, although there are still some of us who remember it well, and still some who experienced it first hand. As a university teacher, I am constantly trying to explain the past to young people whose ties to history seem ever more tenuous. I am often asked why it is important to remember and stress the wrongs and injustices of the American past. "Isn't it better," some of them ask, "to remember the good things that have happened?" Such notions—and they are not confined to young people—are pernicious. The history of a nation should never be, in Richard Hofstadter's phrase, "merely a literature of national self-congratulation." American history, if it is to have any function other than entertainment, must be an ongoing analysis and exploration of both the accomplishments and the mistakes in our past in order better to shape the American present, and the American future. Thus, the essays in this book commemorate the camp at Heart Mountain, and analyze and speculate about its meaning, both in the past and today.

The camp at Heart Mountain was one of ten concentration camps operated by the War Relocation Authority (WRA) during and just after World War II, although, of course, the WRA never called it that. To officialdom, these camps were—and are– relocation centers, but I, and others, have insisted for a long time now that they were concentration camps, places where persons charged with no crimes were made prisoners, not because of what they had done, but because of what they were: men, women, and children who had been born in Japan, or, more often, the children, or in a few cases, grandchildren, of persons who had been born in Japan.

The camp at Heart Mountain was the sixth to open—the first prisoners arrived on August 12, 1942—and the fifth or sixth to close—the last prisoner departed on October 15, 1945. It was in operation for 1,187 days and had a peak population of 10,767 inmates, which made it the fourth largest camp. Five hundred fifty new American citizens were born behind its barbed wire, and 182 of its inmates died while still prisoners. Two hundred twenty three couples at Heart Mountain were married, and only eighteen couples were divorced.

In 1969 when I first put these statistics together—from a volume published by the Department of the Interior in 1946[1]—it seemed to me that Heart Mountain was an "ordinary," "average," American concentration camp. I had wanted to do a book about the incarceration of Japanese Americans for my doctoral dissertation at UCLA, but there was no Freedom of Information Act in the late 1950s, and much of the archival material was restricted under a twenty-five year rule. Thus documents created in 1942 would not be generally available until 1967, etc.; thus for wartime materials, 1970 would be the first time that all archival materials would generally be available. I had signed a contract with a New York publisher, Holt, Rinehart and Winston, to write a book to be called *Concentration Camps, USA: Japanese Americans and World War II*, for delivery in early 1971. My plan called for me to concentrate on the overall story, but examine in some detail the history of one "normal" camp and its interaction with its surrounding community. Tule Lake, because of its acquired special character as a place to segregate those whom the WRA found troublesome, would have been treated differently, but as far as I was concerned, any other camp would have done. Had I remained at UCLA, Manzanar would have been the logical place to examine; had I moved to the University of Colorado, it would have been Granada, etc.

But after the vagaries of an academic career brought me to the University of Wyoming in 1969, Heart Mountain was the natural choice. I quickly discovered that there was a run of the *Heart Mountain Sentinel* in the university library and that a gifted new graduate student at the university, Douglas W. Nelson, was looking for a good topic for an M.A. thesis and he agreed to write a history of the camp at Heart Mountain.[2] Our joint reading of the published literature gave us no reason to believe that Heart Mountain was a place with a special history, although we understood that each camp would have its unique characteristics, as each individual does. Although we never believed the characterization of Heart Mountain as a "happy camp," as one survey of the wartime experience had put it, we understood what its authors meant.[3] That false characterization—none of the camps was, or could have been, "happy camps"—stemmed from the fact that there were no mass disturbances or government homicides at Heart Mountain, as there had been at Manzanar, Topaz, and Tule Lake, and we had no reason to expect that anything special had happened at Heart Mountain.

However, Heart Mountain did have a very special and very important history, a history that had been suppressed by the Japanese American community leaders and had not been written about in the already fairly large literature about one of the most shameful chapters in recent American history. That special history, of course, centered around draft resistance. Not the resistance of those who said "no," or "no, no," to the infamous and stupid questions numbered twenty-seven and twenty-eight, in the loyalty question-

2

naire, labeled "Application for Leave Clearance" that prisoners were instructed to complete in early 1943. That resistance had been chronicled and dealt with, and the data from Heart Mountain were consistent with the "happy camp" stereotype. In answering question twenty-eight, which asked:

> Will you swear unqualified allegiance to the United States of America and faithfully defend the United States from any or all attack from foreign or domestic forces, and forswear any form of allegiance or obedience to the Japanese emperor, to any foreign government, power or organization?

only 181 persons at Heart Mountain said "no." That amounted to 2.25 percent of those registered; a total of 5,376 persons throughout the WRA camps said "no," a total of 6.95 percent. If we restricted the data to male United States citizens age seventeen and over, just thirty-eight of 2,145 at Heart Mountain, said "no," or 1.77 percent, as opposed to 3,421 of 21,061 in all camps, or 16.24 percent. Thus the rate of "no" answers from draft-eligible persons at Heart Mountain was just about 11 percent of the rate for all of the camps. Only Granada, where just ten of 1,580 male citizens said "no" had a lower rate.[4]

What Douglas Nelson and I "discovered," of course, was the draft resistance movement at Heart Mountain. The word "discovered" is in quotation marks, because that "discovery," like Columbus' "discovery" of America, was the "discovery" of something a large number of people already knew about: in Columbus' case, the Native Americans: in the Heart Mountain case, the resisters themselves, many other people in the Nikkei community, government officials, etc. Sometime after our "discovery" of the Heart Mountain resistance, I went back and talked to some of the Heart Mountain people I had interviewed and asked if they had known about the resistance, and all but one said they did. When I then asked those with good memories why they had not mentioned it when I had interviewed them, I got answers like, "Oh Professor, that was so unpleasant. I didn't think that you wanted to be bothered with that." And, when I looked hard for evidence, there was one statistical table and six lines of text about "Selective Service Violations by Disposition and by Center" in one of nine volumes that the Department of the Interior published about the activities of the WRA in 1946.[5] But even if one read the text and looked at the table, there was nothing to indicate that this was an organized draft resistance movement as opposed either to draft evasion, or confused if principled opposition. Nelson and I quickly realized that the resistance movement at Heart Mountain, which eventually spread to six other camps, particularly Poston, was important, and each of us devoted a significant portion of our work to it, he, because of his special focus, more than I.

I am not even going to attempt to retell the story of the draft resistance here: the accounts, first-hand and secondary, that appear in this volume make that superfluous. What I am gong to do is try to explain its greater significance.

*****

When trying to explain the past, one must always keep in mind the circumstances of that time, not the circumstances of today, six decades later. As the wise woman, Yoshiko Uchida, reminded us in one of her last books:

> Today [1982] some of the Nisei, having overcome the traumatizing effects of their incarceration and participation in a wide spectrum of American life with no little success, are approaching retirement. The Sansei children, who experienced the Vietnam War, with its violent confrontations and protest marches, have asked questions about those early World War II years.

> "Why did you let it happen?" they ask of evacuation. "Why didn't you fight for your civil rights? Why did you go without protest to the concentration camps?" They were right to ask these questions, for they made us search for some obscured truths and come to a better understanding of ourselves and of those times. They are the generation who taught us to celebrate our ethnicity and discover our ethnic pride.

> It is my generation, however, who lived through the evacuation of 1942. We are their link to the past and we must provide them all we can remember, so they can better understand the history of their own people. As they listen to our voices from the past, however, I ask that they remember they are listening in a totally different time: in a totally changed world.[6]

Even though she is no longer with us, we should listen to Uchida's voice. We should remember, not only that the 1940s and 1950s were not the 1960s or 1970s, but also that the time in which we now speak is changed again. The enactment of redress and the formal apology that accompanied it have modified and shaped the thrust of our inquiries. Where we once strove to discover what the government did and why it did it, now many of us are more interested in scrutinizing what the community and its leaders did, and why they did it.

The community and its leaders decided to submit to the government's demands, to cooperate in its own incarceration, to go quietly, to be

4

good and obedient citizens, all in a hope not only of surviving, but also of attempting to achieve a place for themselves in America after the war. No prudent person can challenge that decision. One shudders to contemplate, given the conditions and moods of 1942, what the consequences of even mass resistance might have been, no less, confrontation. But whether it was necessary, even in 1942, for some community leaders to vilify individual peaceful protestors such as Gordon Hirabayashi and Min Yasui, who tried to win justice through the legal system, is quite another matter. I am not here criticizing their ends, which were, in the final analysis, nothing less than the preservation of the Japanese American people. The means they chose were undemocratic and essentially authoritarian, but at least the attacks on the early dissidents were done in public. Behind the back of the community, the top leadership of the Japanese American Citizens League (JACL) conspired with some of the chief oppressors of the Japanese American people to silence and thwart dissent. Their chief accomplice was Assistant Secretary of War, John J. McCloy.

The JACL also, more or less publicly, were consistent in urging the army to reinstitute selective service for Japanese American young men and to form special all Japanese American units. The notion was that the Nisei battlefield sacrifices would help insure a future for the Japanese American people. And I cannot quarrel with the ends. But when protest movements began, at Heart Mountain and elsewhere, the JACL leadership again turned on the individual dissidents and conspired with others to blunt their growing movement. Most despicable was the collaboration of the director of the American Civil Liberties Union, (ACLU) Roger Baldwin. When Kiyoshi Okamoto, one of the leaders of the Heart Mountain protesters, wrote privately asking the ACLU to help him to challenge the constitutionality of drafting citizens who were behind barbed wire, Baldwin answered *publicly*, disassociating himself and his organization from the Heart Mountain dissidents and insisting that "men who counsel others to resist military service are not within their rights and just expect severe treatment." Baldwin also had reneged on an earlier promise made by the ACLU to activists in Seattle to support the protest of Gordon Hirabayashi against the curfew established by General DeWitt for enemy aliens and "non-alien" Japanese. ("Non-alien" was the term that the Western Defense Command preferred to use to describe American citizens of Japanese Ancestry.)

The resisters, of course, lost their challenge in the courts. And they probably would have lost it even had the ACLU supported them. But ACLU support would have made it more difficult for their protest to be ignored, as it largely was. The Heart Mountain draft resisters did at least have their day in court. A quick trial in the federal district court in Cheyenne in May 1944 resulted in sixty-three convictions. It is still the largest single trial for draft resistance in American history. The protestors' appeal was rejected by the Tenth Circuit Court in Denver, and the Supreme Court denied certiorari, thus refusing even to listen to their case. At least 263 Japanese American citizen inmates of concentration camps were convicted for draft resistance, 85 of them, 32.3 percent, from Heart Mountain. At least one Japanese American not in a concentration camp, Gordon Hirabayashi, was also convicted of draft resistance. All 264 served time in federal prisons.

By the time they were released, the war was over. Even before that, the exploits of the 100th Battalion and the 442nd Regimental Combat Team were receiving well earned kudos, and the Supreme Court was awakening from its patriotic stupor, at least enough to end the restriction which kept loyal Japanese American citizens from returning to the West Coast. That decision was handed down in *Ex parte Endo* (1944) along with the disgraceful *Korematsu* decision which sanctioned putting citizens in concentration camps merely on the grounds of their ethnicity.

Already in the 1940s, the "model minority" myth, though not yet named, was being propagated. A British historian, E. H. Carr, once noted that "history is written by the victors," and the JACL version of history, the winners' version, was, for a time at least, triumphant. The resisters, by and in the large, went "into the closet," and simply were not heard from. In this, the Japanese American community mirrored the American community as a whole, which was celebrating what we now call "consensus history" and was preparing for what *Life* magazine's Henry Luce called an "American century." Had history ended then, the resisters would have been forgotten. But history doesn't end, and the winners' history, eventually, gets revised. And, to be sure, revisionist history itself is also subject to revision.

How that change came about, so that we today can celebrate *both* those who served and those who resisted is an interesting story. In the process of revision we must never forget that, had the whole community, or even a major fraction of it, resisted, postwar Japanese American history would have been very different, and much more tragic than it was.

Notes

1.War Relocation Authority, United States Department of the Interior, *The Evacuated People: A Quantitative Description* (Washington, D.C.: GPO, 1946), Tables 5, 52, and 56.

2.Douglas W. Nelson, "Heart Mountain: The History of an American Concentration Camp," University of Wyoming, M.A. thesis, 1970. With some revision it was published as *Heart Mountain: The Story of an American Concentration Camp* (Madison: State Historical Society of Wisconsin, 1976).

3.Audrie Girder and Anne Loftis, *The Great Betrayal: The Evacuation of the Japanese Americans during World War II* (New York: Macmillan, 1969), 247.

4.My computations come from War Relocation Authority, United States Department of the Interior, *WRA: A Story of Human Conservation* (Washington, D.C.: GPO, 1946), Table 3, 199- 200.

5.*The Evacuated People*, 126, and Table 50, 128. The text read *en toto*:
> Table 50 reflects in part evacuee reaction against the reestablishment of Selective Service resulting from a feeling that Japanese Americans had been denied many of their constitutional rights and that, if inducted, certain discriminations would still be practiced against them. Of the 315 arrests due to Selective Service violations, 263 resulted in convictions and 28 in releases.

Eric L. Muller. *Free to Die for Their Country: The Story of the Japanese American Draft Resisters in World War II.* Chacago: University of Chicago Press, 2001, is the best book on draft resistance.

6.Yoshiko Uchida, *Desert Exile: The Uprooting of a Japanese American Family* (Seattle: University of Washington Press, 1982), 147.

PART I

BACKGROUND AND ANTECEDENTS

Historical Background and Terminology of Incarceration

by Gail Nomura

The forcible removal and incarceration of Japanese Americans in World War II marked the culmination of a century of a racist policy of discrimination and exclusion of Asians in the United States. Always considered foreign because of their race, even the U.S.-born, American citizen, second-generation Japanese Americans, the Nisei, were incarcerated in inland concentration camps during World War II, along with the immigrant, first generation, the Issei, who were "aliens ineligible to citizenship." This essay will examine prewar anti-Asian exclusion legislation in the United States in order to understand racism and prejudice as a context for the wartime incarceration, of Japanese Americans. This essay then explains the process of removal and incarceration and concludes with an examination of terminology used to describe and (mis)represent the incarceration experience.[1]

Exclusion is a central theme in the early history of all Asian Americans in the United States.[2] Though Asian immigrants provided much of the labor for building the "American" West in the nineteenth and early twentieth centuries, especially for mining, transportation, and agriculture, they were eventually excluded from immigration and naturalization on the basis of a racist assumption that they could never become American, and thus posed a threat to American society. A racialized definition of "American" was constructed which excluded Asians.

The treatment of Chinese immigrants in the nineteenth century set the pattern for the treatment of other Asian immigrants. Exclusionists claimed that Chinese were biologically inferior to whites and incapable of assimilating to democratic self-government. Exclusionists asserted that Chinese were naturally inclined to *oriental despotism* and thus their participation in the political life of the United States posed a threat to the very foundation of American democratic society.[3] In many Western states, Chinese immigrants were denied voting rights, barred from testifying in court cases involving whites, and forced to pay special fees and taxes.[4] But anti-Asian exclusion acts were not limited to state action. On the federal level, immigration exclusion acts were the most damaging of these legal constraints.

The Chinese Exclusion Act of 1882 was the first in a series of exclusion acts passed by the U.S. Congress that stunted the growth of Asian groups in the United States and distorted their population composition. Passed in the midst of an economic recession in which Chinese became the scapegoat for many on the West Coast, the Chinese Exclusion Act set a dangerous precedent that would have far-reaching effects for subsequent Asian immigrants. There were two major provisions of the act. The first suspended the immigration of Chinese laborers, skilled, unskilled, and those engaged in mining, for ten years. The second provision prohibited the naturalization of Chinese. The Chinese Exclusion Act was extended with additional restrictions three times before it was repealed in 1943.

Since very few Chinese women had come to the United States before 1880, and Chinese laborers were not able to send for wives after 1882, there was little hope of having a settled family life for most Chinese immigrants in the United States after the Chinese Exclusion Act.[5] In effect, the Chinese Exclusion Act prevented family formation in the Chinese community, condemning the Chinese in the United States to becoming an aging bachelor society. Since no new Chinese laborers were allowed to immigrate to the United States after 1882, the population decreased dramatically with each census from 1890 to 1920. Further, the anti-Chinese movement intensified after the passage of the Chinese Exclusion Act. The Chinese Exclusion Act seemed to legitimize the assumption that Chinese were not fit to become part of American society. Chinese became an easy scapegoat for white frustrations. The Chinese Exclusion Act set a precedent for the exclusion of all Asian immigrants.[6]

In 1907-08, under pressure by the United States and hoping to halt anti-Japanese agitation in the United States, the Japanese government agreed to prohibit the immigration of Japanese laborers to the United States.[7] This was called the "Gentlemen's Agreement." However, the Japanese Government and the United States differed in their views of Japanese women. The Japanese Government continued to allow the emigration of Japanese wives and children of settled laborers in the United States. More and more Japanese husbands began to send for their wives. Unmarried men who were unable to return to Japan to marry had their families in Japan, or "go-betweens" arrange marriages for them with so-called "picture brides" in Japan. Pictures and information were exchanged between the prospective bride and groom, and they married by proxy. Anti-Japanese exclusionists condemned the picture bride practice as "barbaric," "uncivilized," "immoral," and devoid of "love" and "morality." Exclusionists viewed picture brides as prostitutes who posed a threat to the morals of U.S. society. Initially, picture brides married by proxy had to be wed again in a "Christian" ceremony at the docks before being allowed to land. Later, the men had to go to Japan and marry in person.

Exclusionists also perceived picture brides as an economic threat in the West Coast. Because wives worked side by side with their husbands in the fields, exclusionists claimed that Japanese women were thus laborers and should be barred under the Gentlemen's Agreement's prohibition of Japanese laborers. But the Japanese Government did not view the wives as laborers. Rather, the Japanese Government viewed the immigration of Japanese Americans wives as a necessary means to promote family reunification, "family values," and a settled family life among its emigrants to counter anti-Japanese accusations that Japanese were sojourners who did not commit to life in the United States. Indeed, the coming of picture brides ensured the permanency of Japanese settlement in the United States. With the arrival of the picture brides, there was an increase in the number of children born to the Japanese immigrants. Japanese community life expanded with the establishment of Japanese churches, temples, women's organizations, and Japanese language schools.

In response to exclusionists' attacks on the picture bride system, the Japanese Foreign ministry stopped issuing passports to picture brides in 1920. Forty-two percent of Japanese immigrant males were unmarried at that time. After 1920, Japanese males had to incur the expense of going back to Japan to marry and bring back their wives to the United States.

Exclusionists continued their vociferous attacks on the reproductive role of Japanese immigrant women. To exclusionists, the coming of Japanese wives meant an increase in the population of the hated Japanese. Issei women were portrayed as breeding like rats and producing "unassimilable" children who were, by birth in the United States, U.S. citizens. Exclusionists could never accept the possibility of a person of Japanese ancestry being "American." For exclusionists, race was the key ingredient in determining who could be an American. Exclusionists called for the revoking of citizenship from the Nisei on the grounds that they were being raised by aliens ineligible for citizenship.

Further immigration restrictions were imposed against Asians by the Immigration Act of 1917 that created an Asiatic barred zone from which no immigrants from India, Siam, Indo-China, parts of Siberia, Afghanistan, Arabia, and the islands of Java, Sumatra, Ceylon, Borneo, New Guinea, and Celebes could come. Then, in 1924, Congress passed a major comprehensive immigration law that prohibited the immigration of "aliens ineligible to citizenship." The only "aliens ineligible to citizenship" were Asians. Thus only Asians were prohibited from immigrating to the United States. The 1924 Immigration and Naturalization Act is also known as the Japanese Exclusion Act since it targeted the only Asian alien group not already barred from immigration to the United States.[8]

After 1924, no new immigration of Japanese occurred until the post-World War II period. Still, because the Japanese males had been able to send for wives from 1908 to 1924, the Japanese community continued to grow as a generation of Japanese American citizens, Nisei, were born in this country.

Clearly defined generation and gender cohorts developed as a result the of discriminatory U.S. immigration laws that halted new Japanese immigration early in the century. For example, the typical Nisei was born between 1915 and 1935, and the typical Sansei was born between 1945 and 1965.

The 1924 immigration law used the category "aliens ineligible to citizenship" to exclude Asians. The exclusion of Asians from the right to become naturalized Americans is the key feature that distinguishes the Asian immigrant experience from that of other immigrants to the United States. In 1790, Congress had originally set a racial condition for naturalization by restricting that right to an alien who was a "free white person." However, after the Civil War, in 1870, Congress extended the right of naturalization to former slaves by making aliens of African nativity and descent also eligible. Though naturalizations laws did not specifically deny naturalization to Asian immigrants, the 1882 Chinese Exclusion Act prohibited naturalization for Chinese aliens. The question remained whether non-Chinese Asians had the right of naturalization. Could they be classified within the definition of free white persons? Some lower federal courts had issued naturalization papers to Japanese, for the 1910 census indicates that there were 420 naturalized Japanese. But the U.S. Attorney General ordered federal courts in 1906 to stop issuing naturalization papers to Japanese. Japanese took their case to the U.S. Supreme court in the test case of Takao Ozawa, a Japanese immigrant who met all of the nonracial requirements for naturalization. Ozawa argued in a legal brief for the U.S. Supreme Court, "in name, General Benedict Arnold was an American, but at heart he was a traitor. In name, I am not an American, but at heart I am a true American."[9] In November of 1922, the U.S. Supreme Court heard Ozawa's case but ruled that Ozawa did not have the right of naturalization since he was of the Mongolian race and therefore was not judged to be either a free white person or an African by birth or descent. The Court had affirmed a racial prerequisite for naturalization that excluded those of the "Mongolian race."

It is interesting to note how the court handled the question of naturalization rights of South Asians who by the racial classifications of that time were considered to be Aryan.[10] Between 1914 and 1923, some seventy South Asians had become U.S. citizens based on the criterion that they were "high caste Hindus of Aryan race" and were thus Caucasian and entitled to be considered "white persons" eligible for citizenship. Although in the 1922 *United States v. Ozawa* decision, the court had based its ruling on the racial definition that white person meant Caucasian, in 1923 *United States v. Bhagat Singh Thind* decision, the U.S. Supreme Court further refined its exclusionary definition for naturalization now relying on the "understanding of the common man" rather than on a basis of racial classification. The Court argued that Congress never meant to include South Asians in the definition of white persons since in 1790 Congress associated the term white persons with immigrants from northern and western Europe, and in 1870 Congress, assumed it meant Europeans. The court further reasoned that in denying South Asians immigration privileges in 1917, Congress was opposing their naturalization, too. The Court concluded that neither the public nor Congress ever intended that South Asians be granted naturalization rights.

Thus the U.S. Supreme court affirmed the legality of the useful category of "alien ineligible to citizenship." In making Asians ineligible to citizenship, the *Ozawa* and *Thind* decisions greatly facilitated the total exclusion of all Asian immigration. Congress utilized this category of "alien ineligible to citizenship" to prohibit all Asian immigration in 1924. The denial of their naturalization rights led to the political weakness of the Asian immigrant communities in the prewar period. Asian immigrants were permanently disenfranchised in the United States. No politician sought their political support nor cared for their needs. In fact, politicians found it popular among their voters to call for further restrictions against Asians.

The permanent status of Asian immigrants as "aliens ineligible to citizenship" also served as the basis for further discriminatory laws such as the anti-alien land laws passed in various West Coast states which greatly restricted their economic opportunities by prohibiting the ownership, leasing, renting, and share-cropping of land by "aliens ineligible to citizenship." However, the U.S. born children of the early immigrants, the Nisei, grew up as American citizens and were not subject to anti-alien laws. The Issei parents took special pride in the achievements of their children whose success marked a rectification for past and present injustices. The hopes and aspirations of the immigrants rested in the future of their American children.

Exclusion from naturalization condemned Asian immigrants to the permanent status of being forever foreign in the United States. While Asian immigrants were systematically denied every avenue of legally becoming Americans, they were faulted for being foreign. Exclusionist forces perceived Asian immigrants as being incapable of being American. In the eyes of exclusionists, the fire could never be hot enough to melt Asian immigrants into the melting pot of America. The immigrants were not ignorant of the impossible position in which they were placed by the illogicality of the exclusionists who denied them naturalization, socially discriminated against them, economically restricted them, and yet demanded that Asians assimilate or be excluded.

But despite the hostility and discrimination directed against them, Asian Americans persisted as active agents in the making of their own histories. They challenged the fluctuating boundaries of who was and was not included in the United States. Asian immigrants resisted exclusion and fought for their human and civil rights through diplomatic channels, through the courts, through creative resistance, and through collective action. In the

15

process of resisting exclusion, they laid the foundations for the permanent establishment and growth of their communities in the United States while challenging an exclusive definition of America and American and broadening the inclusiveness of the application of American ideals. Asian American resistance to racist exclusion challenged the United States to fulfill the promise of democracy for all.

The anti-Asian exclusion movement and legislation laid the racist foundation for assuming the "military necessity" for the forcible removal and incarceration of Japanese Americans in World War II. After the outbreak of war between the United States and Japan, Japanese immigrants, who had been denied the right of naturalization, became enemy aliens and were viewed with great suspicion. They and their citizen children were subject to a myriad of restrictions. On February 19, 1942, President Franklin Roosevelt issued Executive Order 9066 (E.O. 9066) which led to the forcible mass round-up, removal, and incarceration under armed guard of more than 110,000 Japanese Americans from the West Coast. Executive Order 9066 authorized the Secretary of War and military commanders he designated to prescribe military areas "from which any or all persons may be excluded," and it authorized the Secretary to provide necessary transportation, food, shelter, and other accommodations. Executive Order 9066 was followed on March 18, 1942 by another executive order which established the War Relocation Authority (WRA), which was put in charge of developing and implementing a program to remove, relocate, maintain and supervise the persons affected by Executive Order 9066. The U.S. Congress was complicit in the exclusion and incarceration of Japanese Americans by funding the establishment of the WRA and by passing Public Law 503 on March 21, 1942, which placed criminal penalties on those who did not comply with the exclusion orders.[11]

Civilian exclusion orders which moved persons of Japanese ancestry "alien and nonalien" first to temporary detention centers, called "assembly centers" followed. The term "nonalien" was a euphemism for U.S. citizen. They were told that they could bring only what they could carry. They were then moved from the temporary detention centers located on existing public fairgrounds and racetracks to permanent inland incarceration camps built specifically for this purpose. For some, wartime incarceration lasted almost four years. In all, more than 110,000 Japanese Americans were forcibly rounded up, removed from their homes on the West Coast, and incarcerated under armed guard in barbed wire enclosures located in California, Idaho, Wyoming, Utah, Colorado, Arizona, and Arkansas. Two-thirds of those incarcerated were U.S. citizens, and the rest resident aliens who had been denied the right of naturalization on the basis of race. The exclusionists' ultimate goal of physical removal had been achieved.

Though the United States was at war with Germany and Italy, there was no mass round-up and incarceration of German and Italian Americans. Clearly, the difference in treatment was based on race. Japanese Americans were never charged with a crime. There were no trials, no convictions, no due process. There are no documented cases of sabotage attributed to Japanese Americans. Moreover, Japanese Americans fought with distinction in the U.S. armed forces in World War II in both the European and Pacific theaters. The 100th Battalion and the 442nd Regimental Combat Team were the most decorated units of their size in U.S. military history. Furthermore, government documents uncovered in 1981 revealed that the initial recommendations for mass internment of Japanese Americans were based on racial considerations, and that in later cases argued before the U.S. Supreme Court, the government knowingly suppressed, altered, and destroyed evidence proving that there existed no military necessity for the removal of Japanese Americans from the West Coast. On the basis of this uncovered evidence of government duplicity, the lower courts finally vacated the convictions of the World War II test cases of Korematsu, Yasui, and Hirabayashi[12] in the mid-1980s and, due to the vigorous educational campaign by the Japanese American redress movement, the legislative and executive branches of the U.S. Government moved to correct this injustice. In 1988 Congress passed, and the president signed legislation to apologize and pay monetary compensation to redress the forcible removal and incarceration of Japanese Americans during World War II.[13]

The government consistently utilized euphemisms to describe the incarceration of Japanese Americans in order to mask the massive violation of civil rights and constitutional due process.[14] The government used the word "evacuation" to refer to the removal of Japanese Americans from the West Coast. "Evacuation" implies removal and temporary relocation of people from hazardous areas for protective purposes in times of imminent danger as in the case of fire or flood. Japanese Americans were not evacuated; they were forcibly rounded up and exiled under armed military guard.

There is much confusion as to the use of the terminology "internment." Historian Roger Daniels has written extensively with regard to the misuse of this term.[15] As Daniels has explained, "Internment" refers to a legal process regulated by the Geneva Convention and described in U.S. statutes that applies to the confinement of selected nationals of a country with which the United States is at war. Although there may have been great injustice in an individual's internment, as prisoners of war, internees had rights under the Geneva Convention and had their cases reviewed by Enemy Alien Hearing Boards. Although about 8000 Japanese nationals were legally interned by the U.S. government during World War II, there was no legal process for the mass incarceration of 110,000 Japanese Americans in 1942. Japanese Americans placed in "relocation centers" did not have any due process. There were no charges brought against them, and no trials. They were not interned. They were incarcerated. Moreover, two-thirds of those incarcerated were U.S. citizens who were taken into custody, not because of their status as nationals of a country with which the United States was at war, but because of their racial/ancestral tie to an enemy nation. Therefore, the mass incarceration of Japanese Americans should not be described with a word, "internment," which describes a legal process applied to nationals of an enemy nation.

There is also a continuing debate as to what to call the sites where the bulk of Japanese Americans were incarcerated. Many Nisei use the ambiguous term "camp," and variously use the terms "evacuation," "relocation," and "internment." However, since most Japanese Americans were not "interned" but rather incarcerated *en masse* based on their ethnicity without any due process, many scholars believe that these sites should be called "concentration camps" rather than internment camps. Others argue that the term "concentration" camp is too harsh a term especially in comparison to the atrocities associated with World War II Nazi death/extermination camps. The government called the sites where Japanese Americans were held "relocation centers" or "evacuation centers," and called the people in these relocation centers "residents" or "colonists," not prisoners or inmates. But government officials like President Roosevelt and Supreme Court Justice Owens did use the term "concentration camp."

In order to understand the underlying reasons for the massive wartime violation of the civil rights of Japanese Americans we must recognize the preceding history of racism and prejudice directed against Asian Americans. And, we must be careful in the usage of the terminology of incarceration, for as Roger Daniels asserts, "words do matter." Euphemism and inaccurate terms cover up the serious constitutional implications for all Americans of the illegal incarceration of Japanese Americans in World War II. The Heart Mountain Fair Play Committee understood what was at stake, and they took action. In their Fair Play Committee bulletin they declared that "If Democracy and Freedom is to exist in this Country, then we must uphold the ideals and principles of the Constitution and right the wrongs committed to a minority group."[16] As Fair Play Committee member, Frank Emi, asserted in a hearing held on April 4, 1944, "you could say that you are fighting for democracy abroad, but if you lose democracy at home what have you won?"[17] The resisters of conscience teach us the importance of fighting for democracy at home.

Background and Terminology of Incarceration

Notes

1.I was asked by the resisters and organizers of the workshop, "Protest and Resistance: An American Tradition," to cover these issues in my introductory presentation.

2.For comprehensive histories of Asian Americans see Sucheng Chan, *Asian Americans: An Interpretive History* (Twayne Publishers,1991), Roger Daniels, *Asian America: Chinese and Japanese in the United States Since 1850* (University of Washington Press, 1988), and Ronald Takaki, *Strangers from a Distant Shore: A History of Asian Americans* (Penguin Books, 1989).

3.See Robert G. Lee, *Orientals: Asian Americans in Popular Culture* (Temple University Press, 1999).

4.For an account of how Chinese challenged racist discrimination see Charles J. McClain, *In Search of Equality: The Chinese Struggle against Discrimination in Nineteenth-Century America* (University of California Press, 1994).

5.For an excellent history of Chinese American women see Judy Yung, *Unbound Feet: A Social History of Chinese Women in San Francisco* (University of California Press, 1995).

6.For further information on the implementation and impact of the Chinese Exclusion Act see Sucheng Chan, ed., *Entry Denied: Exclusion and the Chinese Community in America* (Temple University Press, 1991), Scott K. Wong and Sucheng Chan, eds., *Claiming America: Constructing Chinese American Identities during the Exclusion Era* (Temple University Press, 1998), and Lucy E. Salyer, *Laws Harsh as Tigers: Chinese Immigrants and the Shaping of Modern Immigration Law* (University of North Carolina Press, 1995).

7.For the best account of early Japanese American history see Yuji Ichioka, *The Issei: The World of the First Generation Japanese Immigrants, 1885-1924* (The Free Press, 1988).

8.Although Filipinos were not citizens, they were U.S. nationals since the Philippines was a U.S. possession after the Spanish American War. As U.S. nationals, Filipinos could migrate freely to all U.S. territories. However, Filipino migration from the Philippines to other U.S. territories was restricted to a quota of 50 with the passage of the Tydings-McDuffie Act of 1934.

9.Yuji Ichioka, *The Issei*, 219. See pages 210-226 for a detailed account of the quest by Japanese for naturalization.

10.For a detailed account on naturalization issues concerning South Asian immigrants see Joan Jensen, *Passage From India: Asian Indian Immigrants in North America* (Yale University Press, 1988).

11.For a comprehensive account of the history of the World War II incarceration of

A Matter of Conscience

Japanese Americans see Roger Daniels, *Concentration Camps USA: Japanese Americans in World War II* (Holt, Rinehart and Winston, 1971) and *Concentration Camps: North America, Japanese in the United States and Canada During World War II* (Robert E. Krieger Publishing Company, 1981, 1989 with updating).

12.For a detailed account of the Japanese American wartime cases see Peter Irons, *Justice at War: The Story of the Japanese American Internment Cases* (Oxford University Press, 1983) and Peter Irons, ed., *Justice Delayed: The Record of the Japanese American Internment Cases* (Wesleyan University Press, 1989).

13.For an excellent account of the Japanese American redress movement see Mitchell T. Maki and Harry H. L. Kitano and S. Megan Berthold, *Achieving the Impossible Dream: How Japanese Americans Obtained Redress* (University of Illinois Press, 1999).

14.See Raymond Okamura, "The American Concentration Camps: A Cover-Up Through Euphemistic Terminology," *The Journal of Ethnic Studies* 10:3 (1982) and James Hirabayashi, "Concentration Camp or Relocation Center: What's in a Name?"

15.See Roger Daniels, "The Internment of Japanese Nationals in the United States During World War II," *Halcyon*, 17 (1995), 65-75; and in a forthcoming publication titled "Words Do Matter: A Short Note on Inappropriate Terminology and the Incarceration of the Japanese Americans" to be published in an anthology edited by Louis Fiset and Gail M. Nomura.

16.Fair Play Committee Bulletin, "WE SHOULD KNOW," in Gail M. Nomura, et. al, eds. *Frontiers of Asian American Studies* (Washington State University Press, 1989), 50.

17.Hearing Transcript, Hearing Board For Leave Clearance, Rehearing, April 6, 1944 in Nomura et. al , eds. *Frontiers of Asian American Studies*, 67.

Cultures of Resistance:
Japanese American Draft Resisters in Transnational Perspective

by Takashi Fujitani

RETHINKING THE IDEA OF "CULTURE"

In a thoughtful introduction to a book of essays on culture, modernity, and globalization, Arjun Appadurai remarks on his unease with the word
"culture." "I find myself frequently troubled by the word *culture* as a noun,"
he professes,

> but centrally attached to the adjectival form of the word, that is *cul-
> tural*. When I reflect on why this is so, I realize that much of the prob-
> lem with the noun form has to do with its implication that culture is
> some kind of object, thing, or substance, whether physical or meta-
> physical. This substantialization seems to bring culture back into the
> discursive space of race, the very idea it was originally designed to
> combat.[1]

Appardurai's discomfort with the word "culture" is one that I have
felt for many years, and it is an anxiety that has been expressed by numerous
scholars writing over the last two decades or so.[2] For such critics, commonsensical understandings of culture are problematic because they tend to represent cultures as overly uniform and consistent, apparently impervious to
change, determinative of individual behavior, and essential to the identity of
everyone belonging to a particular collectivity. As Appadurai points out in
the quote, moreover, the idea that a group of people has an essential culture
comes awfully close to the biological determinism of racial thinking—in other
words, just as it used to be openly said that the characteristics of an identifiable collectivity were determined by the racial constitution of its members, it
is now often assumed that members of a particular group behave in prescribed ways because of their culture. Cultural determinism often appears to
stand in for an older form of racial or biological determinism, with many of
the same effects.

In everyday practice people today tend to understand culture in
almost the same way as they, their grandparents or perhaps even their parents used to speak of race. Thus when people think of "Chinese culture,"
"Indian culture," "Japanese culture," "Muslim culture," and so on, they are

21

usually assuming that individuals within each of these groups behave in essentially similar ways and that their cultures have remained intact and unchanged over long stretches of time. In fact, I suspect that most people rarely even consider time or history when they think of culture, except to assume that even though history might produce transformations, culture does not change in any substantial way. Thus, we commonly hear that the Japanese people underwent massive transformations over the course of the last century and a half or so, but have retained their culture. Or sometimes, conversely, the media reports that the Japanese people have undergone such tremendous change that they are getting out of touch with, or they are losing their culture. In either case the assumption about culture is the same: that it is a fixed thing with readily identifiable characteristics that either do not change in fundamental ways, or are so impervious to change that the only alternative to remaining as is, is to die out.

But what do my admittedly abstract thoughts on the word "culture" have to do with Japanese American draft resistance? I begin with this general critique of "culture" to register my dissatisfaction with the way that "Japanese culture" tends to be understood by members of the Japanese American community, as well as by scholars writing on Japanese Americans. In particular, I want to address the issue of how we might understand Japanese American draft resistance and Japanese American history without recourse to ahistorical, inflexible, and simplistic (or even stereotypical) notions of Japanese culture. Along the way I want to consider the historical reasons why the image of "Japanese culture" as a static and politically debilitating inheritance has been so pervasive.

ARE "SHIKATA GA NAI," "GAMAN," AND "THE NAIL THAT STICKS UP GETS HAMMERED" REPRESENTATIVE OF JAPANESE CULTURE?

The workshop on "Protest and Resistance: An American Tradition," was a marvelous gathering of scholars, educators, activists, artists, former draft resisters, and other civic minded people. It provided a welcome and stimulating opportunity to learn about the (mis)treatment and experiences of Japanese American draft resisters, both during the war and after. Moreover, it made a powerful statement about the activism of Japanese Americans during the war years, reminding us that it is at least as important to remember the courage and principled stance of those who resisted the draft as it is to celebrate the heroism of those who joined or were drafted into the armed services. Yet as I sat through the panels, listened, and read up on Japanese American draft resistance, I repeatedly encountered statements suggesting that Japanese culture was and is a deterrent to political or social protest. Some of the most common terms or aphorisms encapsulating this supposed

Cultures of Resistance

Japanese culture of passivity are ones that most Japanese Americans have heard many times over, whether regarding the internment experience or Japanese American behavior more generally. They are "*shikata ga nai*" (it can't be helped), "*gaman suru*" (endure), and "the nail that sticks up gets hammered."

For example, in his otherwise excellent book on the resisters, Eric L. Muller features such Japanese cultural traits as a significant, though to be sure not the only reason for Japanese American reticence in combating the program to remove them from the West Coast. He writes:

> every Nisei had grown up hearing his Issei parents recite the phrases *shikata ganai* and *gaman suru*—"it can't be helped" and "just endure it." It was thus a virtue, or at least a feature, of Japanese culture to accept what could not be changed. It was also a virtue of Japanese culture not to do things that draw the attention of others: "The nail that sticks up," explained the Issei to their children, "gets hammered." [3]

Such characterizations imply that in the public sphere, if not necessarily in private life, Japanese cultural traits must be shed for Japanese Americans to participate fully in American democratic life. While a democratic tradition of protest would seem to require active historical agents who can contest injustices, Japanese culture is portrayed as a culture of resignation that encourages subservience or compliance to authority. While a democratic ethos would seem to require individualism, the old adage about the upright nail getting hammered implies that Japanese society has little tolerance for non-group behavior. Instead, it supposedly celebrates groupism, consensus, or subjection of the self to larger collectivities such as family, neighborhood, community or nation.

Yet even a very cursory overview of Japanese American and Japanese history should give us pause to reconsider such formulations. Pioneering historians of Japanese Americans demonstrated long ago, particularly from the 1970s onward,[4] that Japanese immigrants to the United States and their descendents were anything but passive objects of rule and exploitation, and that the image of them as the "quiet Americans" is a myth. Since Arthur Hansen's contribution to this volume superbly covers the details of this Japanese American tradition of resistance, I will defer the details of this history to him. Here it may suffice to note that from labor organizing to striking against exploitative employment practices and engaging in various forms of resistance in the camps, many Japanese Americans, far from manifesting a predilection to accept things as they were, far from assuming that there was nothing they could do about their situations, regularly chose to shape the

A Matter of Conscience

course of their own futures. Here the most appropriate Japanese phrase would not be *shikata ga nai*, literally meaning, "there's nothing that can be done"[5] but perhaps *ganbaru*, a term that means to persevere in struggle, and suggests dogged determination. It is from this verb that Karl Yoneda, labor organizer, activist, and writer, took the title of his autobiography, *Ganbatte*.[6]

Still, one might object, these were Japanese Americans who had internalized American ways and values. They were not Japanese in Japan. But let us turn to Japan and briefly consider if the people there were afflicted by some kind of "Oriental" fatalism—a character flaw symbolized in the notion of *"shikata ga nai."* Apparently they were not. One might start with the obvious: the act of immigration. Had these would-be emigrants been resigned to their fates in Japan, they might simply have endured, rather than set out for uncertain futures abroad. But more tellingly, the long history of common people who have lived in the place we call Japan is a history of struggles, protests, uprisings, rebellions, strikes, and other everyday forms of resistance to political authority and economic exploitation, [7] just as much as it is a history in which there were periods of relative calm and apparent quiescence.

Over the last several decades, historians have been charting the history of common people's struggles in Japan against exploitation by the state and the wealthy. These historiographical efforts took off in Japan in the 1960s when many scholars began to argue that earlier historical research had focused excessively on elites, and that historians should write histories of the common people. From the 1970s, a fair number of historians writing in English also began to focus on the histories of the Japanese non-elite.[8] From this cumulative research, it is now very clear that commoners in Japan have hardly been passive or fatalistic in their relations with political authorities and the economic elite. For instance, while it was once thought that the Tokugawa period (1600-1868) had been remarkable in a comparative sense for the relative infrequency of peasant uprisings against the ruling class, when historians began to look for evidence of such disturbances, they found that conflict or protests were the norm in rural Japan, not the exception. Thus in a book published in 1966 Aoki Kōji listed more than 2, 800 peasant uprisings that had occurred between 1590 and 1867.[9] Over the years, he and other historians have bumped their numbers upwards, as researchers have continued to turn up more historical documents revealing other uprisings. Peasant uprisings and city riots took different forms throughout the era, but culminated toward the end of the Tokugawa period in what were called "world renewal" (*yonaoshi*) uprisings. In these disturbances, peasants took radical measures, not only criticizing their rulers and engaging in acts of violence, but also often declaring that the world would be a better place, in fact a paradise, with the destruction of the old economic and political elites. As Tatsurō, the leader of one such world renewal uprising was reported to have said to his interrogators, "when those above become perverse, those below become even more so." [10]

The Meiji Restoration (1868)—which was really a revolution resulting at least in part from the legitimation crises engendered by rural and city disturbances—soon led to the establishment of a modern nation-state. This nation-state adopted as its policy the slogan, "rich country, strong army" (*fukoku kyōhei*); but one consequence of the drive to become a wealthy and militarily powerful nation-state was the exaction of tremendous burdens on commoners in the cities and countryside. Tenancy rates in rural Japan skyrocketed after the Restoration, particularly in the 1880s, as a result of a new land tax system, while economic modernization and industrialization produced not simply development, but disparities of wealth. Thus in the late nineteenth and early twentieth centuries, precisely the period of greatest emigration to Hawaii and the mainland United States, the Japanese people continued to be faced with choices about how they might respond to extreme demands of the state and the economic elite.

To reiterate the question we have been pursuing: did Japanese commoners abide by the fatalism of "*shikata ga nai*" in this period? Sometimes, but certainly far from always. Many people in rural Japan felt betrayed by the new Meiji government. Whereas they had looked forward to a world renewed toward greater equality of wealth and overall improvement in the quality of their conditions of life, the new state began to claim even more from them than they had experienced under the Tokugawa period rulers. Commoners repeatedly resisted such new impositions.

Given the theme of this volume, we might offer draft resistance during the Meiji period (1868-1912) as one particularly poignant example. In the Tokugawa period, the samurai class had reserved the right to bear arms and form armies for themselves. However, in 1873 the Japanese government announced that all men over the age of twenty would be subject to military conscription, regardless of social background. But patriotism or loyalty to the nation was not a significant idea to most people in Japan at that time. Their most intimate associations with collectivities were to local communities, not the Japanese nation. Emperor worship was extremely uncommon, and many did not even know who the emperor was.[11] In such a situation, most people in Japan considered the draft an unjustifiable and indeed incomprehensible obligation. Not only did it mean the possibility of death, but few families could afford the loss of one adult male's labor. As a result, draft evasion was rampant. Some negotiated with their acquaintances in the local government offices, maybe getting them to doctor their family registers (*koseki*). Birthdates written in *kanji* (Chinese ideographs) could easily be changed with a few brushstrokes, so that one could claim that one was still too young, or beyond conscriptable age. For instance, the single horizontal line for the number one,

25

ichi, could readily become the start of several alternative numbers. Some peasants even went so far as to maim themselves physically, perhaps lopping off a finger or toe. [12] In other cases, young men simply disappeared. More than a few disappeared to places like Hawaii or the mainland United States. Evidence that some Issei immigrants were actually young men fleeing from the draft is not difficult to find.[13]

Poor farmers also protested and sometimes rebelled *en masse* against tax policies favoring the rural rich and the development of a new economic elite involved in Japan's industrial and commercial revolution. In 1884 near-ly 10,000 poor farmers in the Chichibu area of the Kanto Plain rose up in rebellion against such policies. They formed what was called a "poor people's army" and even resorted to violence against moneylenders and symbols of governmental authority, such as public buildings.[14] Whatever one might think about their use of violence, it can at least be said that *shikata ga nai* can in no way represent the attitude of these people. If they had ever heard that "a nail sticking up gets hammered," it obviously did not prevent them from openly and clearly displaying their anger against perceived injustices.

In the Meiji period, some villagers who were not a part of the cosmopolitan urban elite or the government independently studied Western political theory and wrote constitutions that they felt would be appropriate for Japan's new form of government. In his pathbreaking studies of such individuals,[15] Irokawa Daikichi showed that numerous study groups formed in rural Japan in the 1870s and 1880s to consider the writings of such Enlightenment thinkers as Rousseau and John Locke and to discuss democracy and constitutionalism. To be sure, the opinions of these constitutionalists and political theorists were not heard in any significant way by the Meiji political oligarchs, and their writings, including drafts of constitutions, were literally hidden away for nearly a century until they were rediscovered by Irokawa and his students. Yet it is now clear that a vibrant community of grassroots theorists, living in conditions not so different from those that Issei immigrants had come from, had worked passionately to make their mark on the institutional and ideological forms that their government would take.

Social and political activism did not end with the Meiji era. Labor strikes had already become fairly common in the late 1890s, and in the inter-war years nearly 500 strikes per year took place throughout Japan.[16] Tenant unions also increased over time. In 1913 a "movement to protect constitutional government" reached its climax when thousands of citizens besieged Japan's parliament, the Diet, in protest against a few oligarchs' manipulation of the process by which Japan's prime minister was selected. The universal manhood suffrage movement also reached its peak in the 1920s, and in 1925 all males over the age of twenty, including Korean and Taiwanese residents on the main Japanese islands, received the right to vote and hold office.

I could describe many more instances in which common Japanese people acted as agents in trying to fashion their own futures. Some of these involved women such as Deguchi Nao and Nakayama Miki, who utilized the language of folk religion to articulate their own critiques of the modern state, patriarchy, and economic and social injustice. Women also challenged the state and exploitation of their labor through involvements in the "Freedom and Popular Rights Movement" of the 1870s and 1880s, or through labor organizing and strikes. Kanno Suga, an anarchist executed for her alleged participation in a plot to assassinate the Meiji emperor presents a figure considerably at odds with the stereotype of demure and self-sacrificing Asian women. This section could be filled with many more examples of protest and resistance. Moreover, we could consider the limitations or problems as well as strengths of each of them. But hopefully the main point has already been made well enough. *Shikata ga nai* and *gaman* may reveal partial truths about some Japanese during particular moments in the past, but we can hardly accept them as enduring, constant, and foundational qualities of something that we call "Japanese culture."

THE POLITICS OF HISTORICAL REPRESENTATION: ORIENTALISM AND NATIONALISM

Much of what I have outlined above will not be new to students of Japanese history who have kept up with the literature in the field. Yet somehow, representations of Japanese women and men as passive or subservient objects of rule continue to persist in the popular imagination. Those who appear to have these qualities are regarded as representative products of Japanese culture, while those who do not are understood to be exceptional, and in most cases westernized. In other words, those who fulfill preconceptions about Japanese culture are seen as proof of the truthfulness of the preconception, while those who contradict expectations are considered not authentically or typically Japanese. The assumptions in this line of thinking can never be disproven. In this section I want to consider some of the reasons why such simple and clearly misleading representations about "Japanese culture" have had such a force up to and including the present. To answer this question, we need to begin by considering who has gained from producing and circulating such understandings.

As Edward Said argued in his highly influential book, *Orientalism*,[17] Western representations of the so-called Orient, especially from the nineteenth century onward, were very much entangled with the political stakes that Western powers had in dominating the world outside the West. In *Orientalism* Said referred specifically to the area that we know as the Middle East, but his insight that representations of non-Western cultures and peoples have had a political utility in legitimating Western domination or influence over other peoples is one that we might also consider when we think of Euro-American representations of Japan and Japanese culture. To be sure, Japan is not usually considered a colony of the U.S., but it is important to realize that the representations of Japanese culture as exotic or mysterious, unchanging in essence, groupist, and especially in the post-WWII years lacking in the ethical individualism upon which a modern democratic ethos could be based, have been linked to U.S. political stakes in the Asia-Pacific region. They constitute what Said might call a Euro-American Orientalism about Japan.

In this short commentary I cannot hope to trace the entire genealogy of U.S./Japan relations and how they helped shaped American representations of Japan. But, at a minimum, it might at first be noted that the will to achieve power necessitated simple, one might say stereotypical images of Japan. Simplified representations of Japan were more useful in formulating an American stance toward that nation than were complex understandings that might have revealed a plurality of cultures within Japan's official borders. "Culture" was a tool that allowed sweeping statements and misstatements about an internally diverse and contradictory national collectivity. In the middle of the nineteenth century, the moment that inaugurated the modern U.S./Japan [18] relationship, the place we call Japan was a highly disaggregated place with tremendous cultural differences that varied with status, local language, gender, region as well as from individual to individual. In fact, the actual borders of Japan were highly ambiguous, particularly in the far north and south. People throughout Japan spoke a multitude of languages. A peasant from the north, say the Tōhoku region, would not have been able to converse in any meaningful way with someone from Kyūshū. Modern linguists have called these different local languages dialects of Japanese and have thereby perpetuated the idea that Japan had a uniform language traditionally, but from the speakers' points of view, the bottom line would have been that they simply could not understand each other. A standard Japanese language was created in the late nineteenth century, but linguistic unification took many decades to accomplish and has still not completely erased local languages (or dialects). Although the concept of ethnicity did not exist in Japan in the mid-nineteenth century it could be argued that there was considerable ethnic diversity in Japan at the time—from Okinawans to Ainu and even perhaps between those living in eastern and western Japan—and that this diversity only increased in the twentieth century because of the immigration of millions of colonial subjects, especially Koreans. Conversely, however, it could be argued that we can only imagine ethnic diversity in retrospect in the Tokugawa period because the idea of a unified Japanese ethnicity did not exist. In either case, Japan was not by any means a culturally homogenous place in the mid-nineteenth century.

Cultures of Resistance

And yet, these niceties about diversity within Japan were not prominent in Euro-American representations about Japan—in large part because it was not politically useful to entertain such images. As a result, even those American social scientists who studied particular places within Japan tended to consider their objects of study as so many examples of the nation writ small. Suye Mura, for example, the first village in Japan to be studied by an American anthropologist, was written up as not just a discrete village in Kumamoto Prefecture, but a representative Japanese village. Thus John F. Embree gave his book's title *Suye Mura*, the subtitle *A Japanese Village*. [19]

The political imperative of mapping cultural traits at the national level, rather than of recognizing internal diversity reached its most obvious apogee during the Second World War when the cultural anthropologist Ruth Benedict and others wrote national character studies of Japan. Ruth Benedict worked for the Office of War Information, an agency charged with propaganda and psychological warfare, as well as with informing the American public and the outside world about the status and aims of the war effort. In other words, Benedict was charged to produce knowledge that would be useful in knowing the enemy, Japan. But this was not all, for by the time Benedict began her study, high civilian and military officials were already laying plans for "winning the peace" after Japan's defeat, and her book was actually published in the year after the war's end. Although her primary informants were not even Japanese, but rather Japanese Americans, Benedict made gross generalizations about Japanese cultural patterns and behavior, and she did so in the U.S. national interest. Above all, she argued that the Japanese had a "shame culture" or a culture of extreme situationalism, rather than a culture of internalized guilt. For her, this culture of shame and situationalism could be put to positive uses by the U.S. in achieving its aims for Japan. As she put it, this "strange ethic"[20] was not necessarily only a bad thing. The Japanese had failed in their militaristic efforts and so, because theirs was a situationalist ethic rather than an ethic of internalized principles, in the postwar years they could easily make an about face and work toward becoming a peace loving nation. There is much more that we might say about Ruth Benedict and the national character studies genre, but my main point here is that knowledge produced about Japan as a uniform collectivity was part of a national interest strategy for containing or regulating Japan.

However, this still does not answer the question of why Japanese culture has tended to be associated with some specific and usually less than flattering, sometimes perverse, or at best, quaint or imitative qualities. Even when lauding Japanese "high culture" in the arts, architecture, music, and so on, there is usually more than a touch of exoticism. For example, why have white Americans and other white Westerners, been prone to view the Japanese as inscrutable or mysterious? Even as late as 1990 Karel von

A Matter of Conscience

Wolferen authored a supposedly academic book titled *The Enigma of Japanese Power*, and in it he argued that power worked in mysterious ways in Japan— in a manner that defied Western logic.[21] Furthermore, why has Japanese society been regarded as intolerant of individualism and lacking in an ethos appropriate for modern civic life? Following Edward Said's insights once again, we might conclude that a partial answer lies in the interests of those who have produced and circulated such images.

These often unflattering representations have served to legitimate the export to Japan and to the world more broadly of what have been deemed to be American culture and values. What I mean by this is that whether characterized as exotic, irrational, or independently incapable of democracy, "Japan" was constructed into a place in need of the positive culture, values, and influence that America could provide. If Japan was mysterious and irrational, the West could provide what was necessary to make Japan more normal and rational. If Japanese were lacking in ethical individualism, Americans could help nurture it. Such reasonings helped serve to legitimate the U.S. presence and influence in Japan during the Occupation, and they continued to do so during the Cold War years when the U.S. sought to remake Japan in its own image, albeit as a junior partner.

Paralleling the emergence of a discourse on Japanese Americans as the U.S.'s preeminent "model minority," Japan from the late 1950s and 1960s came to be figured as a kind of global model minority. A school of American scholars commonly known as "modernization" theorists began to argue that Japan was exceptional within the non-Western world, for it had successfully become almost like the modern capitalist West. For this, the Japanese deserved praise. However, this characterization of Japan as *almost*, but not quite like the West, had a condescending dimension that likewise resonated with model minority discourse. For both representations suggested that these groups—one internal, the other external—were a distinct minority, that they had not quite made it, and perhaps never would. In a 1968 publication John Hall, a Japan specialist and one of the leading modernization theorists, openly expressed his fear that although Japan was coming along just fine in the immediate postwar decades, "irrational inheritances out of the past" might still reemerge.[22]

It should also be noted in this connection that the Cold War years witnessed the publication of many books arguing that Japanese culture is group oriented, with consensus valued and conflict denigrated. Some of these works in English were actually authored by Japanese scholars, one of the most influential being Nakane Chie's *Japanese Society*.[23] Yet, in the context of the Cold War, Japan's alleged groupism had a double-edged effect. On the one hand, groupism or a collectivist ethic seemed to have been one of the keys to Japan's modernization successes. This invited praise, especially during the

Cold War because other non-Western nations had turned toward communism or socialism and were regarded as threats, while Japan had successfully built a capitalist economy and liberal-democratic political system and was considered one of the U.S.'s strongest allies. On the other hand, the very cultural values that had turned Japan into a success story economically, appeared to be alien and inferior to the American way of life, which is supposedly based upon a principled individualism. This discourse on groupism and capitalist success thus set up an unfortunate no-win situation for Japan because the very factors that allegedly gave rise to Japan becoming more like "us" in the economic arena, were also those that apparently made Japan seem forever inferior and inadequate in its social and political relations. The discomfort that the collectivist ethic engendered was captured by Herman Kahn in 1970 when he described Japanese society as "Japan, Inc."[24]

In this section I have thus far considered why mainstream Euro-American and especially American representations of Japan have favored sweeping and simplistic statements about the Japanese as homogeneous and group oriented. However, it is also important to consider the ironic complicity of Japanese writers in the production of this discourse on "Japaneseness." Ever since the late nineteenth century, Japanese nationalists, including the political elite in government and their ideologues, have produced images of Japanese cultural unity that transcend time. This unifying core is often called tradition, and it connotes an authentic essence to the Japanese people. Certain cultural traits—such as loyalty to nation, filial piety, understanding one's proper place in society, hard work, and frugality—have been trumpeted as parts of this Japanese tradition. Why?

It is not simply that these traits can be found historically among some people in Japan during different periods of time. In fact, most people in Japan did not manifest such characteristics until fairly recent times in history, namely the nineteenth and twentieth centuries, and many still do not. These supposedly timeless traditions were historical products of modernity and were what might be called "invented traditions."[25] They were manufactured as tradition because successful nationalisms, whether in modern Japan or practically anywhere else in the modern world, have required the creation of the idea that people belonging to one nation have shared a cultural tradition for a very long time. Modern nationalisms have depended upon the belief that the individuals making up the national community have a common, as well as distinctive past, and a future destiny together. When nationalism as an ideology came to the fore in the late nineteenth century, in large part in response to the fear that without national unity and the mobilization of the energies of the common people Japan might become subject to the whims of the western powers, nationalists promoted ideas about Japanese culture that in many cases resonated well with the simple Euro-American representations of Japan

A Matter of Conscience

that I have already criticized above.

The stereotype of Japanese as subservient or blindly loyal to and self-sacrificing in relation to larger collectivities such as nation, community and family; the image of Japanese as lacking individualism; the belief that Japanese culture values consensus over conflict; the notion that it is better to endure (*gaman suru*) than to "stick out"—all of these supposedly authentic Japanese characteristics were promoted by the nationalist political elites because they were the cultural traits that were felt to be most conducive to development as a nation and control over the people. Let us take the example of Ninomiya Sontoku. Ninomiya lived in a specific time period, the late Tokugawa years (1787-1856), during which he encouraged common people to work hard and practice frugality.[26] But Ninomiya did not become a national icon and a representation of Japanese culture until the Meiji government promoted him in elementary schools throughout Japan through such efforts as erecting statues of him carrying a load of firewood on his back. Thus the cultural values represented by Ninomiya were not the core of an authentic Japanese culture—there is no such thing as authentic Japanese culture—they were values that existed among some people and in some places in Japan prior to the Meiji era, that were then taken up and fostered by the Meiji government and its ideologues because they were specific elements within a diverse past that appeared congenial to the program of creating a modern and powerful nation. The figure of Ninomiya Sontoku that one can find today even in Los Angeles's Little Tokyo thus represents not the core traditional culture of all Japanese, but an invented tradition.

The invention of Japanese culture and nationalism required massive forgetfulness about other possible candidates for the Japanese cultural legacy. Taira no Masakado led a longterm rebellion against the imperial court in the tenth century from his stronghold in eastern Japan. Yet for obvious reasons, the modern state did not promote rebellion against imperial authority as an important Japanese cultural tradition. Warfare among regional hegemons was common in Japan throughout its history, and killing became so endemic from the mid-fifteenth to the late-sixteenth centuries that the era is called the Warring States Period. Yet civil war involving the internecine killing of some Japanese by other Japanese is not regarded as a Japanese cultural tradition. Finally, commoners rising up against their rulers, another practice throughout Japanese history, was not constituted into a traditional inheritance. Why? Because all of these were parts of the past that Japan's political leaders in the late nineteenth and twentieth centuries did not wish to see continuing into modern times. These were cultural memories that needed to be marginalized, not revived.

The drive to present a unified history of the Japanese people continued into the Second World War years, and by that time official slogans declared that the "hearts of the one hundred million people" in Japan were beating as one. Of course, this was not true. There was still tremendous diversity within Japan, with numerous dissidents thrown into jail or forced to go along with the wartime system. Moreover, about twenty-five to thirty million of those hearts in the Japanese empire belonged to Korean, Taiwanese, and Micronesian colonial subjects—most of which undoubtedly beat to a different rhythm than those belonging to residents of the main Japanese islands.

Thus Japanese nationalist discourse tended to create an image of Japanese tradition that confirmed, and at times, even helped produce many Euro-American understandings of Japanese culture. If official wartime ideology declared to the world that all Japanese hearts beat as one, this confirmed the Western belief that Japanese culture denigrated individualism. If the modern Japanese state fostered the notion that loyalty to employer and nation was traditional while strikes and incomplete conformity were not, these ideas were taken up by American propagandists who declared that the Japanese people were unthinking automatons enslaved by their rulers. As Frank Capra put it in his wartime propaganda movie, *Know Your Enemy: Japan*, the Japanese people were like "prints off of the same negative."[27] And in the postwar decades of high economic growth, when Japanese scholars such as Nakane Chie described Japan as a groupist society—just the idea of tradition that big business interests wished were true—this was readily consumed and regurgitated by American commentators who, as we have already seen, praised Japanese efficiency based on these social relations, but usually with the implication that Americans would never tolerate such a sacrifice of the self, even if it meant the prosperity of the whole.

CONCLUDING THOUGHTS

Japanese nationalism and Euro-American Orientalism thus worked hand in glove to produce confident and sweeping generalizations about the Japanese people. They simplified a complex and conflict ridden history, and left many Japanese Americans and their observers with very stereotypical representations of what constitutes Japanese culture. This is not to say that aphorisms such as "there's nothing that can be done," "just endure," or "the nail that sticks up gets hammered," were never uttered or believed by anyone in Japan. And it is certainly possible that Issei parents told their children that these were core Japanese values. It is to say, however, that these expressions symbolize only a small range of the multiple cultural legacies that historians and others have rediscovered in the Japanese past.

Therefore, I hope that we can once and for all stop speaking and writing as if something called Japanese culture has been an obstacle to a democratic life, or that Japanese Americans had to overcome Japanese culture in order to engage in political and social criticism. At the same time, I am not arguing that Japanese Americans should go back to their Japanese roots to recuperate hidden but somehow ethnically authentic legacies of protest and resistance. For me, one of the great lessons proffered by the Japanese American draft resisters is that resistance to inequity need not be based on a complete identification with an ethnic past, but on commonsensical and principled understandings of justice that can be shared across communities for the future. The symbolic as well as legal resources for the draft resisters' protests were the U.S. Constitution and the values that it represents; and their heroic efforts and victories should serve as a source of inspiration for Americans and non-Americans alike. But it is also important to keep in mind that Americans and something we call American culture do not have a monopoly on struggles for justice and democracy. Peoples throughout the world have their own diverse legacies of struggle and resistance. These have sometimes been couched in the language and philosophy of Euro-American constitutionalism, but they have at other times and places looked into alternative traditions to construct other visions of a modern civic life.

Notes

1. Arjun Appadurai, *Modernity at Large: Cultural Dimensions of Globalization* (Minneapolis: University of Minnesota Press, 1996), 12.

2. For example, James Clifford, *The Predicament of Culture* (Cambridge, MA: Harvard University Press, 1988).

3. Eric L. Muller, *Free to Die for Their Country: The Story of the Japanese American Draft Resisters in World War II* (Chicago: University of Chicago Press, 2001), 26.

4. The works of Art Hansen, Yuji Ichioka, and Gary Okihiro come immediately to mind.

5. In a volume authored with Mits Koshiyama, Yoshi Kuromiya, Takashi Hoshizaki, and Frank Seishi Emi, William Minoru Hohri, also notes the contradiction between the often heard phrase, *shikata ga nai,* and the resistance of some Issei and Nisei to government actions against them during the war (*Resistance: Challenging America's Wartime Internment of Japanese-Americans* [Lomita, CA: the Epistolarian, 2001]), 41-44.

6. Karl G. Yoneda, *Ganbatte: Sixty-Year Struggle of a Kibei Worker* (Los Angeles: Asian American Studies Center, University of California, Los Angeles, 1983).

7. Mikiso Hane's *Peasants, Rebels, & Outcastes: The Underside of Modern Japan* (New York: Pantheon Books, 1982) provides a good overview of common people's protests and rebellions since the late nineteenth century.

8. For some more detailed thoughts on the emergence of one such school of historians, that of "People's History" or *minshūshi*, see T. Fujitani, *"Minshūshi* as Critique of Orientalist Knowledges," *positions* 6:2 (Fall 1998): 303-22.

9. Aoki Kōji, *Hyakushō ikki no nenjiteki kenkyū* [A Chronilogicle Study of Peasant Uprisings] (Tokyo: Shinseisha, 1966), p.13.

10. Cited in Aoki Michio, ed., *Tempō sōdōki* [A Chronicle of the Tempō Disturbance] (Tokyo: Sanseido, 1979), 221.

11. On the relatively recent invention of emperor worship and nationalism in Japan, see T. Fujitani, *Splendid Monarchy: Power and Pageantry in Modern Japan* (Berkeley: University of California Press, 1996).

12. Unless otherwise noted, the information on draft evasion in Japan is based upon T. Fujitani, "Kindai Nihon ni okeru kenryoku no tekunorojii: guntai, `chihō ', shintai (Technologies of Power in Modern Japan: The Military, The 'Local', The Body), translated by Umemori Naoyuki, <u>Shisō</u> 845 (November): 163-76.

13. Oral histories of Japanese Americans are filled with examples of men who gave draft evasion as the reason for their emigrating to the United States. For example, in Eileen Sunada Sarasohn's, *The Issei: Portrait of a Pioneer* (Palo Alto, California: Pacific Books, 1983), one Mitsumori Nisuke, born in Yamanashi Prefecture on Feb. 15, 1888, notes that he had immigrated to the United States after the outbreak of the Russo-Japanese War in order to escape being drafted. He noted that, "In those days anybody who wished to come to the United States was considered an unpatriotic person. When a person became eighteen, he received a physical examination for conscription. From mid-March no one could leave the country, because the physicals were conducted from March 15 until July. The government said that every citizen should participate in the war between Japan and Russia, and all the eighteen-year olds were hidden by their families. Therefore, I thought I had to leave as quickly as possible and applied for a passport immediately after New Year's Day. I must have received my passport in two or three weeks, because I left Japan in February. I did not have any particular idea of what I would do in the States. I had a vague idea that something would work out once I arrived." [p.18]

14. Roger W. Bowen, *Rebellion and Democracy in Meiji Japan* (Berkeley: University of California Press, 1980).

15. Irokawa Daikichi's relevant writings in Japanese are too numerous to mention here, but in English the reader can consult *The Culture of the Meiji Period*, trans. and ed., Marius Jansen (Princeton: Princeton University Press, 1985).

16. See the figures in Hane, *Peasants, Rebels, & Outcastes,* 285, note 95.

17. Edward Said, *Orientalism* (New York: Pantheon Books, 1978).

18. Some have argued that the idea of culture was itself born out of colonialism because it was a necessary concept for the colonial powers to categorize, order, and regulate those they encountered in their colonial projects. See for example, Nicholas B. Dirks, "Introduction: Colonialism and Culture," in *Colonialism and Culture*, ed., Nicholas B. Dirks (Ann Arbor: University of Michigan Press, 1992), 1-25.

19. John F. Embree, *Suye Mura: A Japanese Village* (Chicago: The University of Chicago Press, 1939).

20. Ruth Benedict, *The Chrysanthemum and the Sword: Patterns of Japan Culture* (New York: Houghton Mifflin, 1946), p.306.

21. Karel van Wolferen, *The Enigma of Japanese Power*, Vintage Edition (New York: Vintage Books, 1990).

22. John Whitney Hall, "A Monarch for Modern Japan," in *Political Development in Modern Japan*, ed. Robert E. Ward (Princeton: Princeton University Press, 1968), 64. I have written at some length on the linkages between model minority discourse and modernization theory in "'Go for Broke', The Movie: Japanese American Soldiers in U.S. National, Military and Racial Discourses," in T. Fujitani, Geoffrey White, and Lisa Yoneyama, ed., *Perilous Memories: The Asia Pacific War(s)* (Durham and London: Duke University Press), 239-66

23. Nakane Chie, *Japanese Society* (Berkeley: University of California Press, 1970). Two informative critiques of the groupism model for Japan are Harumi Befu's *Hegemony of Homogeneity* (Melbourne: Trans Pacific Press, 2001); and Ross Moeur and Yoshio Sugimoto, *Images of Japanese Society* (London: Kegan Paul International, 1986).

24. Herman Kahn, *The Emerging Japanese Superstate: Challenge and Response* (Englewood, NJ: Prentice-Hall, 1970).

25. The classic book on "invented traditions" is Eric Hobsbawm and Terence Ranger, eds., *The Invention of Tradition* (Cambridge: Cambridge University Press, 1983). For the invention of various traditions in modern Japan, see T. Fujitani, *Splendid Monarchy* and Stephen Vlastos, ed., *Mirror of Modernity: Invented Traditions of Modern Japan* (Berkeley: University of California Press, 1998).

26. In *Tokugawa Religion: the Values of Pre-Industrial Japan* (Glencoe, IL: Free Press, 1957), the sociologist Robert N. Bellah describes Ninomiya's activities and beliefs. However, he tends to treat Ninomiya as part of an apparently timeless tradition found in the Tokugawa period. Yasumaru Yoshio, one of the founding figures in the "People's History" movement in Japan, however, argues that Bellah's interpretation is ahistorical and that Ninomiya should be properly situated in the decades immediately preceding the Meiji Restoration.

27. Capra's film was not released until August 9, 1945 and was not in circulation for long because the war ended the following week. However, it is regarded as a classic World War II film. John Dower has some interesting things to say about this film in his *War Without Mercy: Race and Power in the Pacific* (New York: Pantheon Books, 1986), esp. 18-23.

Speaking of the Opposition

by William Hohri

This essays discusses two parts of the opposition to the draft resistance movement: first, the organized and vocal opposition by the Japanese American Citizens League (JACL), and second, the need for the Nisei to prove their loyalty to a suspicious and hostile America (the two are interdependent).

LOYALTY AND THE JAPANESE AMERICAN CITIZENS LEAGUE

The Japanese American Citizens League was formed in two stages. An informal gathering of antecedent organizations, including the American Loyalty League, and Seattle Progressive Citizens League, was convened in San Francisco in April 1929. Note that neither of these predecessor groups used "Japanese" in its name. Bill Hosokawa, in his book, *JACL in Quest of Justice*, reports that at this meeting, "The only point to stir discussion was the proposed name of the organization. Some delegate, particulary from areas where American Loyalty League sentiment was strong objected to the word 'Japanese' in the name, contending it carried a connotation of split loyalty."[1] Loyalty to the United States and pride in U.S. citizenship would become ingredients of the new League. The new organization agreed to call itself the "Japanese-American Citizens League," with a hyphen between "Japanese" and "American."

In August 1930, founding convention met and voted to delete this hyphen. The hyphen's removal was intended to stress "American" by making "Japanese" an adjective that modified "American." "Japanese American" was to name only U.S. citizens of Japanese ancestry. This usage was consistent with the League's rule that excluded from its membership Japanese-Americans who were not U.S. citizens.[2] Sadly, while the League was formed to protect the civil rights of a minority, this rule excluded Japanese-Americans who were born in Japan and came to America as children with their parents and were peers to the League's members. The rule also excluded immigrants who *chose* America as their home—the "Pilgrims" from Asia. At its founding, the League's sense of loyalty was discriminatory and divisive.

The League's emphasis on loyalty and citizenship also did not well serve the larger Japanese American community when war erupted between the U.S. and Japan in 1941. Japanese-Americans served as scapegoats for the devastating defeat America suffered when the Japanese Imperial Navy attacked the U.S. Pacific Fleet as Pearl Harbor. That attack gained advantage by its complete surprise coupled with the series of mistakes by the U.S. military leadership.[3] In testimony given in November 1981 before the Commission on Wartime Relocation and Internment of Civilians, the wartime Assistant Secretary of War, John J. McCloy, who was given to switching clauses in mid-sentence, said of his key role in the exclusion and detention program, "I don't think the Japanese population was unduly subjugated, considering the exigencies to which—the amount it did share in the way of retribution for the attack that was made on Pearl Harbor." He was challenged by Commissioner Judge Marutani. Marutani asked the court reporter to read back McCloy's testimony. The court reporter, perhaps sensing the dramatic moment, instead fiddled with the tape recorder and played back the audio for all to rehear: ". . . the amount it did share in the way of retribution for Pearl Harbor." McCloy was quick to change "retribution" to "consequences." But he did not withdraw his judgement. Japanese-Americans did suffer the consequences of the attack by their ethnic kin on Pearl Harbor. McCloy admitted and confirmed the war's racial dimension. He was probably speaking for most Americans.[4] McCloy, we should note, used "Japanese" to name Japanese-Americans, and in my judgment, he probably did mean retribution.

By February 15, 1942, 3,113 Japanese-American resident aliens had been rounded up as suspect enemy aliens. Instead of rushing to the their defense, members of the League participated in the roundup.[5] They were affirming their citizenship by proving their loyalty to the United States.

The League also opposed the constitutional test cases. On April 7, 1942, ten days after Minoru Yasui challenged the constitutionality of the curfew orders that descended on Japanese-American communities on the West Coast, the League issued *Bulletin # 142*, which stated, "**National Headquarters is unalterably opposed to test cases to determine the constitutionality of military regulations at this time.** We have reached this decision unanimously after examining all the facts in light of our national policy of: 'the greatest good for the greatest number.'"[6] The opposition is emphatic and categorical. Note, too, that the policy is an odd one for a minority group. It seems to rationalize invidious discrimination against minorities. For such discrimination does favor the greatest number. It does make sense if the League, hearing the message of acculturation, believed its mission was to join and become part of the majority. Fortunately, other individuals were undeterred by this unalterable opposition. Gordon Hirabayashi, Fred Korematsu, and Mitsuye Endo followed Yasui with their test cases that went to the U.S. Supreme Court. And altered the course of history.[7]

On November 17, 1942, after all ten permanent detention camps had been built and filled, the League gathered in Salt Lake City, Utah in a national conference of League representatives from the tem camps, plus several persons from what I call "free America."[8] During this week- long meeting, the League enacted a resolution to seek reinstatement of the Selective Service for Japanese-Americans, including those interned. Selective Service had been discontinued for Japanese-Americans on June 17, 1942. But instead of reinstating military conscription, on January 28, 1943 the War Department announced the formation of an all-volunteer and segregated combat team for Japanese-Americans. The League had opposed volunteering for military service; it wanted U.S. citizens of Japanese ancestry to be treated like other U.S. citizens and be subject to conscription. Curiously, the League seemed not to notice that exclusion and detention were not part of normal life in America. Nevertheless, as soon as the January announcement was made, the League reversed itself and supported volunteering.

When Selective Service for Japanese-Americans was finally reinstated on January 14, 1944, the League returned to its staunch support for conscription. Within weeks, it was faced with a public relations nightmare: organized draft resistance emerged in the camp at Heart Mountain, Wyoming. On February 24, a mimeographed flyer was distributed by the Heart Mountain Fair Play Committee. The flyer stated that,

> The Fair Play Committee was organized for the purpose of opposing all unfair practices that violate Constitutional rights . . . and *occur* within our present concentration camp, state, territory, or Union. It has come out strongly in recent weeks in regards to the discrimination features of the new selective service program as it applies to Japanese Americans . . . .[9]

In the following month, sixty-three men refused to report for their pre-induction physical examinations and were arrested. The rationale for this resistance was spelled out in a long statement issued by members of the Fair Play Committee on March 4, which said in part: "we feel that the present program of drafting us from this concentration camp is unjust, unconstitutional, and against all principles of civilized usage."[10]

The League responded with a volley in its weekly newspaper, the *Pacific Citizen*. On March 25, 1944, Saburo Kido, the League's president, and an attorney wrote:

> Any person who incites or encourages any citizen to evade the draft is assuming a grave responsibility. It is needless to say the offense constitutes sedition. One must remember theat one of the most serious offenses a person can commit is to become a "draft dodger." A nation will not easily forgive or quickly forget anyone who refuses to

A Matter of Conscience

serve when his country calls in a national emergency. It will be a tragic mistake to have young men who are 18 or thereabouts to become
stigmatized as a "draft dodger" for the rest of their lives.[11]

"Sedition" is a short step away from "treason." It is a serious exaggeration by
Mr. Kido. The Fair Play Committee position affirmed the primacy of the U.S.
Constitution, the same Constitution that public office holders, from the president on down, are sworn to uphold and which lies at the heart of American
democracy. As for being stigmatized for a lifetime, three years later, on
December 23, 1947 President Truman pardoned 1,523 draft resisters, including 282 Japanese-Americans.

Likewise, "draft dodger" is inappropriate. It is not the same as "draft
resister." A draft dodger escapes conscription by evading the law, by, for
example, leaving the country and the reach of the law. A draft resister challenges conscription by engaging the law and accepting the consequences.
These young men were engaging, not evading, the law and also trying to
challenge the constitutionality of their detention. Moreover, given the circumstances, leaving the camps was impossible, to say nothing of leaving the
country. So draft dodging was not an option.[12]

A week later, on April 1, Bill Hosokawa, *Pacific Citizen* columnist,
wrote:

> At first glance it would seem that the committees that have sprung
> up in the various relocation centers are all motivated by a sincere
> desire to seek a showdown, once and for all, as to the legal status of
> the nisei. Undoubtedly many of the individuals behind these com-
> mittees are sincere, and their loyalty is beyond question. But there are
> others who can be identified only as periodical patriots, individuals
> who protest their Americanism and demand their rights as citizens
> only when they are confronted with the task of fulfilling the respon-
> sibilities of that citizenship.[13]

The way this statement opposes the demand for rights with the responsibilities of citizenship is interesting. I am inclined to pair the two, not oppose
them. When is there a more critical time to demand one's rights than when
those rights are being violated? Conscription was adding insult to the injury
of unlawful detention and of being denied what the preamble to the
Constitution calls, "the Blessings of Liberty."

Still another week later on April 8, Larry Tajiri, editor of the *Pacific
Citizen*, wrote:

> This act of defiance by 41 young men is the result of a combination of

42

circumstances, misguided leadership and information, and strong pressures and influences. Its effect may be that of negating the victory of loyal Japanese Americans in winning the reinstitution of selective service, and may retard the eventual full restoration to Japanese Americans of the privileges of freedom which are the birthright of every American. By their action these men, and those who prompted their action, have injured the cause of loyal Japanese everywhere.[14]

The expression, "the victory of loyal Japanese Americans in winning the reinstitution of selective service," is a myth that endures. There was a fairly close coincidence between the week-long conference at Salt Lake City, which occurred on November 17, 1942, and deliberation within the War Department to reinstate the draft. A memorandum of the same date was drafted by Colonel M. W. Pettigrew to Assistant Secretary of War John McCloy, which argued in favor of reinstating the draft. However, the motion to support this reinstatement at the conference occurred at least three days later.[15] So the reinstatement was initiated with the War Department independently of the League. Of course, there is serious doubt whether any civilian organization, much less one that was Japanese-American, could influence a military decision within the U.S. War Department.

The position of the League should be clear, but it did not cover the matter of how Japanese-Americans felt, and continue to feel, about proving their loyalty. One June 29, 2001, there was a formal opening in Washington, just north of the Capitol, of "The Japanese American Memorial to Patriotism During World War II." More than thirteen million dollars was raised from around twenty thousand individuals, mainly Nisei, to erect this memorial, which is a monument to the demonstration of loyalty of Japanese-Americans through military service during the war. These numbers clearly indicate where the sentiments of most Japanese-Americans reside.

At best, it seems, many would record resistance as a footnote, as a minor strain of counterpoint to the heroic theme of the exploits and sacrifices of the Nisei soldiers of the 100th Infantry Battalion and the 442nd Regimental Combat Team, many of whom volunteered for military service in order to prove their loyalty to the United States. Few doubt that the heroics of the all-Nisei Combat Team won more than military victories; they won the public relations battle as well.

For U.S. citizens of Japanese descent, America was their homeland. If America had known them, America would have known their culture and loyalties. But America did not know them, and consequently it segregated them with restrictive housing covenants, discrimination in hiring practices, and the racially motivated degradation of anti-miscegenation laws. Many of the majority whose hearts were warmed by their heroics also applauded the program of exclusion and detention.

However, the proof of loyalty through volunteering for military service is, in part, an illusion. The 100th Battalion was formed in June of 1942, months before the 442nd Regimental Combat Team came into being as an all-volunteer unit. The 100th was largely composed of draftees from Hawaii. Most of the Nisei soldiers from the camps were conscripts; of the 3,600 inducted, only 805 were volunteers.[16]

A widely held belief by many is that thousands volunteered from the camps in spite of their treatment. Actually, only 1,208 volunteered from a population of 120,000, or one per cent. In Hawaii, around 10,000 volunteered from a population of 160,000, more than six per cent. Thus, as a percentage, six times as many persons of Japanese ancestry volunteered from Hawaii as from the camps. So, instead of being a demonstration of loyalty, this demonstrates the reluctance of Nisei to volunteer while interned.

Also, if we compare draft resistance as a percentage of the population, thirty times as many Nisei were convicted of violating the draft from the camps as from Hawaii. Of the 282 Nisei pardoned, eleven were from Hawaii. The camps not only failed to produce volunteers, they produced dramatic opposition to military service.

Finally, the proof of loyalty through military service turns lame when we realize that hundreds of Japanese-Americans who served in combat in the U.S. Army during the First World War, were excluded and detained along with the rest. Their military service proved nothing.

Yet a loyalty oath was established as, in official jargon, a "pre-clearance" requirement for all draft-age Japanese-American males to determine their eligibility for Selective Service.[17] These men filled out form DSS 304A, with its ethnic "Statement of United States Citizenship of Japanese Ancestry."[18]

The loyalty oath is contained in the form's final questions, 27 and 28. Question 27 asks, "Are you willing to serve in the armed forces of the United States on combat duty, wherever ordered?" In affirming their loyalty here, Japanese-Americans are thereby denied the right to alternative services as conscientious objectors in Civilian Public Service camps or as noncombatants in the armed forces. It was combat duty or disloyalty. In addition, some respondents wondered whether "wherever ordered" implied one was volunteering for hazardous duty without limitations.[19]

Question 28 asks, "Will you swear unqualified allegiance to the United States of America and faithfully defend the United Sates from any or all attack by foreign or domestic forces, and forswear any form of allegiance or obedience to the Japanese emperor, or any other foreign government, power, or organization?" "Unqualified allegiance" is, ironically, comparable to the Japanese military's commitment of absolute obedience to the Emperor that served as rationale for, among other things, the commission of atrocities.[20] The term "forswear" in its first meaning of "renounce" or "give up" led many to be properly suspicious of the oath: were they being trapped into affirming the prior existence of allegiance or obedience to the Japanese emperor?

"Unqualified allegiance" has other implications. Question 28 was also used on the remaining Jpanese-American internee population to determine whether an internee was disloyal and should be segregated into a permanent detention camp apart from the rest of the internee population. In order to be released, Japanese-Americans had to affirm their unqualified allegiance. Some feared that by affirming this, one thereby said, "All is forgiven. Whatever you, the government, has done or will do to me is acceptable, including your unconstitutional exclusion and detention of me." One thereby absolved the government of all wrongdoing.

Much of the excess of the loyalty questionnaire may be understood when we realize that it was crafted to serve the army. Selective Service for Japanese-Americans had been suspended on June 17, 1942.[21] In late 1942, the army reconsidered reinstating Selective Service; it needed the division it could field with Japanese-American volunteers and conscripts. In his November 17, 1942 memo, as revised November 21, 1942, to Assistant Secretary of War John J. McCloy, Colonel M. W. Pettigrew provided statistics and wrote: "Summarized briefly, the figures indicate that resumption of conscription alone should produce a total of an additional 16,800 which, with the approximately 4,000 now in service[,] (after deducting for special language use) would be ample to provide and sustain a division . . . ."[22]

These figures, we should note, include Hawaii and "free America," as well as the camps. The projection was fairly accurate. According to the War Department, 25,778 Japanese-Americans were inducted into the Armed Forces between November 1940 and December 1945.[23]

Two purposes were served by the questionnaire. On the one hand, the army, obviously, did not want to induct men who were disloyal to America. On the other hand, it did not want disloyals to dissuade others from enlisting. This dissuasion could be blocked by segregation, according to the reasoning in a November 17, 1942 memo from within the War Department, form Chief Economist Calvert L. Dedrick to Assistant Secretary of War McCloy and Colonel Karl R. Bendetsen:

> The segregation of at least the anti-American elements must be a first step for any volunteer recruiting. Not only must the Nisei be relieved from jibes and threats of the Kibei and pro-Japanese Issei, but the prospective volunteers must given the assurance that these groups will not run the Centers and dominate their wives, children, and parents during their absence.[24]

A Matter of Conscience

Dedrick confines his proposal to volunteers. The program to segregate began in 1943, the year of the War Department's effort to recruit volunteers. Conscription began in 1944. The military's use of the loyalty questionnaire continued through 1945.

In summation, the decision to reinstate military service for Japanese-Americans was military; it came from the War Department. It was not a victory by loyal Japanese Americans. It was done to add a division to our armed forces, not as a test of loyalty for inmates of the ten detention camps.

What was at stake here was not the demonstration of Japanese American loyalty. The conscription of the inmates from the ten internment camps was a serious, in-the-gut challenge to the viability and applicability of the Constitution to all Americans in time of war. Courts were still operating and laws still had to be obeyed. The Selective Service and Training Act of 1940 explicitly forbade the registration of inmates of penitentiaries or similar institutions to be registered for the draft. It is obvious, even without knowing what the Act states, that a person who was serving, say, a ten-year prison term could not escape imprisonment by volunteering or simply being conscripted for military service. It is also clear that public proclamation WD 1 makes the camps institutions comparable to penitentiaries. The term "War Relocation Authority" and "War Relocation Center" and "evacuation" are euphemisms that only tried to hide the reality of imprisonment, even though we continue to use these terms. Those interned were not free to leave. Their living quarters were Spartan. Their toilet facilities and mess halls were communal. Family life dissolved. The Blessings of Liberty were no longer secured. Their constitutional rights had been grossly abused. The call for military service, for a demonstration of patriotism rang hollow.

I am not scholarly enough to know who first said that the genius of democracy lies in its proximity to our human instinct for freedom. It was Fred Korematsu's instinct for freedom that initiated his resistance, and his resistance led, of course, to the landmark decision—and mistake—by our Supreme Court. The same, I believe, can be said for the draft resisters. Liberty is a necessary precondition for military service. One fights for the Blessings of Liberty. While the challenges by the resisters failed to get into the Supreme Court, it has been installed in our history as a lesson in courage to our progeny. It is courage as I extrapolate from Confucius's definition of cowardice: "To see what is right and not to do it is cowardice."[25] The courage of the resisters was to see what was right, and to do it.

Notes

1.Bill Hosokawa, *JACL in Quest of Justice* (New York: William Morrow and Company, Inc., 1982).

2.Ibid. In reaction, I hyphenate "Japanese-American" in order to include permanent residents who were not citizens.

3.Gordon W. Prange, *At Dawn We Slept: The Untold Story of Pearl Harbor* (New York: McGraw Hill Book Company, 1981).

4.McCloy was more unrepentant than most. In the same colloquy, he declined to forgo mass exclusion and detention as a means of ensuring our nation's internal security. William Minoru Hohri, *Repairing America: An Account of the Movement for Japanese-American Redress* (Pullman: Washington State University Press, 1988), 162-63.

5.For example, I refer the reader to "The Lim Report," available on the internet at *resisters.com* and *javoice.com*.

6.The Japanese American Citizens League Archives.

7.The Supreme Court's decision in the *Korematsu* case set a very high bar for racial discrimination, while its nearly concurrent decision on *Endo* persuaded the government to end mass exclusion and detention.

8.Hosokawa, *JACL in Quest of Justice*, 196-97.

9.Hohri, *Repairing America*, 13.

10.Fair Play Steering Committee, "Fair Play Committee Bulletin # 3, March 4, 1944.

11.Saburo Kido, *Pacific Citizen*, March 25, 1944.

12.There was another way of avoiding the draft that I discovered when I turned 18 in 1945. I answered no to the loyalty questions and was classified IV-C, as an alien unsuited for military service and not drafted. Until the end of 1945, Nisei males had to answer the loyalty questionnaire even while living in what I call "free America." I answered not to 27 because I wished to serve in a non-combatant capacity. I answered no to 28 because I believed that no government deserves one's unqualified allegiance, especially not the United States of America after what it had done to me. But I was complying with the draft, not dodging it and not resisting it.

13.Hosokawa, *Pacific Citizen*, April 1, 1944.

14.Larry Tajiri, *Pacific Citizen*, April 8, 1944.

15.Hosokawa, *JACL in Quest of Justice*, 197.

16.*The Evacuated People*, Table 49.

17.*Selective Service and Victory: The 4th Report of the Director of Selective Service, 1944-1945* (Washington D.C.: U.S. Government Printing Office, 1948). This pre-clearance was abolished on December 27, 1945,18.Selective Service DSS FORM 304A, January 23, 1943.

19.This concern was not farfetched. In April 1944, Mike Masaoka, National Secretary for the Japanese American Citizens League, issued his "Final Report" in which he reveals the League's discussion with "a high military official" on forming an all-volunteer suicide battalion, "which would go anywhere to spearhead the most dangerous missions." This proposal is said to have been made and rebuffed by military officers before the exclusion and detention of Japanese-Americans. See Masaoka, "Final Report."

20.Haruko Taya Cook and Theodore F. Cook, *Japan at War: An Oral History* (New York: The New Press, 1992).

21.Earlier, on March 30, 1942, the War Department ordered the suspension of induction. Both dates are from *Personal Justice Denied: Report of the Commission on Wartime Relocation and Internment of Civilians* (Washington D.C.: U.S. Government Printing Office, 1983), 187.

22.National Archives and Records Administration, Washington D.C., Record Group 107.

23.*The Evacuated People*, Table 49.

24.Memo, Calvert L. Dedrick, Chief Economist, War Department, to John J. McCloy and Colonel Karl R. Bendetsen, 111742, National Archives, Record Group 107.

25.*Analects*, 2:24.

PART II

THE RESISTERS

Protest and Resistance: An American Tradition

by Frank S. Emi

On November 17, 1942, after all ten permanent detention camps had been built and filled, the Japanese American Citizen League (JACL) passed a resolution to seek reinstatement of Selective Service for Japanese Americans, including those interned in concentration camps. Selective Service had been discontinued for all Nisei on June 17, 1942, after they were reclassified 4-C (an alien ineligible for military duty). But instead of re-instituting the draft, the War Department, on January 28, 1943, announced the formation of an all volunteer, segregated combat team for Japanese Americans. The JACL had opposed volunteering for military service; it wanted U.S. citizens of Japanese ancestry to be treated normally, like other American citizens, and be subjected to the draft. The JACL, in its continued collaboration with the federal government, apparently felt that the exclusion and detention of Japanese Americans was part of normal life in America. Nevertheless, it reversed its stance and supported volunteering for military service.

The Army had expected thousands to volunteer from the camps because of the overwhelming response from Japanese Americans in Hawaii. However, in Hawaii there had been no wholesale exclusion or detention. Japanese Americans living in that territory still had their freedom; therefore, they were more eager and willing to volunteer for service in the segregated army unit. Selective Service was reinstated for all Japanese Americans, including inmates of the camps, on January 14, 1944.

Resistance to military service by an incarcerated people was not far beneath the surface. Insult was added to injury when the so-called "Loyalty Questionnaire" was imposed on the internees confined in the camps. The two controversial questions were number 27 and number 28, number 27 asked, "Are you willing to serve in the Armed Forces of the United States on combat duty, wherever ordered?" If a Nisei answered "Yes," the implication was that he would volunteer for the army because the questionnaire had the Selective Service logo on top of the sheet and a box with the words, "Local Board Date Stamp With Code." On question 28, the second part read, "and forswear any form of allegiance or obedience to the Japanese Emperor or any other foreign government or organization." If a Nisei answered, "Yes," he or she would be admitting a previous allegiance to the Japanese Emperor, which was ridiculous. If an Issei, a Japanese immigrant, answered "Yes," he or she

51

would become a stateless person because immigration laws during that time prohibited the Issei from becoming citizens of this country.

As an internee at Heart Mountain, the more I studied the two questions, the more disgusted I became. The questions were ambiguous, ill advised, and demeaning to me. I finally came up with my response to the two questions. I wrote in, "Under the present conditions and circumstances, I cannot answer these questions." After all, we were not free agents. We were under duress, confined in concentration camps.

My first act of resistance began innocently enough. I felt that some inmates might be in a quandary as how to answer those questions, so with the help of my younger brother, Art, we hand printed copies of my answers to the two questions on sheets of paper and posted them on mess hall doors, and other public places, with a notation that these were suggested answers to the two controversial questions.

The Fair Play Committee (FPC), as an organization, was formed in the spring of 1943, almost one year before the military draft was implemented in the camps. A public meeting was held in one of the mess halls at which the associate editor of the *Heart Mountain Sentinel*, the camp newspaper, was the speaker. His name was Nobu Kawai, a past president of the Pasadena JACL. He was urging the internees to cooperate with the government and answer "Yes" to the two controversial questions. This was the same Nobu Kawai who, as a chapter president of the JACL, wrote on February 28, 1942, "We can turn the tragedy of the evacuation into a display of loyalty."[1] I had a long acrimonious debate with him via the camp newspaper. The text of this heated discussion is included in William Hohri's book, *Resistance: Challenging America's Wartime Internment of Japanese-Americans*.

After Nobu Kawai finished speaking and sat down, an older Nisei man stood up and identified himself as Kiyoshi Okamoto, a forty-ish soil testing engineer from Hawaii. Okamoto called himself the "Fair Play Committee of One." He was a subscriber to the *Open Forum*, an American Civil Liberties Publication, so he might have been a member of the American Civil Liberties Union (ACLU). He spoke about the Constitution and the Bill of Rights, and how the government had trampled on our constitutional rights. Okamoto told us that as American citizens we should not follow a policy of appeasement, but stand up for our rights. He was an inspiration to some of us who felt very strongly about the government's arbitrary actions.

After the public meeting ended, a few of us met with Okamoto and had a long discussion. We were impressed with his knowledge of the law and the Constitution. A few days later, the Fair Play Committee of one became the Heart Mountain Fair Play Committee, an organization of many who were committed to fight for civil rights. We formed a steering committee with Okamoto serving as chairman. The rest of the committee was made up of individuals who had met with Okamoto following the Nobu Kawai mess hall meeting, and others who had attended subsequent meetings. We met intermittently to discuss ways of improving the quality of life in camp, such as obtaining better food, stopping abuses by the internal police, and communicating with outside sources. While we discussed internal problems, Okamoto corresponded with the ACLU, reviewing the government's violations of our various constitutional rights, and discussed those violations with the committee.

When news that the draft was going to be instituted in the detention centers reached the camps, the shock was understandably great. We had been forcibly uprooted from our homes and businesses (our life savings lost), and put into desolate areas of the country bounded with barbed wire fences and watch towers, and with our families still imprisoned with no certain future, the government was going to draft the young men from the camps into a segregated combat unit on the same basis as it conscripted free men living in a free America. It was unbelievable! While the JACL lobbied for the reinstatement of the draft in November of 1942, and then applauded its reinstatement, no one I knew at Heart Mountain joined in the applause. The draft became the main topic of contention. Men who were affected complained bitterly about the injustice of the government conscripting internees.

The Fair Play Committee took up the draft issue and organized public meetings to discuss its ramifications. In the beginning, the administration gave us permits to exercise our right to free speech and assembly, but once they got wind of the topic under discussion, they ceased the further issuing of permits. However, we continued to hold public meetings and exercised our First Amendment rights without interference from the administration. We held nightly meetings in various blocks to standing-room-only crowds. The imposition of the military draft within the interment camp was of great concern to all Heart Mountain residents.

The steering committee drafted bulletins outlining what we were going to discuss, and circulated them before each meeting. Our two main speakers were Kiyoshi Okamoto and Paul Nakadate. Okamoto was blunt in his speech, rather bombastic, and sometimes used "salty expressions." Paul Nakadate, on the other hand, was a polished and smooth speaker. Guntaro Kubota, an Issei, translated the English text of the meetings into Japanese for the Issei parents of the young men.

The audience largely shared the sentiments of the Fair Play Committee. They agreed with our stand on Selective Service, namely that drafting Nisei from the concentration camps was morally wrong and legally indefensible, and furthermore, that the government should first restore to all internees, their freedom and civil rights, and compensate them for their economic pauperization. Only then, they felt, should the Nisei be subjected to the same Selective Service requirements as other, but *free*, Americans. The FPC acquired approximately 200 dues-paying members over the course of our campaign from audiences that numbered nearly 400.

It was during this period, actually on March 29, 1944, that Minoru Tamesa and I attempted to walk out of the camp through the front gate to see if we had freedom of egress or ingress. We were stopped by the armed military policeman at the gate and ordered to turn back. When we tried to explain that we were American citizens who had not committed any crime and were imprisoned illegally, and that we were going out to a nearby town to do some shopping, the guard's reply was, "If you want to get shot, go ahead." We knew he was not kidding because some internees at other camps had been shot and killed by the military police. Since we saw no point in getting ourselves shot, we submitted to being arrested, at which point we were lodged in the military brig where, at least, we enjoyed good food for a change.

Several days later we were summoned to the Heart Mountain Project Director's office for a hearing on our attempt to walk out of the camp. We were surprised to see a large group of official looking men sitting in a semi-circle behind Director Guy Robertson's desk. There was the project attorney, the Chief of Internal Security, a representative of the Heart Mountain Military Police, and a second Internal Security officer. Nobu Kawai of the *Heart Mountain Sentinel* was also sitting next to the military police officer, presumably to witness the proceedings. A friend of Tamesa's was also there as a witness for us. The hearing went on for approximately two hours, but the charges against us were dismissed after we agreed not to try walking out of the camp again. We had made our point that there was no freedom of movement in or out of the relocation centers, which we felt might be of some value should we be involved in any litigation in the future.

The first few meetings and the bulletins we circulated were primarily informational. The third and final bulletin circulated was to be a challenge, a call to action. Since we were an organization committed to fight for civil rights, some of us wanted the FPC to take a more active stand on the draft issue. We felt that we had to challenge the legality of conscripting inmates held in concentration camps. After a heated discussion in the steering committee, we drafted our third and final bulletin. That bulletin was our manifesto on the military draft.

We presented our resolution, the final paragraph of the manifesto, at our next public meeting, to a standing-room-only crowd of approximately 400. About one-half of those in attendance were dues-paying members of the FPC. The resolution we presented was unanimously approved. But as things played out, not all of those who supported the resolution (including some FPC members) resisted the draft. However, we held no ill will toward the non-resisters.

Protest and Resistance: An American Tradition

The following are excerpts from that fateful, final bulletin, which expressed our innermost desire for justice. Eventually the document was used in evidence against the seven most visible leaders of the FPC when they were indicted on a charges of conspiracy to violate the Selective Service Act, and counseling others to resist the draft. Of the seven leaders, only three men were eligible for the draft. Okamoto was past the draft age, Kubota was also overage, and a non-citizen as well. Nakadate and I had families with children. The Army was not drafting men with children at that time. The common bond that brought us altogether was the feeling that we had been betrayed by our own government. We felt anger and frustration at the unjust and unconstitutional acts perpetrated against us.

Excerpts From The Bulletin Of March 4, 1944:

We, the Nisei, have been complacent and too inarticulate to the unconstitutional acts that we were subjected to. If ever there was time or cause for decisive action, IT IS NOW!! We, the members of the FPC, are not afraid to go to war. We are not afraid to risk our lives for our country. We would gladly sacrifice our lives to protect and uphold the principles and ideals of our country as set forth in the Constitution and Bill of Rights, for on its inviolability depends the freedom, liberty, justice, and protection of all people, including Japanese Americans and all other minority groups. But, have we been given such freedom, such liberty, such justice, such protection? No!! Without any hearings, without due process of law as guaranteed by the Constitution and Bill of Rights, without any charges filed against us, one hundred and ten thousand innocent people were kicked out of their homes, literally uprooted from where they have lived for the greater part of their lives, and herded like dangerous criminals into concentration camps with barb wire fence and military police guarding it, and then, without rectification of the injustices committed against us nor without restoration of our rights as guaranteed by the Constitution, we are ordered to join the army thru discriminatory procedures into a segregated combat unit. Is that the American way? NO! The FPC believes that unless such actions are opposed NOW, and steps taken to remedy such injustices and discriminations IMMEDIATELY, the future of all minorities and the future of this democratic nation is in danger.

Thus the members of the FPC unanimously decided at their last open meeting that until we are restored all our rights, all discriminatory features of the Selective Service abolished, and measures are taken to remedy the past injustices thru Judicial pronouncement or Congressional Act, we feel that the present program of drafting us from this concentration camp is unjust, unconstitutional, and against all principles of civilized usage, therefore, WE MEMBERS OF THE FAIR PLAY COMMITTEE HEREBY REFUSE TO GO TO THE PHYS-ICAL EXAMINATION OR TO THE INDUCTION, IF AND WHEN CALLED, IN ORDER TO CONTEST THE ISSUE.[2]

In March 1944, sixty-three male internees at heart Mountain refused to take their physical examinations and resisted the draft. They were arrested and incarcerated in the jail at Cheyenne, Wyoming, and other jails in nearby towns. The Fair Play Committee sought help from the American Civil Liberties Union, but ACLU director, Roger Baldwin, in his letter of April 6, 1944 to Kiyoshi Okamoto advised;

1. The men who have refused to accept military draft are within their rights, but they of course must take the consequences. They doubt-less have a strong moral case, but no legal case at all.

2. Men who counsel others to resist military service are not within their rights and must expect severe treatment, whatever justification they feel.[3]

We did not know that from May through June of 1942, the board of the ACLU, voting by mail, supported President Roosevelt's Executive Order 9066 and the government's right during wartime.

If the ACLU supported E. O. 9066, it could hardly have agreed with the arguments of the Fair Play Committee and the Heart Mountain draft resisters. However, history would prove Baldwin wrong on both points.

During the trial of the sixty-three resisters, the Cheyenne *Wyoming Eagle* quoted a leading Wyoming newsman as saying "He'd be damned if he would serve in the army if he were treated like the evacuees." The War Relocation Authority (WRA) had to send a public relations man to Cheyenne to convince the newspapermen that the resisters were not representative of the entire population at Heart Mountain. The newsmen had been surprising-ly sympathetic to the resisters.

The trial of the sixty-three began on June 12, 1944 and ended on June 20 with their conviction, and their sentencing to three-year prison terms in a federal penitentiary. They were denied parole at the request of Dillon Myer, Director of the WRA. Later, an additional twenty-two men from Heart Mountain resisted, were convicted, and sent to prison, bringing the total number of Heart Mountain draft resisters to eighty-five. It is important to note that among the resisters were men with physical disabilities, which would have prevented them from passing a physical and qualifying for induction into the army. But they stood on principle and refused to accede to the government's demands, thus casting doubt on the those naysayers who called them cowards and draft-dodgers.

During that same time period, the leadership of the Fair Play Committee was being attacked in the *Heart Mountain Sentinel* and the *Pacific Citizen* (the JACL newspaper). Their malicious, virulent editorials were disgusting. They called us "dim-witted cowards," "provocateurs," and said we should be charged with sedition. The *Pacific Citizen* made a similar attack on James Omura, the English language editor of the *Rocky Shimpo*, a Japanese American newspaper based in Denver, Colorado. The FBI was not far behind.

Approximately one month after the sixty-three draft resisters were convicted, the FBI arrested five of the most visible leaders of the Fair Play Committee still residing in the camps. In addition, the FBI brought two of the resisters (also leaders of the Fair Play Committee) who were imprisoned and serving three sentences at Fort Leavenworth Federal Penitentiary back to Cheyenne for trial. The FBI also arrested newspaper editor James Omura. On July 21, 1944, eight men, including myself, were charged with conspiracy to violate the Selective Service Act, and with counseling others to resist the draft. We were held in the dark, gloomy jail in Cheyenne for several weeks. Then some of us were transferred to the much nicer jail in Laramie, Wyoming (of course no jail is nice).

The inclusion of Omura in our group was somewhat of a surprise to us. We had never met the man, and none of us had even spoken to him over the telephone. The only connection we had with Omura was through the press releases concerning our activities in camp, which I had been sending to him at *Rocky Shimpo*, as well as to several other newspapers. At times Omura had written editorials dealing with our efforts to challenge the constitutionality of detention. Of course, Omura believed that comments made in his editorials were protected within a newspaper's right to free speech.

Our trial began on October 23, 1944, in the Federal District Court in Cheyenne. We had retained A. L. Wirin, a famous Constitutional lawyer for the Los Angeles branch of the ACLU. However, since the ACLU did not support us, Wirin was working as a private attorney. Since James Omura was not a member of the Fair Play Committee, he retained a separate attorney. Omura's lawyer requested, and received a separate trial for his client.

We opted for a jury trial. The original Heart Mountain sixty-three did not request a jury trial, but had their case heard by Judge T. Blake Kennedy. Since the newspapermen covering that trial had been so sympathetic to the resister's cause, we felt that we stood a better chance having our case decided by a jury.

A Matter of Conscience

During our trial a surprise witness for the prosecution appeared on the stand. His name was Jack Nishimoto. Nishimoto was a man in his late thirties who had been one of my neighbors at Heart Mountain. We all wondered what he was doing at the trial. It did not take us long to find out. His testimony was directed against me, and most of it consisted of bare-faced lies. I had done some favors for him when I was driving a truck in camp and he had visited with me a few times. I believe to this day that the reason the prosecution brought Nishimoto to testify against me was because a few days prior to my arrest by the FBI, they had interrogated me and the other leaders of the Fair Play Committee, and I had not given them any information. Nishimoto apparently thought he would provide the necessary connection to the conspiracy with his false testimony.

As it turned out, Nishimoto's perjured testimony was of no consequence. He only succeeded in exposing himself as "Inu" or informer. His role was clearly exposed when I obtained a copy of the declassified FBI files, and there it was in black and white. In a report filed by FBI agent Harry W. McMillen, the Heart Mountain Community Analyst, Asael T. Hansen, reports in detail to WRA Director Dillon S. Myer on Nishimoto's attempts to purposely get close to me, by befriending me, visiting me in my quarters, and so on. He then conjured up conversations with me and reported them to the FBI through Hansen. The man's duplicity was unbelievable.

Our trial lasted approximately two weeks, and when our attorney requested that certain instructions be given to the jury, the judge denied most of them. Right then we felt that we were not going to have much of chance in that court. Mr. Wirin had previously told us that our chances at the District Court level were not good, and that we would likely have to appeal the case to a higher court because of the constitutional issue involved.

Several days later the jury reached a verdict. We did not fare any better than the Heart Mountain sixty-three. All seven of us were pronounced "guilty as charged." The judge sentenced Okamoto, Nakadate, Horino, and me, to four years in the Federal Penitentiary at Leavenworth, Kansas. Kubota, Tamesa, and Wakaye, who had been convicted of draft evasion in an earlier trial and were already serving three-year terms, were sentenced to an additional two years for this conviction.

James Omura, the newspaperman whose defense was based on his First Amendment rights of "Freedom of the Press," was acquitted. We were very happy for him, but the trial nearly ruined him financially. He should never have been charged with participating in the conspiracy.

Our next move was to file an appeal to the United States Court of Appeals for the Tenth Circuit. Wirin, our attorney, requested that we be released on bail and returned to the concentration camp pending our appeal. However, Judge Rice refused that request stating that we were agitators and that the camp was better off without us. Rice's decision mirrored that of Dillon Myer in the latter's request that the Justice Department deny parole to the draft resisters form the camps because he felt it would be bad for the moral of other internees still in camp.

Leavenworth was a high security federal prison. Among the inmates were murderers, bank robbers, drug dealers, crooked lawyers, and even some medical doctors who had run afoul of the law. There were three groups of prisoners that I remember quite well. There was one group of about thirty American citizens of German decsent who were members of the German American Bund. They had been court-martialed and sentenced to be executed because, while guarding a prisoner-of-war camp holding captured German soldiers, they had helped some of the prisoners to escape. Their sentences were later commuted to thirty years in prison. Another group consisted of seven German spies who were captured when they were left on shore by a German submarine which had been operating off the East Coast. The strange thing about this group was that there was one man who always walked about six feet behind the others. We asked one of the prisoners why this man seemed to be shunned by the others in the group. We were told that the man trailing the group had been the first fellow ashore but was quickly captured, after which time he ratted on the others, resulting in the capture of all seven. Since that time he had been ostracized by the others in the group. The third group, like the first, was also made up of American soldiers. It consisted of eight Japanese American soldiers who were serving in the army prior to the outbreak of war. After America entered the war, the army stripped them of their weapons and other military equipment, and put the entire group on latrine duty. The soldiers endured this for a time, but then began making repeated requests that they be treated as U. S. soldiers should be treated. When their requests were ignored, the men wrote a petition which they all signed with blood drawn from their fingers. They then went on a hunger strike. That action resulted in the soldiers being court-martialed and sentenced to be executed. That sentence was later commuted to thirty years in prison, and by the time we entered Leavenworth, it had been further reduced to fifteen years. It is my understanding that they were all released from prison when the war ended.

While still awaiting our appeal, prison officials asked us if we would like to participate in "Sports Day," which was held on the athletic field. We had some black belts in the martial art of Judo in our group, so we agreed to participate and to put on a Judo demonstration. We used the denim prison jackets as Judo jackets and the officials put several cotton mattresses together for us to fall on. We choreographed the action so that the smaller men would throw the bigger fellows with spectacular throws. We also demonstrated choking techniques and arm locks. The crowd of inmates sitting on the bleachers gave us a great ovation. This was their first look at the martial arts and they were very impressed. We also felt that this was why we were not bothered by other prisoners. In fact, when the other prisoners learned the details of our case, they were very sympathetic toward us. The prison officials also seemed to be very understanding of the stand taken by the resisters.

The appellate court was taking longer than we had anticipated. A decision was not rendered until the war in the Pacific had ended. On December 16, 1945, the U. S. Court of Appeals in Denver reversed the conviction of all seven of us. After serving nearly one-half of our three year prison sentence, we had finally won our battle. In speaking for the majority, Judge Bratton quoted from the Supreme Court decision in *Keegan vs. The United States,* reached earlier in 1945, which said, "one with innocent motives, who honestly believes a law is unconstitutional and, therefore, not obligatory, may well counsel that the law shall not be obeyed."

We proved Roger Baldwin wrong on his second point. This was only one of two cases won by Nisei in the appellate courts at the time.

As for the resisters, their outcomes were mixed. On identical draft resistance charges, decisions ranged from complete dismissal of charges, to sentences of a one cent fine and no jail time, up to three to four-year prison terms. Twenty-seven resisters from the Tule Lake camp in California were tried before Judge Louis A Goodman. Judge Goodman dismissed the charges against the twenty-seven with this statement: "It is shocking to the conscience that an American citizen be confined on the ground of disloyalty and then, while so under duress and restraint, be compelled to serve in the armed forces, or be prosecuted for not yielding to such compulsion."[4]
Judge Goodman thereby disproved Roger Baldwin's first point.

The varied sentences meted out by the judges for the very same infraction of the law seemed to reflect the sense of justice and fairness of each judge hearing the case. The scales of justice were certainly unbalanced.

The records of Nisei draft resisters were cleared through a Presidential Pardon signed by Harry S. Truman following the war, and their fight for principle was vindicated. The government acknowledged in the wording of the pardon that the resisters had legitimate reasons for their actions. The leaders of the Fair Play Committee had been challenged and charged in the courts, and successfully rebuffed the charges.

The Constitution and Bill of Rights is alive and well. It is the men and women who interpret it that sometimes stumble and lose sight of its ideals and principles.

[Editor's] Notes

1.William Minoru Hohri, *Resistance: Challenging America's Wartime Internment of*

Japanese-Americans (Lomita, CA:, the Epistolarian, 2001), 119-128.

2.Hohri, *Resistance*, 103-05.

3.Hohri, *Resistance*, 106.

4.Eric L. Muller, *Free to Die for Their Country: The Story of the Japanese American Draft Resisters in World War II* (Chicago: The University of Chicago Press, 2001), 143.

Jack Tono: The Journey of a "Light-footed Felon"

by Mike Mackey

On Monday, June 12, 1944, Jack Tono, along with sixty-two other men from the Heart Mountain Relocation Center, were brought together in a Cheyenne, Wyoming courtroom. The Heart Mountain Sixty-three were charged, in what became the largest mass trial in Wyoming's history, with the willful violation of Section 311, Title 50, U.S.C.A. Selective Service and Training Act of 1940. The young men were draft resisters who had failed to report to the local draft board when so ordered.[1] Although Jack Tono's stand, and that of the other Heart Mountain draft resisters, would result in incarceration in a federal penitentiary for two years, his journey began like that of 110,000 other West Coast Japanese and Japanese Americans, with the bombing of Pearl Harbor.

Jack Kiyoto Tono was born in November of 1920 in Gilroy, California, approximately thirty-five miles south of San Jose. He was the eldest of ten children. His father had emigrated to the United States in 1903. His mother, a "Picture Bride" from an arranged marriage, arrived in California in 1919. The Tonos were share-croppers who had grown strawberries for as long as Jack could remember. Since farm work occupied his parents year-round, they never had time to learn to speak English. One year before it was time to enroll Jack in elementary school, his father would send him to the neighbor's house after dinner for English lessons. The neighbors, also a Japanese family, had older children who were in school and who taught Jack to speak English.[2]

Tono graduated from high school in 1939 and helped his family by working on the farm. When the Selective Service Act was passed into law, Tono registered and was designated 1-A. During December of 1941, Tono was working at the Durio Brothers packinghouse in Edenville, California. Approximately two-thirds of the packinghouse employees were Caucasian, the remainder were of Japanese ancestry. In spite of the racial mix of employees at Durio Brothers, Tono said everyone got along well, and that he did not recall any acts of prejudice. In fact, when everyone returned to work on Monday, December 8, the day after Pearl Harbor had been bombed, the talk around the packinghouse focused on the defense of the country. All of the younger employees, both Japanese and Caucasian, felt that they would soon be leaving to enlist in the army, or some other branch of service.[3]

The calm which Tono had enjoyed at work was soon erased. California politicians, patriotic groups within the state (American Legion,

A Matter of Conscience

The Native Sons of the Golden West), and groups and individuals who could benefit economically from the removal of Japanese Americans from California and the West Coast wasted little time in contributing to the growing "war hysteria." That hysteria was compounded by Lieutenant General John DeWitt, the man in charge of defending the West Coast against invasion. The paranoid Dewitt, who had seen his counterparts in Hawaii (Admiral Husband Kimmel and General Walter Short) relieved of command, contributed exponentially to the anti-Japanese attitude in California by passing false reports of radio transmissions from within California to Japanese ships cruising just off the West Coast, on to the public. A result of that hysteria was President Franklin Roosevelt's signing of Executive Order 9066 on February 19, 1942.[4]

General DeWitt, and the federal government used E. O. 9066 to remove everyone of Japanese ancestry from designated military zones on the West Coast and in parts of Arizona. After the Tono family had been informed (during the spring of 1942) that they would be evacuated, they began packing to leave. Following a visit with the "junk man" concerning the purchase of items that the family could not take along, the Tonos decided it would be better to store what they had, or to loan some items to Caucasian neighbors. For example, the family had, only weeks earlier, purchased a new refrigerator for the sum of ninety dollars. When the "junk man" told them the most he would pay for it was ten dollars, the refrigerator was given to a neighbor lady.[5]

Being one of the first families to be evacuated from the San Jose area, the Tonos were sent to the Santa Anita Assembly Center and housed in the stable area. The horse stable in which the family of twelve was housed also had a walled-in walking area just outside. The stable and walking area were divided in two, with the male members of the family staying on one side, and the female members on the other. Tono said that it was while constructing camouflage netting for the army during his internment at Santa Anita, with his family living in a horse stall, that he began giving serious thought to the ideas of democracy and the supposed rights of all American citizens set forth in the Constitution.[6]

During the month of September, 1942, the Tono family was put on a train and told that they were being sent to a permanent camp in Wyoming. Arriving at the Heart Mountain Relocation Center, the members of the Tono family stepped off of the train onto snow-covered ground. The family was taken by truck to their new "home" in the camp. Each barrack building was divided into six "apartments," but since the there were twelve members of the Tono family, they were give the two middle apartments, which they later tied together by cutting a doorway in the wall separating the two rooms.[7]

Wanting to escape the confines of the camp, Jack Tono applied for a

Jack Tono: The Journey of a "Light-footed Felon"

work release permit almost immediately upon arrival at Heart Mountain. With most young men volunteering or being drafted into the army, the resulting labor shortage was Tono's way out of camp. Jack, a brother, and eight other Heart Mountain internees traveled to a farm near Billings, Montana where they worked topping and harvesting sugar beets for Harold Glantz. Tono enjoyed being out of camp and working for Glantz. He got along with the farmer so well that when the beet harvest had been completed, he and his brother stayed on and continued to work for Glantz through the winter feeding sheep.[8]

By the time Jack and his brother returned to Heart Mountain in the spring of 1943, several events which would affect Tono's life had taken place. Following the bombing of Pearl Harbor, many draft boards began classifying Japanese Americans as 4-F, mentally or physically unfit for service. A short time later, the Selective Service sent out notices to all draft boards stating that all men of Japanese ancestry, whether they were American citizens or not, were to be classified as 4-C, enemy aliens. These changes to his draft status, and that of other Japanese Americans, had all taken place without a medical examination, or security interview by any military intelligence or law enforcement organization.[9]

During the summer of 1942, the all-Nisei 100th Battalion had been organized and its ranks filled with volunteers from Hawaii. Amazed at the number of Nisei volunteers from Hawaii (with a few exceptions, Japanese Americans in Hawaii had not been interned), the federal government believed it could recruit just as many Nisei volunteers from the ten relocation centers on the mainland, and use those men to build the all-Nisei, 442nd Regimental Combat Team. With that in mind, the government was once again looking to change the draft status of Nisei men.[10]

Upon his return to Heart Mountain in the Spring of 1943, Jack Tono had found that the Nisei volunteers were all required to fill out a "Statement of United States Citizen of Japanese Ancestry" form (this was an early version of the much discussed "Loyalty Questionnaire"). Despite the draft designation of 4-C, all draft age Nisei men were still required to register with Selective Service. For example, the sixth such registration for eighteen and nineteen year olds was completed at Heart Mountain on December 31, 1942. On February 6, 1943, army Lieutenant Ray McDaniels arrived at Heart Mountain in search of volunteers. At a recruiting meeting, McDaniels was interrupted by Frank T. Inouye, who asked why the Nisei should volunteer for service in the army while family members were still confined behind barbed wire. The majority of those in the audience supported Inouye, who went on to organize what came to be known as "The Heart Mountain Congress of American Citizens." Inouye's gatherings were attended by individuals who later made up the leadership of the Fair Play Committee.[11]

A Matter of Conscience

Back in camp, Tono read Inouye's many letters to the editor of the *Heart Mountain Sentinel* and was in complete support of the stand taken by the latter. Following McDaniels' recruiting drive at Heart Mountain, Tono was happy that the majority of the camp's population felt as he and Inouye did. This was made evident in that, by March 6, 1943 McDaniels had succeeded in recruiting only thirty-eight volunteers from an overall camp population of approximately 10,000.[12]

During the summer months of 1943, the Nisei volunteer controversy died down as it appeared that the federal government was not going to press the issue. By the autumn of that same year, Jack Tono and a number of other young men from Heart Mountain volunteered to harvest sugar beets and potatoes near Idaho Falls, Idaho. Although Tono and nine others had to ride to Idaho Falls in the back of a beet truck, they traveled via Yellowstone National Park, a trip Tono described as "quite memorable." Once in the park, the driver gave the volunteers the option of taking a short-cut, or the scenic route through Geyser Basin. They unanimously chose the scenic route. Upon reaching Idaho Falls, Tono and the others worked long hours harvesting sugar beets and potatoes. With little leisure time, the volunteers returned to Heart Mountain with their pockets full of cash.[13]

When Tono returned to Heart Mountain, he found that the issue of military service had come up once again. This time the government was not looking for volunteers from the relocation centers, instead it had decided to forego the recruiting missions and simply draft internees directly from the camps. Tono and the other young men at Heart Mountain found that their draft designation had been changed back to 1-A. Other than filling out the "Loyalty Questionnaire," Tono and the other Nisei had their draft status changed three times in two years, at the government's discretion, without ever having been interviewed by anyone.[14] Upset with the evacuation and incarceration of his family and other Japanese Americans, and being further enraged by the continual change in his draft status at the government's convenience, Tono said, "When I give up my life for democracy, I want to see the goddamn thing first."[15]

In early February, 1944, young men at Heart Mountain began receiving notices to report for preinduction physicals. A few days later, on February 8, the first meeting of the Fair Play Committee (FPC) was held. That committee, whose leadership was made up primarily of individuals involved with Frank Inouye's short-lived "Heart Mountain Congress," began holding public meetings where it discussed democratic principles, the Constitution, and the government's legal right, if indeed that right existed, to draft men directly out of concentration camps where the government had placed them.[16]

During an investigation of the FPC several weeks later, FBI agent Harry McMillen pointed out that the reinstatement of a 1-A draft status, and

Jack Tono: The Journey of a "Light-footed Felon"

the decision by the government to begin drafting Nisei men out of the camps led the residents of Heart Mountain to develop three different points of view regarding the issue. The first point of view was taken by a small minority who welcomed the draft and saw it as a step toward the restoration of full civil rights. The second minority view point was taken by members of the FPC. Those individuals felt that the Nisei had no obligation to meet the requirements of the Selective Service Act until all of the injustices perpetrated upon them and their families during the relocation process had been rectified. McMillen said that the majority of those interned at Heart Mountain felt that it was unfair of the government to draft evacuees from a camp where they had been placed without their consent. However, those internees also believed that if they did not go along with the draft, they would be punished, and that anti-Japanese sentiment on the outside would increase.[17]

Jack Tono was among many of the draft-age Nisei in camp who decided to attend an FPC meeting to see what that group had to offer. Tono said that there were approximately 200 young men in attendance at the first meeting he attended. There was nothing anti-American going on. The discussions focused primarily on the Constitution, due process, and civil rights. Tono felt that with so many men in attendance, the War Relocation Authority (WRA) would simply cancel their work permits and not allow any of the FPC members to leave camp. He did not believe that the government would arrest and try 200 men. However, if they were arrested, Tono believed that their refusal to report for preinduction physicals would lead to the courts addressing the larger issues of due process and the illegality of relocation itself.[18]

Guy Robertson, the camp director at Heart Mountain, was moving to put an end to the FPC's influence as quickly as possible. The FBI was called in, and arrest warrants were issued for all of those Nisei who had refused to report for preinduction physicals. Tono's initial excitement at the large number of individuals attending FPC meetings was dashed when, in the end, only sixty-four men were arrested for resisting the draft, and one of those was found to be "mentally deficient" and released (later in the year a much smaller group of resisters was also arrested at Heart Mountain).[19]

Word traveled through the camp quickly, and the resisters knew of their impending arrest. On April 4, 1944 an FBI agent and a U. S. Marshall appeared at the door of the Tono family barrack apartment. Jack answered the knock at the door. He remembered that the FBI agent identified himself and then asked, "Is your name Jack Tono?"[20] Tono said "yes," and picked up his shaving gear and some clothes which he had already packed and followed the two men to a vehicle which was waiting in front of the barrack. Tono's arrest experience was similar to that of the other resisters. Yosh Kuromiya recalled his arrest. "I said quick goodbyes to my father, mother, and sister. Curious neighbors stood a discrete distance, whispering and pointing. . . . There were six other fellow internees in the limo. I was the final catch of the day."[21]

Tono and the other resisters who had been arrested with him, were taken to the county jail at nearby Cody. Upon arrival at the jail, he was fingerprinted and interrogated by FBI agents. Tono was, to a point, correct in his earlier belief that 200 resisters would be too many for the authorities to deal with. Even though there were only sixty-three men arrested in the original round up, that number taxed the available accommodations in Wyoming's small county jails. By the time all sixty-three were arrested, the resisters were incarcerated in county jails in Cheyenne, Laramie, Casper, and Rawlins. Tono was sent to the Natrona County Jail in Casper, where one of the larger groups of resisters was held.[22]

Other than the resisters, there was hardly anyone else incarcerated at the Natrona County jail. Tono and the others got along well with the sheriff, and, for the most part, actually enjoyed their stay in Casper. When Tono and some of his fellow prisoners offered to relieve the sheriff's wife of her cooking responsibilities, the sheriff unlocked the kitchen and gave the resisters freedom in the area. The cells were not locked, and the kitchen and recreation area were left open during their entire stay. That little bit of freedom meant a great deal to the men, and they hold fond memories of the sheriff who treated them so humanely.[23]

While spending time in the Casper jail, Tono and the others would talk through the windows with Heart Mountain Nisei who were passing through town on their way to take preinduction physicals. Mostly, they just passed the time talking about their upcoming trial and guessed as to its outcome. Even though some of the resisters felt that they had a good case, and were optimistic,[24] Tono said that during their discussions in the Casper jail, many of the men believed they would lose in court. There were men who had refused induction into the army for religious or political beliefs and had been sent to prison. Tono was sure that resisters with "the face of the enemy" would be convicted. During one discussion Tono told his fellow prisoners, "You know, when we do these things, you don't want to have a rosy outlook, more so in time of war, the situation the way it is. We're not going to get any break, so forget it."[25]

Tono and the other resisters scattered throughout the state, were gathered together and placed in the jail in Cheyenne to await their trial. Even though the Cheyenne jail had cells with "double bunks" on two walls, there was not enough room for all sixty-three men. Many of the prisoners were told to sleep of the floor of the recreation area. The accommodations were not nearly as comfortable as those in Casper. Tono said the men were given mattresses and blankets when they arrived.[26] Another prisoner in Cheyenne, Yosh Kuromiya, said that, "The ancient mattress and threadbare blanket reeked of urine and vomit of former residents."[27]

On May 8, 1944, the grand jury was convened in Cheyenne and brought indictments against the sixty-three Heart Mountain draft resisters. The charges brought against the resisters, according to U. S. District Attorney Carl Sackett, were for failure to report to the local draft board in Powell, Wyoming. The official charge was violation of Section 311, Title 50, U.S.C.A. Selective Service and Training Act of 1940. In a pretrial motion the defendants agreed to be tried as a group and waived a jury trial. The largest trial in Wyoming's history began on Monday, June 12, 1944, before District Judge T. Blake Kennedy. While going over the trial agenda with the defendants, Kennedy addressed the group as "You Jap Boys."[28] Even though Kennedy quickly corrected himself, Tono told those around him, "This son of bitch, he's got it in for us. Don't have high hopes. This guy, he's going to give it to us."[29]

The Heart Mountain Sixty-three were defended by Samuel Menin, a Denver, Colorado Civil Liberties attorney, and Clyde Watts of Cheyenne. Tono said that Menin told the defendants all to get similar short-cropped haircuts, and not to answer when their names were called. The idea was that it would be up to the court to identify each defendant. Tono said that on top of everyone looking like a bunch of Buddhist monks, if the court wanted to identify each individual, all they had to do was check fingerprints.[30]

The trial itself had its share of interesting moments. Prosecuting attorney Carl Sackett stated that the act of resisting the draft was itself, proof of disloyalty. Sackett called several FBI agents who had interrogated the resisters to testify. The agents all testified that the resisters said they would serve in the army if their civil and constitutional rights were restored. Under cross examination, all of the agents told Menin that they believed each and every one of the resisters to be loyal Americans. Menin was also able to point out that at least one of the defendants had tried to enlist in the army in California before the evacuation, and had been refused.[31] Menin and Sackett turned the case into a personal battle. According to Mits Koshiyama, during one of Menin's many objections, Sackett turned and "said that if our lawyer didn't sit down, he would personally set him down. Our lawyer took off his coat and dared the prosecutor to try it."[32] Later, when Sackett felt sure that he was going to win the case, he was leaning back in his chair rocking on the two back legs when he tipped over and crashed to floor. The younger defendants all started laughing. Koshiyama said Sackett "got up red-faced, pointed his finger at us, and said that we wouldn't be laughing when we heard the verdict."[33]

The trial lasted only four days and came to an end on June 16, 1944. However, the verdict was not handed down until July 25. In the meantime, Tono and the others were returned to the jail in Cheyenne to await a summons from Judge Kennedy. While sitting in jail, Tono and his fellow inmates discussed the trial in great detail, but Tono knew what the verdict would be. On July 25, 1944, Judge Kennedy brought the Heart Mountain Sixty-three together and read his verdict. All sixty-three men were found guilty of violating the Selective Service and Training Act. Each man was sentenced to three years in a federal penitentiary. Thirty-three of the defendants, aged twenty-five and under, were to serve their sentences at the federal penitentiary at McNeil Island, near Tacoma, Washington. The other thirty resisters were to serve their time at the federal penitentiary at Fort Leavenworth, Kansas. Although the case was appealed, the higher court based its review on the technical interpretation of the law and upheld the Kennedy decision.[34]

Tono and the other prisoners arrived in Washington and traveled over to McNeil Island via ferryboat. One of the resisters, Tak Hoshizaki, remembered the island being approximately three miles by four miles in size. The complex was made up of two separate facilities, the "Big House," for hardened criminals, and the prison farm.[35] Upon arrival, Tono and the others spent their first month at the prison in quarantine. There, they were interviewed by a psychiatrist, doctor, parole officer, and finally, the prison chaplain. While speaking with the chaplain, Tono said, "Reverend, you know, you look like a pretty decent guy. What do think? You think we did the right thing?" The chaplain thought for a moment, and then replied, "I probably would have done the same thing you guys did."[36]

Unlike the hardened criminals in the Big House, Tono described the resisters as minor criminals, more along the line of "light-footed felons." Tono and the others were soon transferred to the prison farm. There, they were housed in buildings similar to dormitories, with large open bays that were filled with bunks for the prisoners. The prisoners were up at 6:15 AM, had breakfast at 7:00, and were off to work by 8:00 AM. The prisoners worked at various tasks, though most spent their days laboring in the fields. Lunch was served at noon, and then they went back to work until 4:30 PM with dinner at 6:00 and lights-out at 9:30. After spending two years at Heart Mountain, the resisters were easily acclimatized to life on the prison farm.[37]

Although all the prisoners on the farm were required to work, life at McNeil Island was not hard. Instead of receiving financial compensation for the work they did, the prisoners on the farm earned three days per month of "good time." The second year, good time payments were increased to five days per month. If a prisoner's earned good time was combined with the 254 days of statutory good time that each resister received, he would serve slightly less than two years of his three year sentence. But good time could also be taken away by prison officials for misconduct.[38]

When the position opened up, Tono accepted the job of athletic director at the prison farm. The other prisoners worked forty-four hours per week,

Jack Tono: The Journey of a "Light-footed Felon"

but Tono had to make sure that the leisure time available to the inmates was enjoyable. Baseball was the pastime most enjoyed by the prisoners. The resisters fielded two teams, another group of resisters from Heart Mountain, who were convicted in a trial several months after that of the Heart Mountain Sixty-three, had a team, and so did a group of resisters from the Minidoka camp in Idaho. In addition, there were two teams made up of black prisoners, and two others made up of Caucasian prisoners, most of whom were Jehovah's Witnesses. Tono would maintain the limited amount of athletic equipment, rake the field every day, and mark out the diamond.[39]

Tono was upset with the poor quality of the athletic equipment, and the lack of interest the prison farm's superintendent had focused on requests for new equipment. Tono was constantly sewing gloves back together as his requests went unanswered. One of the black prisoners, named Ewing, drove a truck back and forth between the farm and the Big House. Tono knew that Ewing was friends with the athletic director at the Big House and asked Ewing to see if they had enough used baseball equipment, for two full teams, that could be sent to the farm. Ewing returned that evening with two boxes full of equipment. Although the baseball gloves were "raggedy," they were in much better shape than the ones the prisoners on the farm had been using.[40]

Annoyed that Tono had gone over his head, and succeeded, the superintendent of the farm called Jack into his office. After receiving a severe reprimand, Tono went on the offensive and said, "Hey listen! I talked to you people I don't know how many times to get equipment. Some of these fellows [are] going to get hurt, and we shouldn't be penalize[d] . . . because of your shortcoming." Tono knew that he had crossed a line with the superintendent, so he continued on the offensive and quit as athletic director before he could be fired. As punishment for verbally assaulting the superintendent, Tono was sent to work in the fields under the supervision of the "worst guard" on the farm.[41]

Tono was sent to the field with seventeen other prisoners to weed the tomato plants. Two of the other prisoners had been verbally abused by the guard so Tono told them, "Hey, let's give this guy the works." Tono said the three of them made quite a team (Tono, Rosenthal, and Hardy), a Japanese, a Jew, and an Irishman. While the Jehovah's Witnesses weeded one row after another, Tono and his two companions would slowly pull one blade of grass at a time, to see if they could aggravate the guard, and they did. All three men were "pink slipped," which meant that they had to go to court. In court, the superintendent was the judge, with the psychiatrist, doctor, parole officer, and lieutenant of the guard serving as the jury. The loss of movie privileges was the penalty for conviction on one's first offense. And Tono was found guilty of not working up to his capabilities.[42]

After losing his movie privileges, Tono continued his defiance. The black prisoners were the first to attend the movies the next weekend, and knowing all of the prisoners through his work as athletic director, Tono told the black inmates to keep the line tight as they filed passed the guard into the movie room. In the meantime, Tono sneaked along the outside of the line and into the theater. After the movie ended, Tono walked out of the building in line with the black inmates. When they passed through the door, the guard yelled, "Hey, Tono, you're supposed to be in the dormitory." Jack looked at the guard, smiled, and said, "Yeah, I know."[43]

Tono did his best to aggravate the superintendent throughout the remainder of his stay at McNeil Island. However, the punishments moved from a loss of movie privileges, to a loss of good time. In the meantime, Tono and the other resisters would have been eligible for parole after serving one year of the three year sentence. The guards and other inmates told the resisters "Oh, hell, you guys are clean as a whistle, no record. If you guys don't get paroled, there's something wrong."[44] However, Guy Robertson felt that returning the resisters to Heart Mountain would be a bad influence on the other internees. He had been discussing the possibility of parole with Dillon Myer, head of the WRA, for some time. Due to influence from Myer's office, parole was denied.[45]

After serving two years of his three year prison term, Jack Tono was released from McNeil Island, Federal Penitentiary on August 5, 1946. The other Heart Mountain internees, who had not lost any good time days, had been released twenty-three days earlier. On December 23, 1947, President Harry S. Truman signed Presidential Proclamation 2762. That instrument granted a full pardon to all Nisei draft resisters and wiped their records clean.[46]

Upon his release from prison, Tono joined his family near Philadelphia where they were working on a farm. He later married, and in the early 1960's, relocated with his wife and children to Chicago, Illinois, where he resides today. Over the years, Tono spent much of his vacation time combing the records of the National Archives, and the Wyoming State Archives in search of information concerning the case of the Heart Mountain Sixty-three. Tono said that his choice to join the resisters was the right one. And when asked if he were bitter about relocation and the prison term he was forced to serve, he said, "I'm not bitter, only disappointed sometimes."

Notes

1.*The Wyoming Eagle*, May 11, and June 12, 1944. *United States vs. Fujii*, Criminal Case No. 4928, U. S. District Courts of the United States, Record Group 21, National Archives-Rocky Mountain Region, Denver, Colorado. Mike Mackey, *Heart Mountain: Life in Wyoming's Concentration Camp* (Powell, WY., Western History Publications, 2000), 115.

Jack Tono: The Journey of a "Light-footed Felon"

2.Jack Tono interview with Jean Brainard, May 13, 1992, Cheyenne, Wyoming, 4-8, Wyoming State Archives. John Tateishi, *And Justice for All: An Oral History of the Japanese American Detention Camps* (New York: Random House, 1984, (reprinted) Seattle: University of Washington Press, 1999), 168.

3.Ibid., 168.

4.Roger Daniels, *Prisoners Without Trial: Japanese Americans in World War II* (New York: Hill and Wang, 1993), 27-34. Jack Tono, "Heart Mountain 63," paper presented at the Heart Mountain Symposium, Powell, Wyoming, May, 1995, (paper in author's possession).

5.Jack Tono to author, February 11, 1993, 2. Jack Tono and Jean Brainard interview, 10.

6.Jack Tono to author, February 11, 1993, 2-3. Tono and Brainard interview, 23.

7.Jack Tono to author, February 11, 1993, 3. Tono and Brainard interview, 3.

8.Jack Tono to author, February 11, 1993, 3. Tono and Brainard interview, 25.

9.Daniels, *Prisoners Without Trial*, 35. Jack Tono, statement to the Subcommittee on Administrative Law and Governmental Relations, Judiciary Committee, United States House of Representatives, April 28, 1986, 2-3.

10.Frank T. Inouye, "Immediate Origins of the Heart Mountain Draft Resistance Movement," Mike Mackey, ed. in, *Remembering Heart Mountain: Essays on Japanese American Internment in Wyoming* (Powell, WY: Western History Publications, 1998), 124.

11.Mike Mackey, *Heart Mountain: Life in Wyoming's Concentration Camp* (Powell, WY: Western History Publications, 2000), 101. Inouye, "Draft Resistance Movement," 125-26. Chizu Omori, "The Loyalty Questionnaire," in Mike Mackey ed., *Guilt by Association: Essays on Japanese Settlement, Internment, and Relocation in the Rocky Mountain West* (Powell, WY: Western History Publications, 2001), 277.

12.Mackey, *Heart Mountain*, 103.

13.Jack Tono to author, February 11, 1993, 3.

14.Jack Tono to author, February 11, 1993, 3-4. Jack Tono interview with Jean Brainard, 28-29.

15.Tateishi, *And Justice for All*, 170.

16.Eric L. Muller, *Free to Die for Their Country: The Story of the Japanese American Draft Resisters in World War II* (Chicago: The University of Chicago Press, 2001), 78. Jack Tono and Jean Brainard interview, 28-29.

17.Mackey, *Heart Mountain*, 111-12.

18.Jack Tono and Jean Brainard interview, 30-31. Jack Tono, paper presented at Northeastern University, November 12, 1978, 1.

19.Jack Tono and Jean Brainard interview, 31. Mackey, *Heart Mountain*, 112-15.

20.Jack Tono and Jean Brainard interview, 31. Tateishi, *And Justice for All*, 170.

21.William Hohri, *Resistance: Challenging America's Wartime Internment of Japanese-Americans* (Lomita, CA:, the Epistolarian, 2001), 63.

22.Jack Tono and Jean Brainard interview, 31. Tateishi, *And Justice for All*, 170. Hohri, *Resistance*, 51, 63.

23.Jack Tono and Jean Brainard interview, 31.

24.Hohri, *Resistance*, 52.

25.Ibid., 34-35.

26.Jack Tono and Jean Brainard interview, 36.

27.Hohri, *Resistance*, 64.

28.Mackey, *Heart Mountain*, 115. Jack Tono and Jean Brainard interview, 38. Muller, *Free to Die for Their Country*, 104. In *Free to Die for Their Country*, Eric Muller discusses in some detail, Judge Kennedy's racist attitudes, 104-07.

29.Tateishi, *And Justice for All*, 171.

30.Jack Tono, lecture at the University of Wyoming, October 19, 1993. Mits Koshiyama to author, August 25, 1993. *The Wyoming Eagle*, June 13, 1944.

31.*The Wyoming Eagle*, June 15 and 16, 1944. William Minoru Hohri, *Repairing America: An Account of the Movement for Japanese-American Redress* (Pullman: Washington State University Press, 1988), 173-74.

32.Hohri, *Resistance*, 52.

33.Ibid., 52.

34.Mackey, *Heart Mountain*, 116. Tateishi, *And Justice for All*, 171. Jack Tono and Jean Brainard interview, 46-47. For an excellent review and legal interpretation of the Heart Mountain draft resister's case, see Eric Muller, *Free to Die for Their Country: The Story of* Japanese *American Draft Resisters in World War II*. For an outstanding lesson plan for use in teaching this subject in the classroom, see Arthur A. Hansen's, "The 1944 Nisei

Jack Tono: The Journey of a "Light-footed Felon"

Draft at Heart Mountain, Wyoming: Its Relationship to the Historical Representation of the World War II Japanese American Evacuation," *Magazine of History*, 10 (Summer 1996).

35. Hohri, *Resistance*, 87.

36. Jack Tono and Jean Brainard interview, 53. *Tateishi, And Justice for All*, 172.

37. Jack Tono and Jean Brainard interview, 54. Hohri, *Resistance*, 88-89.

38. Jack Tono and Jean Brainard interview, 54.

39. Jack Tono and Jean Brainard Interview, 65-57.

40. Ibid., 60.

41. Ibid., 60-61.

42. Ibid., 61-62.

43. Ibid., 62-63.

44. Tateishi, *And Justice for All*, 174.

45. Dillon Myer to Edward Ennis, May 15, 1944, and Edward Ennis to James Bennet, June 1, 1944, Japanese Relocation, Department of Justice Files, National Archives and Records Administration, Washington D. C. Mackey, *Heart Mountain*, 117.

46. Jack Tono and Jean Brainard interview, 59, 64. Presidential Proclamation 2762.

The Fourth Option

by Yosh Kuromiya

After war with Japan was declared, we of Japanese descent were notified by the government that U.S. citizens and non-citizens alike were restricted to an 8:00 PM to 6:00 AM curfew. We were also prohibited from traveling more than five miles from our homes. This did not apply to those of German or Italian descent, even though we were also at war with those countries. Nonetheless, we complied.

In the spring of 1942, we were to be sent to an "assembly center" at the Pomona Fair Grounds. There was much confusion as to the reason for this. Were we suspected as potential saboteurs? Or were we to be detained for our own protection? We were, however, assured that this was merely a precautionary wartime measure, and all citizens' rights and interests would be reinstated in due time. Meanwhile, it was our patriotic duty to abide by these temporary measures in the interest of national security. So said our self-appointed "leaders," the Japanese American Citizens League. So again, we complied.

Later that same year, we were to be transported further inland. This new location was in Wyoming, a place called Heart Mountain. We had had no hearings, and there had been no accusations nor proof of any wrongdoing. The same questions again arose. But, during our brief stay in Pomona, many began suggesting that in spite of our citizenship, somehow the Constitution and Bill of Rights did not apply to us. Our future survival in a country which now viewed us as the enemy, had become our primary concern. We felt that we had to demonstrate our loyalty and dedication to this country for our very survival. So again, we complied.

Heart Mountain was a grim and inhospitable strip of prairie. It was located between two movie-set like western towns, Cody and Powell. Both seemed to turn their backs on the prison camp hastily constructed on land nobody wanted. This orphan-like cluster of tar-papered barracks in the middle of nowhere seemed to express its own self-hate through its guard towers armed with weapons pointed inward, and placed at intervals along a barbed-wire fence.

It took a few weeks to orient myself to my new home, but as the everyday survival needs became more commonplace, the full import of the betrayal by our government began to sink in. I finally had to face the reality I tried so desperately to avoid. Because of the trust we had placed in our government and the cowardly, misguided leadership of our JACL, we had become war-prisoners in our very own country.

Early in 1943, the infamous "loyalty questionnaire" was circulated, causing much confusion, disbelief, and outrage. The Fair Play Committee, which I was only vaguely aware of at the time, warned that the "questionnaire" could be a precursor to imposing the military draft onto those in the camps. If answered carelessly, it could be interpreted as a willingness to be inducted into an already formed, racially segregated army unit.

I naively reasoned that perhaps this was yet another clumsy attempt by the government to determine our trustworthiness, a prelude to our clearance and release. Besides, if I answered "No" out of anger or spite, I might jeopardize whatever was left of my citizenship status. Also, it might tend to justify the government's wholesale detention program as a reasonable wartime contingency.

I finally heeded the FPC mimeographed warning and answered with a *conditional* "Yes" on question 27, as to my willingness to serve in the armed forces, and "Yes" to 28, forswearing allegiance to the Emperor of Japan, even though I had never sworn allegiance to him in the first place.

The FPC was right, of course. Early in 1944, without further hearings nor explanations, my draft classification was changed form 4-C to 1-A. It was a relief to know that I was no longer considered sinister, but the condition of the prior reinstatement of my civil rights seemed to have been ignored.

Shortly thereafter, I received a notice to report for a physical exam prior to induction into the army. I regarded the notice as yet another insult, the first being the curfew, which now seemed so long ago.

What of my family still detained in this infernal prison camp? What of our suspended Constitutional rights? What of our past cooperation with the government in surrendering those rights in the name of "national security"? What of the democratic principles which had been denied us; the very principles we were then asked to defend on foreign soil?

I thought, "NO! This is MY country! This is MY Constitution! This MY Bill of Rights! I am here finally to defend them. I regret I had surrendered my freedom. I will not continue to surrender my dignity nor the dignity of the U.S. Constitution!" Thus, after receiving the notice to report for the pre-induction exams, I REFUSED TO COMPLY!

Had the mainland United States been threatened with probable invasion, I would not have taken this stand. But to join in the killing and maiming in foreign lands, not because they were the enemy, but ostensibly to prove my loyalty to a government who imprisoned me and my family without hearings or charges, I felt would be self-serving, irresponsible, and totally without conscience. Indeed, the real threat to our democracy was at my very doorstep.

Subsequently I, along with sixty-two others, was indicted, tried, and found guilty of violating the Selective Service Act. We were sentenced to three years in prison. An appeal to a higher court was turned down. We were also denied parole, as an early release might encourage others still in the camps to defy the draft. However, after completing two years of our sentence, we were released on good behavior. The war had ended by then, the camps were closed, and we were no longer considered a threat.

A year and one-half after our release, we were *unexpectedly* granted a presidential pardon, erasing all criminal records and reinstating full citizenship rights.

After fifty-seven years of introspection, and with the saner vision of hindsight, I have gained some insights about those events and the on-going misconceptions about the entire internment debacle that still plagues the Japanese American community. The internee reaction to governmental abuses seemed to fall generally into three conflicting catagories: There were those who believed in cooperation and sacrifice without question as a means of regaining the trust and acceptance of our government and the public at large, as proffered by the JACL. Their position seemed to imply that the camps were, in fact, sanctuaries, given the ugly wartime hysteria that prevailed "outside." Any spectacle, such as a court challenge questioning the constitutionality of the camps and other on-going infringements of our civil rights, would only cause unwanted notoriety and bad publicity which they felt we could ill-afford. They endorsed conspicuous acts of patriotism, regardless of their sincerity, in order to project an image of unfaltering loyalty.

On the other hand, there were the co-called "dissidents", the "No-Nos" and those who had become disenchanted with the government's professed "ideals and good intentions." They were basically, anti-administration and anti-JACL. Some were openly pro-Japan, although most were not. Many were Kibei, and a few were WW I veterans outraged with the treatment they received in spite of their previously proven loyalty. They held in common, a righteous anger and resentment resulting from years of racial injustice and had apparently given up all hope of ever attaining equity under what they perceived as a racist government.

The vast majority, however, for various personal reasons, vacillated somewhere between the two extremes, committing themselves to neither position. They remained generally, ineffective victims with a wait-and-see attitude, cautious and prone to finger-pointing, with a general intolerance of those who dared to take a stand. They were, and still remain, smugly cloaked in the anonymity of the "Quiet American."

All three groups, in their own way, had in essence, abandoned that which should have been their greatest asset and source of inspiration—the U.S. Constitution; the first, out of a misguided patriotic fanaticism, the second, out of anger and despair, and the third, out of a culturally ingrained blind deference to authority, no matter what the circumstance.

In that climate of confusion, despair and paralysis, pitting victim against victim, neighbor against neighbor, and brother against brother, the Fair Play Committee provided a fourth option; one which demanded absolute faith in the principles of the U.S. Constitution while challenging, in the courts, government policies which were blatantly in violation of those principles. Indeed, what appeared initially as a reasonable fourth option, emerged, after careful study, as a citizen's *inescapable primary duty*—the spirit of which lay at the very foundation of our country. It was, indeed, more than a simple option.

We lost our case, of course, and in a sense, so did the Constitution and democracy itself. But through subsequent acts like the presidential pardon, the success of the Corum-Nobis cases, and the passage of the Civil Liberties Act of 1988 with the historic acknowledgment by the government of its massive civil rights violations, I feel our actions in placing our faith in the U.S. Constitution and the basic principles of our democracy have been more than vindicated. As the saying goes, "With so much manure, there HAD to be a pony in there somewhere." Happily, I think we found the pony.

Protest-Resistance and the Heart Mountain Experience:
The Revitalization of a Robust Nikkei Tradition

by Arthur A. Hansen

In Lane Hirabayashi's luminous essay for Mike Mackey's edited 1998 anthology, *Remembering Heart Mountain*, he cautioned Japanese American Internment scholars not to over-generalize about Japanese American "resistance" to oppression within the War Relocation Authority (WRA)-administered camps. But Hirabayashi, a nephew of widely reputed World War II Nisei resister Gordon Hirabayashi, at once mitigated his warning: "My reading of the archival record confirms, repeatedly, . . . the frequency and tenacity of resistance on multiple occasions and multiple levels."[1]

Having researched the wartime social catastrophe of Nikkei via archival documents and oral history interviews over the past three decades, I find Hirabayashi's trenchant assessment of Japanese American wartime resistance activity on target. Moreover, I strongly feel that such resistance to oppression not only was frequent and tenacious and operated on multiple occasions and levels during World War II, but also prior to and after the war. Indeed, I would argue that resistance within this racial-ethnic community, while never predominant, has always been widespread (and often consequential), and that resistance and protest have been a Japanese American tradition as well as a generic American one.

Before illustrating this contention by specific reference to historical developments, especially during World War II in relation to events at or associated with the Heart Mountain Relocation Center in northwest Wyoming, I would like briefly to catechize the concept of resistance. Hopefully, this (albeit schematic) discussion, which borrows liberally from the strikingly original theoretical work of Roger Gottlieb pertinent to Jewish resistance during the Holocaust,[2] will provide a broadly suggestive context for the meaningful consumption of my subsequent commentary and examples.

ROGER GOTTLIEB'S CONCEPT OF RESISTANCE

Resistance, according to Roger Gottlieb, necessarily functions within a context of oppression. Styling an action to be one of resistance implicates us in a moral evaluation of a specific set of power relations, and places us in a partisan position as regards a given social conflict. For Gottlieb, the term "resistance" categorically has no "neutral" application: we either root for the success or for the failure of the aims expressed in a resistance action. However, even if we favor the outcome of such an action, we may be too cowed, fearful, or indifferent to actually help out the resisters in question.

"A relation of oppression," Gottlieb avers, "is typically based in certain norms."[3] Thus, in the present-day United States, acts of resistance to sexual and racial discrimination characteristically have to do with resistance to the legitimating norms of those forms of oppression. In Nazi-controlled Europe, on the other hand, acts by Jews exhibiting pride and self-respect served as species of resistance to the Nazi campaign to devalue and abase them. Rarely do relations of oppression consist only of physical aggression. Instead, explains Gottlieb, it is customary for an oppressed group to be controlled or assaulted in various ways: "life, property, religion, family, self-respect, culture, and community."[4]

To qualify as authentic acts of resistance, Gottlieb argues, their motivation must be to prevent, restrict, or terminate the oppressor group's exercise of power over the oppressed, not simply to transfer oppression from oneself to another of the oppressed group's members. In short, "the goal of resistance must be to lessen the total quantity of oppression, not just to shift it around. Otherwise one is not resisting, but simply trying to avoid personal suffering."[5]

Intention, theorizes Gottlieb, is indispensable to the concept of resistance. What we need to know is not whether an oppressed group resisted effectively, but rather whether they sought to resist. Stressing intention, though, hardly means that resistance exists whenever someone simply declares him or herself to be resisting. Intending to resist oppression ipso facto involves confronting the oppressor's superior power in order to thwart, limit, or end his oppressive actions. "The existence and application of this power," Gottlieb argues, "entails that resisters choose among acts, some of which are resistance and some of which are passivity or collaboration. . . . To obstruct the power of an oppressor is to place oneself in jeopardy."[6]

Resisters, in Gottlieb's formulation, must possess two sorts of beliefs. The first concerns their identity: they need to understand implicitly the defining elements of the individual's or group's existence. Beliefs of this type are necessary to the oppressed "recognizing that a part of themselves can be threatened, dominated or destroyed in the relationship of oppression."[7] The second kind of beliefs resisters must hold relates to the manner in which a given oppressor is exercising its domination, about how that particular individual or group is conducting an assault on their identity.

Although the intentions and beliefs manifested through resistance actions may be held in diverse ways and in differing degrees, it is sometimes hard to discern, as with so-called "tacit resistance," whether in fact they are even held. Gottlieb sees the expressed intentions and beliefs in acts of resistance as ranged along a spectrum. At one extreme are found completely formulated political-moral critiques of oppression coupled with a far-reaching determination to overcoming it, such as when an individual or group possesses a plan for overthrowing what one regards as a thoroughgoing domination system. Moving away from this end of the spectrum toward the other end, we find situations wherein an individual or group merely refuses to comply with a discrete order or rule, out of a combined feeling of hatred and guilt rather than because of self-righteous conviction. Cases in point are uprisings or "riots" in racial-ethnic enclaves or ghettos, which appear to be prompted by a sense of oppression, but frequently do not flow from an overarching strategy and are bracketed by long periods of passive accommodation to a racist social order. "When a person's beliefs and intentions become too tacit," Gottlieb opines, "a particular refusal or rebelliousness fails to qualify as an act of resistance. Other things being equal, an act is more fully an act of resistance the more fully the agent understands it as such."[8]

Gottlieb posits two other modes of resistance, both of which pose more difficulty respecting placement on a spectrum: "self-deceptive non-resistance" and "unconscious resistance." The first relates to self-proclaimed resisters whose intentions and beliefs cannot be easily or clearly fathomed. To illustrate this brand of "resistance," Gottlieb draws upon his research into the Nazi invasion of Poland and their enforced concentration of Jews into urban ghettos. "In each ghetto," he writes,

> [the Nazis] appointed a Judenrat, a council of (usually) influential Jews . . . for . . . day-to-day administration. . . . In most cases, the Judenrat administered deportations to the death camps; and members . . . often opposed, sometimes even betrayed, militant resistance groups. Yet . . . the Judenrat generally expressed the belief that they were engaged in an . . . effective strategy of resistance, that their surface cooperation was part of a larger strategy of saving as many Jewish lives as possible. . . . It is clear [however] that in some instances Judenrat members were not telling the truth about their intentions. Sometimes they sought self-protection at the expense of . . . the collective safety of their people. They were not engaged in a resistance effort that was shaped by different beliefs than those possessed by the militants. . . . What they claimed as conscious resistance could be more accurately described as unconscious complicity.[9]

"Unconscious resistance" represents for Gottlieb practically the reverse of "self-deceptive non-resistance." This behavior is associated with an oppressed person or group outwardly complying with an oppressor and foreswearing all intention to resist. Notwithstanding the oppressed party's projection of apprehension, defenselessness, or willing submission, the actions taken can be seen, upon examination, to impede the oppressive intentions and acts of the agent of oppression. The oppressed party may claim that the behavior at issue results from error, timidity, or chance, but it is more likely to constitute either an unacknowledged form of resistance or one to which the party is oblivious. Unconscious resistance is common among oppressed groups. For example, the allegedly "neurotic" behavior of females is, in reality, unconscious resistance to oppressive male domination. Such unconscious resistance behavior, while it thwarts the oppressor from getting the oppressed to fulfill a conventional subservient role on demand, falls well short of actual resistance. Unconscious resistance, after all, is ambivalent resistance. Moreover, because the desire to topple oppression is typically accompanied by fear or acceptance of the oppressor, unconscious resistance is frequently expressed in ways more damaging to the oppressed than to the oppressor. If the oppressing agent does not get what is wanted, the oppressed too often must pay a steep price for refusing to accede to the oppressor. Still, allows Gottlieb, "unconscious resistance behavior may provide direction to and mobilize support for political organizing, the goal of which is to convert unconscious resistance into open rebellion."[10]

PRE-WORLD WAR II JAPANESE AMERICAN PROTEST AND RESISTANCE

With this theoretical framework in place, we are now ready to turn our attention to a historical sketch of Japanese American resistance and to consider, along the way, the nature and degree of the resistance manifested at different times and in different contexts.

Let's begin at the beginning, using the scholarship of Professor Gary Okihiro, the leading historian of Japanese American resistance activity, to guide us on our historical journey.[11] As early as 1868, we find outcroppings of resistance among the members of the 153-party of Japanese labors who sailed from Yokohama to Hawaii for employment on the sugar plantations. Okihiro notes that within a month after landing in Hawaii, this first mass emigration of Japanese overseas, known as the *gannen-mono*, "lodged complaints with the government . . . protesting the withholding of half their $4 monthly wage and the slave-like selling of their contracts between planters . . . [and] even asking for pay for days lost because of foul weather."[12] Well before the termination of their three-year contracts, forty of these *gannen-mono* returned to Japan and, save for one of them, issued a signed public statement charging Hawaii's planters with malice and multiple violations of the contractual terms.

Whether they went to work in Hawaii or on the U.S. mainland,

The Revitalization of a Robust Nikkei Tradition

Japanese American migrants confronted substantial and seemingly unremitting oppression: legal, paralegal, and extralegal. In Hawaii, the combination of plantation *lunas*, police, and the courts enforced rules, levied fines, dished out corporal punishment, and jailed laborers viewed as recalcitrant, lazy, or homeless. On the mainland, Japanese Americans were cursed with vicious racist names and beaten by vigilante mobs, severely discriminated against in the workplace, consigned to segregated neighborhoods, schools, and certain public facilities, and sometimes even had their homes and businesses burned by arsonists or were chased by mobs out of their respective places of settlement.

If the majority of immigrant-generation Issei were passive and compliant in the face of such discrimination, some protested their racist exploitation and took steps to redress it through the courts. As early as 1891, one Japanese worker appeared before the Hawaiian Supreme Court to protest against the contract labor system for being tantamount to slavery, while that same year an Issei woman in San Francisco filed a writ of habeus corpus against the immigration commissioner for refusing her entry into that city and making her suffer the indignity of port detainment. "Although both cases were denied," observes Okihiro, "they were heard in the highest courts of the kingdom and nation, and revealed a feisty spirit of resistance from among a people frequently depicted as fatalistic and passive."[13]

Collective action was joined to individual acts of resistance. In 1903, to cite one particularly dramatic example, 500 Japanese and 200 Mexican sugar beet workers in Oxnard, California, coalesced as the Japanese-Mexican Labor Association to attack the contracting/subcontracting system and the policy mandating them to buy solely from designated stores. After this union struck, a settlement was arrived at through negotiations.

On Hawaii, collective action by plantation workers entailed perennial protests against especially punitive *lunas*, over wages and conditions of employment, and against irrational regulations and edicts. During 1900 alone, there were officially recorded at least twenty strikes involving nearly eight thousand Japanese plantation laborers. Five years later, workers banded together in the Japanese Reform Association to rescue through concerted action a total of 70,000 Japanese from the combined clutches of the Keihin Bank (which was closed down by Japan's government) and the immigration companies (whose agents met with governmental restriction). In 1909, however, the most significant protest of the period occurred when 7,000 Japanese workers on Oahu's main plantations struck, collectively, for higher wages. During this four-month-long strike, laborers complained of their wages not keeping pace with inflation and of earning salaries that were below those paid to white laborers doing the same work. Condemned by the planters as well as some from the Hawaiian Japanese community as being inspired by "agitators" and supported by a "criminal organization," the strike was curtailed and the association leaders arrested, imprisoned, and ultimately convicted on conspiracy charges. In Professor Okihiro's considered opinion, this 1909 strike marked the ending of the migrant stage for Japanese Americans.

During the ensuing settlement stage in Japanese American history, which extended to the outbreak of World War II in 1941, resistance activity in response to oppression remained very much in evidence among the Nikkei. As the major site of the mainland anti-Japanese movement, California was the first state, in 1913, to enact an Alien Land Law. This measure prevented ownership of land by "aliens ineligible for citizenship." Since Japanese (along with other Asian immigrants) were prohibited from becoming naturalized U.S. citizens, the law applied chiefly to them. Issei farmers were partially successful on their own in circumventing this law and subsequent ones that reinforced it, while the Japanese Association of America utilized a number of test cases to challenge these land laws' constitutionality. Notwithstanding that these challenges failed, some Issei frustrated their intended consequences by registering land in the names of their U.S.-born citizen Nisei children.

Oppression occurred not only with respect to those Japanese who worked the land in California, but also those who made a living harvesting the sea. In the fourteen-year interval between 1919 and 1933, the California legislature considered seven separate bills aimed at prohibiting the issuance of commercial fishing licenses to Japanese Americans. All such legislation rested upon the use of U.S. citizenship as the basis for receiving a commercial fishing license. Given the Issei's status as "aliens ineligible for citizenship," the legislation was clearly aimed at them. However, Tokunosuke Abe of San Diego, who ran the largest privately managed fishing fleet in southern California during this time, played a leading role in defeating each incarnation of this anti-Japanese legislation. Abe fought his final battle in 1938 when Democratic assemblyman Samuel Yorty of Los Angeles introduced a bill that, if passed, would have practically removed all Issei from the industry. According to historian Donald Estes, "Abe and his allies ultimately defeated the bill, but not without a long and intense battle that saw the state's Japanese American fishermen pitted against Naval Intelligence, the Congress of Industrial Organizations, the U.S. Attorney for Southern California, the American Legion, and the Native Sons of the Golden West, to name only a few."[14] Here, then, was another example, among many, where protracted Japanese American resistance paid dividends in the war against anti-Japanese oppression.

The Revitalization of a Robust Nikkei Tradition

POST-PEARL HARBOR JAPANESE AMERICAN PROTEST AND RESISTANCE

The most profound oppression directed against Japanese Americans, of course, was set in motion by the aftermath of Pearl Harbor, and this development led to the wartime eviction and incarceration of some 120,000 Nikkei. This story is too detailed and complex to even summarize here. What can be said is that the massive oppression called forth an abundance of resistance activity, resulting in the refurbishment of the Japanese American tradition of protest and dissent. Some of the resistance is well known, particularly the constitutional challenges to the curfew, exclusion, and mass detention mounted by four Nisei– Minoru Yasui, Gordon Hirabayashi, Fred Korematsu, and Mitsuye Endo–and the spectacular strikes and riots that occurred at the Santa Anita, Poston, Manzanar, and Tule Lake camps.[15]

But there was also informal resistance activity that occurred in comparatively quiet and less dramatic ways. This resistance even preceded the enforced mass movement into their wartime concentration camps, such as the destruction by some Japanese Americans of their possessions rather than the sale of them at much reduced prices to avaricious buyers, and the transfer by other Nikkei of their farms to friends and neighbors instead of submitting to a takeover by the Farm Security Administration.

What about resistance activity by Japanese Americans in the Wartime Civil Control Administration (WCCA)-administered "assembly centers" and the War Relocation Authority (WRA)-run "relocation centers?" Although this question cries out for systematic and sustained historical treatment, a useful starting point for such an inquiry is Gary Okihiro's unpublished anthology, "Resistance in America's Concentration Camps."[16]

As Okihiro's perceptive introduction establishes, the character of WRA camp resistance was shaped by the orientation of the U.S. government and power structure toward those of Japanese ancestry during the interval bracketed by the growing threat of war with Japan in the early 1930s and the immediate post-Pearl Harbor roundup of suspected Japanese American community leaders. Summoning Bob Kumamoto's selection, "The Search for Spies: American Counterintelligence and the Japanese American Community, 1931-1942"[17] as documentary evidence, Okihiro states that during this critical decade, the concern for military security was made subordinate to ridding American society of Japanese culture. Instead of seeing Issei patriotism toward Japan as a natural form of ethnic identity and pride (which was especially understandable given that they were barred from becoming naturalized Americans) compatible with the immigrant generation's residential status in America, the U.S. counterintelligence community chose to view it as anti-American. Thus, all Japanese American ethnic distinctions such as language and religion that were previously viewed as being merely inferior, were now construed to be potentially subversive and threatening. This racist outlook led during the post-Pearl Harbor roundup of Issei leadership to a concerted assault on all the institutions through which Japanese culture had been transmitted and preserved in Japanese America. "In effect," concludes Okihiro, "by undermining Japanese clubs and civic organizations and by removing the leaders of the cultural community, including Buddhist and Shinto priests, language school teachers, and journalists, they [counterintelligence] planned the destruction of the ethnic community and ultimately the elimination of Japanese culture in America."[18]

Because of this pervasive cultural oppression of Japanese Americans, much of their resistance activity in the WRA camps was driven by a desire to preserve their ethnic heritage and to recreate their prewar ethnic institutions, practices, and values in their new "homes." In support of this argument, Okihiro references selections in his anthology wherein the authors, such as David Hacker in his study of cultural resistance in Manzanar following the 1942 riot at that camp, emphasize how internees resisted the "Americanization" campaigns foisted upon them by WRA administrators with reassertions of "Japanization." According to Hacker, explains Okihiro, "cultural resistance [at Manzanar] was successful largely because of the collective group, the family and the wider ethnic community, which sought to channel behavior into acceptable Japanese forms."[19] Okihiro also draws upon one of his own studies in the anthology to show how the revival of traditional Japanese religious beliefs and practices in the camps formed the basis for a wider network of cultural resistance. Here, instead of resistance sentiment being channeled into open rebellion as in the case of the Manzanar Revolt, it was funneled into a revitalization of Buddhism and religious folk beliefs and associated Japanese aesthetic expressions (landscape gardening, flower arrangement, *sumo*, music, drama, and poetry) and core Meiji cultural and ethical practices (filial piety and ancestor worship).[20]

As early as 1955, ten years after the end of World War II, sociologist Norman Jackman wrote a study about collective protest in the WRA camps. In it Jackman cataloged and analyzed the myriad protest activity that he uncovered in his research. Characterizing this protest as either "passive resistance and insubordination" or "overt rebellion," he situated his findings relative to extant theoretical and descriptive literature related to imprisoned people. Forty years later, anthropologist Lane Hirabayashi built upon Jackman's stockpile of camp protest incidents in an edited volume of the resistance field reports that participant-observer Richard Nishimoto had compiled at the Poston camp in Arizona for the University of California, Berkeley-sponsored Japanese American Evacuation and Resettlement Study.[21]

The Revitalization of a Robust Nikkei Tradition

In introducing one of Nishimoto's research reports for his 1995 edited volume–that on the All Center Conference held in Salt Lake City, Utah, during February 16-22, 1945–Hirabayashi treated it within the context of "popular resistance" as partially disclosed by Okihiro in his published resistance writings. This conference, explained Hirabayashi, had been called into being in response to the WRA's precipitous unilateral announcement in late 1944 that all WRA camps, save for the segregation center at Tule Lake, would be closed by the end of 1945 (by force if necessary). At this conference, representatives from seven of the camps made it clear that, while they were certainly not against being returned to mainstream America, they nonetheless resented "that the proposal was yet another instance of the WRA trying to push Japanese Americans around without consulting them and without paying sufficient attention to the needs of specific groups within the overall population."[22]

The implied physical coercion exacerbated the representatives' unanimous indignation that such an arbitrary closure date would work an extreme hardship on some Issei and older Nisei who had been pauperized by their eviction/detention experience. Declaring that such persons, as with the disabled, could not make it on their own within the larger society on the twenty-five dollars and the one-way train ticket back to their point of origin in the country that the WRA promised, the representatives lodged a staunch protest. The government, after all, had been responsible for the mass expulsion and imprisonment of Japanese Americans, and it was therefore incumbent upon the government to ensure their secure and sound return back into American society.

Accordingly, as Hirabayshi depicted, "the All Center representatives hammered out . . . [a] document . . . demanding [governmental] consideration of three key points: (1) monetary reparations for losses and damage, (2) special support for the elderly and needy, and (3) a full guaranty of the rights and safety of individuals."[23] Although such popular resistance action did not deter the WRA from proceeding with their closure policy, it did pay dividends at a future date. Clearly, as Hirabayashi argued, these demands foreshadowed similar ones put forward three decades later within the Redress/Reparations movement, and the result was the passage of the Civil Liberties Act of 1988.

JAPANESE AMERICAN PROTEST AND RESISTANCE WITHIN THE HEART MOUNTAIN CONCENTRATION CAMP

The Heart Mountain Concentration Camp in Wyoming has attracted the critical attention of a substantial number of commentators. Among them have been historians like T. A. Larson,[24] Rogers Daniels,[25] Douglas Nelson,[26]

Mike Mackey,[27] Louis Fiset,[28] Frank Chin,[29] William Hohri,[30] Eric Muller,[31] Gwenn Jensen,[32] Susan Smith,[33] and Frank Inouye;[34] social scientists such as Aasel Hansen[35] and Rita Takahashi Cates,[36] journalists and journalist historians like Bill Hosokawa[37] and Lauren Kessler,[38] artists such as Estelle Peck Ishigo,[39] photographers like Masumi Hayashi[40] and Hansel Mieth and Otto Hagel,[41] filmmakers such as Steven Okazaki,[42] Emiko Omori,[43] and Frank Abe,[44] novelists like Gretel Erlich,[45] oral historians like John Tateishi[46] and Susan McKay,[47] archivists such as Eric Bittner,[48] and even firsthand participants and observers like Frank Emi,[49] James Omura,[50] Velma Kessel,[51] and Peter Simpson.[52] With the possible exception of the Tule Lake center, Heart Mountain is probably the best documented of all the wartime Japanese American imprisonment facilities, including so-called assembly centers, relocation centers, segregation centers, isolation centers, and internment camps. Accordingly, it is possible to gain a pretty clear picture of the oppression that existed there as well as the resistance that developed in response to it.

Although Heart Mountain was located outside the Western Defense Command's "Restricted Area," it nonetheless was subject to controls similar to those War Relocation Authority centers sited within that area, such as Manzanar and Tule Lake in California, and Poston and Gila in Arizona. In addition, the same public hostilities were directed at its residents.

In common with those camps in the "Restricted Area," Heart Mountain, as Rita Takahashi Cates has reported, was surrounded by barbed wire fence and watched over by sentry-manned guard towers. The imprisoned population collectively protested these unnecessary indignities. Indeed, a November 1942 petition, signed by half of all the adults in the camp, over 3,000 people, denounced the fence and guard towers as "ridiculous in every respect. . . . a barrier to a full understanding between the Administration and residents" and as "devoid of humanitarian principles . . . an insult to any free human being."[53] The petition was sent to WRA Director Dillon Myer charging that the fence proved that Heart Mountain was a "concentration camp" and that internees were "prisoners of war." Internees supplemented such written indirect protest against oppression with direct oral resistance to and outright defiance of military authority. As recalled by one noted resistance leader, Nisei Frank Inouye, "on several occasions Nisei men found near the fence . . . were pushed or shoved by guards, and they retaliated with angry cries of 'Go ahead, shoot me.'"[54]

Then, in December 1942, the military police patrolling the camp boundaries arrested thirty-two persons for security violations. The culprits the U.S. army took into custody on this occasion were all children eleven or under in age, who had been sledding on a hill just outside of camp. Although released later the same day, this callous treatment of children, in the words of

The Revitalization of a Robust Nikkei Tradition

Roger Daniels, "understandably inflamed many of the Japanese Americans and sparked a general protest against the whole theory and practice of the evacuation."[55]

This protest extended to the camp authorities' practice of searching outgoing internee mail and the imposition of a "pass system" for center ingress and egress. This sense of oppression was compounded by the actions of the nearby Park County towns of Powell and Cody, both of whom passed resolutions barring internees.[56] This particular oppression was further exacerbated by Wyoming's governor, Lester Hunt, declaring that these resolutions were well reasoned and in the interest of the internees' safety and welfare. Heart Mountaineers viewed it as a matter of rank hypocrisy that, while they were not permitted in Cody or Powell, they were permitted, without screening or investigation, to be released from Heart Mountain to harvest crops for beleaguered farmers within the region surrounding the camp. To add to the internees' sense of being a despised and persecuted people, the major metropolitan newspaper serving the camp population, the *Denver Post*, was stridently anti-Japanese and, in March 1943, leveled flagrant and unfounded charges that Heart Mountain had excessive foodstuffs and that the internees were guilty of wantonly wasting these supplies.[57]

More oppression emanated from Heart Mountain's appointed staff, a portion of whom referred to their Nikkei charges as "Japs," and both viewed and treated them contemptuously. Some of these Caucasian employees even threatened to resign from their administrative positions if certain demands of theirs were not heeded. Included in a petition signed by them were the following two offenses: (1) "We object to sharing our dorm with the Japs"; and (2) "We ask that a woman janitor be appointed and that the rest of the Japanese be compelled to keep out of our living rooms. They have their own quarters, [and] we feel that we are entitled to ours. WE MEAN IT!"[58]

Another source of internee oppression included the use at Heart Mountain, as at other WRA camps, of informers. A related problem that contributed to a loss of internee autonomy was that Heart Mountain authorities strategically placed pro-administration internees into desired leadership positions so as to enable them to rally support for the actions, programs, and goals of the camp and the WRA administration. A prime case in point, according to Rita Takahashi Cates and Roger Daniels, was the appointment of accommodationist JACL supporter Bill Hosokawa, a *Heart Mountain Sentinel* editor: "During the height of discontent at the camp, Hosokawa's paper 'reacted typically . . . by assuring the Heart Mountaineers that Director Dillon Myer's WRA was doing "everything possible" under the circumstances.'"[59]

Internal factors that influenced internee perceptions and responses encompassed Heart Mountain's physical conditions, including the provision of basic amenities and support services. In common with other WRA camps,

A Matter of Conscience

Heart Mountain was beset with problems related to food services. Internees complained that food intended for them was either not being delivered to them or else was being diverted to some other destination. This led to a series of investigations, some of which were launched by internee groups. Food supplies ultimately were normalized. However, because some internees feared that under conditions of heavy snows the camp population could become isolated and starve, camp chefs stowed surplus supplies in the block mess hall storerooms once the all-center warehouses were filled to capacity.

In December 1942, Earl Best, the assistant camp steward and a former Army man notorious for his undiplomatic dealings with Japanese Americans, undertook an inventory of Heart Mountain food supplies. When he uncovered a cache of food stored in one block mess hall's attic, he heatedly confronted the chef responsible, a Mr. Haraguchi. Best later formally complained that Haraguchi "had a cleaver in his hand . . . [and] threw a case of applesauce at me when I was leaving."[60] In his solicitude for the people in his block, Haraguchi had become distraught and distempered. Apparently, the situation was even worse than Best had described. Other witnesses divulged that Haraguchi had been wielding a butcher knife, and only the timely intervention of some Japanese women kitchen workers prevented him from killing Best's internee assistant. Furthermore, Heart Mountain's director of internal security noted in a report on this incident that "all [of the camp] cooks appear to be banded together in some type of union," while a spokesman for the cooks was alleged to have said, "If the soldiers try to prevent a strike someone would be killed and he would also kill someone."[61]

Internees, well beyond this particular incident, continued their anguished concern over camp food service, including the quality and the quantity of the food dished up to them. A January 1943 investigation of the camp's thirty-three mess halls, undertaken by the Block Managers Evacuees Food Committee, reported that menus were unfit for children, unbalanced, too starchy, lacked adequate fruits and vegetables, and included dishes that were far too greasy to be eaten by those on regular diets, to say nothing of those on restricted ones.

As with the other WRA camps, Heart Mountain's housing situation was dismal, especially during the opening phase of the center's existence when the barracks quarters were unfinished and the "apartments" congested by an overabundance of occupants. If shelter from the elements was a cause for concern, so too was clothing. Despite repeated promises from the camp's administration for the delivery of clothing allowances, none arrived at Heart Mountain until November 1942. In the meantime, the agitated camp population reacted to this oppressive delay by repeated requests, petitions, and even a strike.

A strike also occurred at the Heart Mountain hospital in June 1943.

The Revitalization of a Robust Nikkei Tradition

The medical historian Louis Fiset, in a fascinating 1998 article, has covered this incident in compelling detail.[62] In October 1942, the *Heart Mountain Sentinel* had lauded the hospital, describing the seventeen-wing facility, which was staffed by 150 employees (including nine physicians, ten registered nurses, three graduate nurses, and forty-nine nurses' aides), among Wyoming's best hospitals. But the *Sentinel* picture was a misleading one. The hospital's comparative lack of equipment and acutely limited supplies obliged its doctors to move patients to nearby Cody and Powell, or even to transport them as far away as Billings, Montana, for surgeries or special treatments. When supplies that had been ordered failed to arrive, the chief medical officer had to round up basic supplies (e.g., swabs, needles, and drugs) locally.

Of still greater significance, the WRA's tardiness in recruiting a head nurse for the hospital meant that the non-professional staff, which would expand to over three hundred in number, was deficient in organization, wanting in professionalism, and practically unmanageable. Not only the chief medical officer, but also the appointed hospital personnel were culturally obtuse and demonstrated unsound judgment when interacting with the Nikkei medical staff (most of whom were already smarting from having lost much of their lofty prewar status and being paid insultingly miniscule camp wages for their professional services). Given this overall situation, morale suffered greatly, and eventually resentments built up against the Caucasian personnel in authority to the point where two hospital walkouts occurred in 1943.

Earlier in 1943, dissent at Heart Mountain was precipitated by the WRA's announced plans to convert the government-owned and operated Community Enterprises stores in the camps into internee-owned and operated cooperatives. The seemingly benign purpose for this change was to put internees at the helm of the camp's largest operation. But rather than embracing this change of affairs with gratitude, the internees overwhelmingly rejected it. The opposition's most vociferous spokesperson was the fifty-four-year-old, Hawaii-born Kiyoshi Okamoto.

Okamoto, in the words of fellow camp activist Frank Inouye, "had previously been a sharp critic of the Japanese American Citizens League, which he considered a Quisling organization because of its earlier cooperation and collaboration with the federal authorities during the 1942 removal of West Coast Japanese Americans."[63] Openly denigrating the WRA cooperation plan, Okamoto vented his antipathy at block meetings and in letters to the *Heart Mountain Sentinel*. Through the mechanism of the cooperative plan, reasoned Okamoto, the U.S. government sought to legitimize their unconstitutional eviction and detention of Japanese Americans. Accepting direct responsibility for operating the cooperatives was tantamount to accepting their wartime mistreatment as a valid and necessary move. Precisely because the internment was patently illegal, declared Okamoto, "the government and only the government was fully responsible for the welfare of the camp population."[64] Okamoto's viewpoint prevailed at Heart Mountain. The WRA's subsequent abandonment of its plan represented, to quote Frank Inouye once again, "the first in a series of 'victories' by the Heart Mountain internees over the WRA. It gave them a sense of limited control over their circumstances and encouraged later and more far-reaching dissident movements."[65]

Susan McKay's recent–and very discerning–article on the "everyday resistance" of young Nisei women at the Heart Mountain camp[66] divulges a subtle way in which a portion of the internee population there achieved, in Inouye's formulation, "limited control over their circumstances" and stimulated long-range dissent (not only during the war in camp, but even much later as within the 1970s-1980s redress and reparations movement). Based upon open-ended, generalized oral history interviews conducted by McKay in the late 1990s with twenty-four former Heart Mountain Nisei women (mostly married mothers while in camp) who were born between 1911 and 1923, this article concludes that these women, in non-public ways (what McKay styles "infrapolitics") and largely within the sphere of "informal networks of kin, neighbors, family, and friends," resisted by "speaking up, defying rules, and protesting."[67] Much of their resistance activity typically involved efforts to improve family life, particularly as it affected their children. Some other of it was directed at affronts to their ethnic and social class identity. Still other resistance and protest was directed at improving housing (e.g., demands for separate space) and food conditions (e.g., challenging mess hall managers for disallowing food to be prepared in family barracks for those children reluctant to eat in a communal facility) related to their family's well-being. Some of the means they used involved risk, such as a hospital nurse defying her Caucasian superior's orders, while others, such as simply acting "normal" in a concentration camp environment (dressing up, wearing cosmetics, and indulging in gossip), opposed their circumstances in less obtrusive yet nonetheless effective ways.

Up until early 1943, notwithstanding what has been described above in the way of protest and resistance activity, some Heart Mountain administrators insisted on characterizing their detention center as a "happy camp." After this point in time, with the emergence of the registration/segregation crisis, dissent became so dramatically manifest as to render such a sanguine label utterly out of touch with the reality at Heart Mountain. With this development, the latent discontents within the camp burst into the open, and the internee population's opposition to U.S. government, WRA, and center authorities so intensified and ramified to where it could justifiably be said that Heart Mountain became, at least for a spell, the least "happy" WRA camp.

The Revitalization of a Robust Nikkei Tradition

The registration program was initiated throughout the Japanese American camps in February 1943 by the issuance of the Army-WRA "Leave Clearance" questionnaires. At Heart Mountain this program, as aptly phrased by Rita Takahashi Cates, "was implemented with less than 'deliberate speed' and 'desirable results' due to widespread resistance and protest."[68]

Encouraged by the success of the 100th Batallion, rooted in prewar Japanese American volunteers and Hawaii draftees, the government, in order to create an all-Nisei 442nd Infantry Regimental Combat Team, "adjusted" the Selective Service Act barring Nisei enlistees. The military had expected to obtain fifteen hundred volunteers from Hawaii, but instead was overwhelmed by more than ten thousand of them. On the other hand, the Army's belief that an equal number would volunteer for military service from the mainland camps proved embarrassingly wide of the mark. Nevertheless, Secretary of War Henry Stimson, the Cabinet officer who most strongly supported Nikkei exclusion and imprisonment, now became a fugleman for camp volunteerism. To separate the "traitors" or "rotten apples" from the "patriots," he devised a screening system. "It is only by mutual confidence and cooperation," he exclaimed, "that the loyal Japanese Americans can be restored to their civil rights."[69] The irony of Stimson's exclamation, as Frank Inouye has astutely observed, was not lost on the Nisei in Heart Mountain and the other camps.

> [The] "mutual confidence" Stimson mentioned would be manifested on their part by their being allowed to die for their country. America's confidence had already been demonstrated in indicting, judging, convicting, sentencing, imprisoning, and dispossessing one-hundred thousand people without evidence or legal formalization.[70]

Because the WRA had been looking for a quick and effective way of distinguishing which of their charges should be permitted to work outside the camps, they capitalized upon a War Department-developed form to be used for recruiting soldiers as the basis for their own questionnaire for leave clearance. The use of these two overlapping documents caused a series of escalating confrontations between the government and the internees at all of the camps, including Heart Mountain.

Two questions, especially, provoked internee resentment:

No. 27. Are you willing to serve in the Armed Forces of the United States on combat duty wherever ordered?

No. 28. Will you swear unqualified allegiance to the United States of America?

Adult males and females were obliged to respond to the form. Issei, ineligible to become naturalized U.S. citizens, were indignant because swearing unqualified allegiance to the U.S., as question 28 demanded, would mean a repudiation of their Japanese citizenship that would render them stateless people. The Nisei, on the other hand, were upset over this question because it implied that they were foreign nationals seeking American citizenship. In fact, both questions infuriated Nisei males because they saw in them a clever trap. "By signing the questionnaire 'yes/yes,'" explains Frank Inouye, "they could be immediately drafted into the Armed Service as volunteers without further processing or exemptions. They would then be forced to leave their aging Issei parents in camp at the mercy of a government that had already proven its disregard for basic human rights."[71] Nor were Nisei females happy with these questions, since their signing them would indicate a willingness to serve in the military.

The registration crisis was especially acute at Heart Mountain. The responsibility for this state of affairs started at the top with the camp's director, Guy Robertson. Instead of proceeding with deliberation and due caution and collaboration, he threatened the internees with severe consequences if they did not respond as expected. Feeling that the government expected the camps to produce army recruits in the same abundance as in Hawaii, he championed the cause of registration in the *Heart Mountain Sentinel* and bullied block leaders to ensure compliance in the process by all of their respective adult denizens.

When the Army Registration Team visited Heart Mountain, they encountered stiff opposition at their first major meeting, on February 6, with internees (overwhelmingly Nisei men). Led by Frank Inouye, a prewar UCLA senior student, a small group of these Nisei men had been holding advance meetings for the explicit purpose of resisting the registration process. Their intention, plainly, was to "disrupt the meeting by challenging the government's right to recruit volunteers without first clarifying and restoring the Nisei's constitutional rights."[72]

The head of the Army Registration Team began the meeting by reiterating Stimson's line: "Our mission is to return you to a normal way of life. . . . Its fundamental purpose is to put your situation on a plane which is consistent with the dignity of American citizenship. Not all Japanese Americans are loyal to their government . . . and individuals who will not accept any obligation to the land which gives them their opportunity . . . are the disloyal ones."[73] This address called forth, by way of a rejoinder, a Nisei manifesto read by Inouye. He referred to the degradation and discrimination suffered by earlier Nisei draftees in the Army, he assailed the U.S. government for the enforced mass eviction and detention of his ethnic community, and ridiculed the irony of the government now asking these same victims to shed their blood for America. Before requesting the Nisei's military enlistment, Inouye concluded his oration, the government should first acknowledge their rights as American citizens.

The Revitalization of a Robust Nikkei Tradition

This "manifesto" was roundly received among camp Nisei, who effectively sabotaged every subsequent attempt by the army team to implement its registration at Heart Mountain. Meanwhile, Inouye called for the creation of an elected central body to explore how best, under the present circumstances, to ensure the best interests of the camp's citizens. And on that very evening, each block chose two representatives to serve in the new organization.

On February 11, the group held its first meeting. All of those in attendance were Nisei males, including two who would become well known the following year as the leaders of the Heart Mountain Fair Play Committee: the aforementioned Kiyoshi Okamoto and Paul Nakadate. Frank Inouye was elected to chair this group, which adopted the name of the Heart Mountain Congress of American Citizens, while Nakdate was chosen to be its secretary. At this meeting, Inouye has recollected, "the delegates submitted fourteen resolutions which were eventually distilled into four main subjects: (1) clarification of Nisei citizenship status; (2) publicizing of clarification by the U.S. President, the Secretary of War and the Attorney General; (3) postponement of further registration until clarification was obtained; and (4) implied consent of the Nisei to serve in the armed forces upon clarification of their citizenship status."[74]

The Congress, as an initial order of business, had to reconcile a paradox associated with the registration. Many camp Nisei were against serving in the armed forces, but at the same time they did not want to lose their U.S. citizenship. The Congress resolved, after considerable deliberation, to recommend that Nisei give a "Yes" response to question 27. "This," according to Inouye, "was felt to be the most expedient means of attaining the Congress' main goal: clarification of Nisei citizenship status. Unless the men indicated their willingness to serve, they would have little bargaining power with the federal government."[75]

Camp activities during this time came effectively to a halt. Dissident voices were heard, loud and clear, within the community. Frank Emi, destined to be a prominent leader, like Okamoto and Nakadate, within the Fair Play Committee, posted hand-printed copies of his answers to Question 27 and 28 in public places throughout the camp: "Under the present conditions and circumstances, I am unable to answer these questions." Okamoto, who opposed all appeasement of authorities as long as Nisei were illegally detained, spoke out advising Nisei to resist all camp recruiting activities while they were still illegally detained. So alarmed were camp administrators at these activities that they tried to prevent the *Sentinel* from covering the Congress's activities, while Director Robertson "threatened to invoke the espionage and sedition laws against those seeking to derail the registration process."[76]

Notwithstanding this opposition, the Heart Mountain Congress of

A Matter of Conscience

American Citizens continued with its campaign. On February 19 it even sent President Franklin Roosevelt a formal petition of protest, plus telegrams to the other nine camps recommending them to act similarly.

Although the WRA/army registration process eventually proceeded, the Congress scored an important triumph when the army conceded that internees could answer Questions 27 and 28 with qualified or conditional responses. Moreover, the final tally of registration showed what a bust it had been in all of the WRA camps. Rather than the Army achieving the 1,500 volunteers sought, it received merely 805. The situation at Heart Mountain was still more pathetic: whereas 2,000 volunteers were expected, only 38 signed on, and a scant 19 of these were eventually inducted.

Then, too, the Heart Mountain Congress produced an unexpected–and certainly unwanted–result: 800 Nisei in camp renounced their American citizenship. "The body had been formed to protest the registration process and clarify Nisei rights," Frank Inouye has written. "What emerged [however] was a massive vote for repatriation to Japan."[77]

While the Congress assuredly did not realize its stated demands, it laid down a legacy that was carried on in the early months of 1944 by a group headed by Kiyoshi Okamoto, Paul Nakadate, and Frank Emi. This new group, the Heart Mountain Fair Play Committee, coalesced once the government decided to "honor" the American citizenship rights of the Nisei by reopening the military to them through making them eligible to be drafted into the Army. Since many of the other articles in this anthology are devoted to this organization and its corporate and individual members' trials, tribulations, and triumphs, the balance of this essay will be reserved for surveying the protest and resistance activities of the sole newspaper editor who publicly supported the Fair Play Committee–Jimmie Omura.

THE 1944 CONSPIRACY TRIAL OF *ROCKY SHIMPO* (PROTEST-RESISTANCE) EDITOR JAMES MATSUMOTO OMURA [78]

Four days after the Feburary 19, 1942, issuance of Executive Order 9066, James Matsumoto Omura and Fumiko Caryl Okuma (the business manager of *Current Life* magazine to whom Omura had been secretly married) appeared in San Francisco at hearings sponsored by a House of Representatives select committee. The committee's chair was Congressman John Tolan of California and its purpose was to investigate "national defense migration." Earlier, a parade of Japanese American Citizens League leaders had informed the Tolan Committee that the government could count on their complete support should mass eviction and detention of their entire ethnic population, two-thirds of them U. S. citizens, be viewed as imperative for prosecuting the war. To this position, whereby loyalty was equated with the sacrifice of rights and accommodation to authority, Omura and Okuma flatly dissented. While the fiercely patriotic Omura agreed with JACLers that subversive actions within the Japanese American community should be reported to government officials, he denigrated their notion that mass evacuation was a necessary evil and disparaged their chauvinistic policy of "constructive cooperation." Chairman Tolan closed the day's hearings before Omura, the last witness, could complete his full testimony, but it was afterwards entered into the official committee record and included his famous lines of protest. "I would like to ask the committee: Has the Gestapo come to America? Have we not risen in righteous anger at Hitler's mistreatment of Jews? Then is it not incongruous that citizen Americans of Japanese descent should be mistreated and persecuted?"

On March 27, 1942, the army issued a proclamation declaring that in two days the free movement of Japanese Americans out of the strategic defense areas of the West Coast would be frozen, and their enforced movement into assembly centers begun. Omura, who had determined not to linger in San Francisco for internment orders, fled to the "free zone" of Denver, Colorado, where his wife had already rented space to house *Current Life*. Unable to continue the magazine's publication, Omura started an employment placement bureau. In addition to assisting Denver's burgeoning war refugee population find jobs free of charge, Omura filed several racial discrimination cases through the War Manpower Commission that led to Nisei defense jobs. To pay his bills, Omura took gardening jobs, worked in a munitions factory, and wrote free-lance articles for Denver's several vernacular newspapers. On January 28, 1944, he accepted the position of English language-editor and business manager for one of these papers, the *Rocky Shimpo*.

Almost a year prior to editing the *Rocky Shimpo*, Omura had contested the JACL-supported Nisei combat unit because it was segregated and, therefore, a symbol of racism. Omura's appointment to his new post closely followed Secretary of War Stimson's announcement about Nisei draft resumption, another policy that Omura knew the JACL had urged upon the government. When this measure caused the Heart Mountain Fair Play Committee to mushroom, Omura opened the *Rocky Shimpo*'s pages to that organization for news releases. Then, on February 28, 1944, Omura wrote his first editorial about draft reinstitution and the reaction to it by those detained in WRA camps. His concern at this point was not Heart Mountain, but the actions taken at the Granada, Colorado, and Minidoka, Idaho, centers. There draft resistance had been sporadic and punctuated with denunciations of democracy and avowals of expatriation to Japan. Whereas Omura believed that the government should restore a large share of the Nisei's rights before asking them to sacrifice their lives on the battlefield, he could not condone impulsive, reckless, and irresponsible draft resistance.

A Matter of Conscience

It soon became plain to Omura that the Fair Play Committee represented an organized draft resistance movement dedicated to the principle that citizen Japanese should do their duty as Americans, equally, but not before being treated equally by the U.S. government. Thereafter in his *Rocky Shimpo* editorials he supported the FPC, not as an organization, but solely on the issue of restoration as a prelude to induction. That the *Heart Mountain Sentinel*, the camp newspaper, was staunchly pro-JACL (and, as such, censorious of the FPC for placing Japanese American loyalty and patriotism at risk) assuredly added fuel to Omura's fiery editorials. These gained members for the FPC and dramatically increased *Rocky Shimpo* sales in Heart Mountain and the other camps (where, opined Omura, "at least 90 percent of the people . . . are opposed to the JACL"). But Omura's hard-hitting editorials also caused the government to oblige him to sever his connection with the paper in mid-April 1944 and then, three months later, prompted the Wyoming grand jury to indict him plus the seven FPC leaders.

But I am going to leave the remainder of Omura's trial by fire for him to tell via the memoir he researched and wrote between 1982 and his death in 1994 (and which I am currently editing for publication).[79]

* * * * *

On the 20th day of July 1944, I arose at 4:30 a.m. with the notion of getting an early start on my Denver-area gardening route and to enjoy an extended weekend to take my show dog for a run in a mountain meadow and to rest. One thing was certain: it would be hot again. The sun had beaten down relentlessly since the beginning of summer. I had felt the need to recharge my battery from this intense heat wave. Breakfast dishes had been cleared and the dog fed, and as I picked up the dish to give the dog water, a surprise knock came at the cabin door. It was still dark outside and I wondered who would be knocking at this ungodly hour. The man at the door identified himself as an FBI agent. I could barely make out the shadowy figures of three other men behind him.

"James Omura?" the man asked.

"Yes," I said.

"We're FBI agents and United States marshals.
You're under arrest."

He then held out a sheet of paper before him and someone behind him held a flashlight so he could read. While the agent read the opening indictment, the Doberman Pincher nudged forward against my right leg and I lightly grasped the collar to restrain him.

The count on which I was charged along with the leaders of the Fair Play Committee was conspiracy to aid and abet violation of the Selective Service laws. The United States Attorneys in Cheyenne brought the action in a secret indictment issued by the Grand Jurors of Wyoming on the 10th of May. The actual case got underway on October 23, 1944, in a Federal District Court in Cheyenne, Wyoming. Coincidentally American troops were advancing upon the homeland of Japan, following a death-blow administered to the Imperial fleet in June of 1942 at Midway.

"Can I give the dog water and chain him up outside?" I asked and the agent assented.

The lead FBI agent entered the house and began a search of the boxes, taking a slender bunch of documents. Later, I was provided with a list of materials removed from my home. As I locked the door, I noticed that the kitchen light next door was on, and I was given permission to ask my neighbor, Mrs. Severson, to provide water for the Doberman. It was going to be a hot day. When I crossed over to Mrs. Severson's house, I spied the second FBI agent stationed behind the house. I was not allowed to take anything with me.

Although I had resigned as English editor of the Rocky Shimpo *on the evening of April 18, it was not considered enough by Tom C. Clark, Assistant Attorney General. My voice had to be discredited. Conviction was a sure method of discrediting me. It was what the Japanese American Citizens League had been clamoring about. The government bureaucrats were strongly influenced by what appeared in the* Pacific Citizen *and took their lead thereby.*

I was driven to the United States Marshal's building, finger-printed, and taken to the top floor and incarcerated in the nearest free-standing cage of which there were two. Other cages lined the north and east walls in a semi-circular fashion. I asked for the use of a phone but was refused. I repeated the request each time a marshal showed up.

Forty-five minutes after being caged, a reporter from the Denver Post *showed up. He was a slender, short person and wore a disconcerted smirk on his face. I took a dislike to him. The reporter walked slowly around the cage, sizing me up.*

"So, you're a fifth columnist," he inquired.

"I'm not guilty of the charge," I responded.

"That's what they all say," he retorted.

He returned a half hour later.

"I'd like to take a picture of you," he said.

"Not in this condition," I stated. "Not unless I get a shave."

"You people are all alike," was his parting shot.

Here was a reporter with a closed racist mind. In fact, the newspaper he worked for was also bigoted. The Denver Post *was a carbon copy of the Hearst "Yellow Journalism" of California.*

A Matter of Conscience

At 1:30 p.m., a deputy marshal escorted me to the City & County Building, where I was motioned to take a seat half way down the courtroom. The courtroom was split in half with bright sunlight in the back and the front half in gloom. Barely discernible was a figure of a man on the bench. I could make him out by the white shirt he wore. He was leaning to his left, conversing with some people below him. They were only visible briefly when someone opened the rear door in exiting.

"Mr. Omura, do you understand what you are charged with?" the judge asked.

"Yes," I replied.

"How do you plead?" he asked.

"Not guilty of the charge," I answered.

More discussions were held at the bench. I was then led out by the deputy marshal.

"There's a bank of telephones to the right near the entrance," he said. "You can make your phone call now."

I made my call to my wife Caryl at the house where she worked as a domestic and informed her of the situation and asked her to call the lawyer Sidney Jacobs and see to the dog. I was returned to confinement.

Twenty minutes later I was taken out again, placed in a car and whisked from Denver to Cheyenne by a marshal and a deputy. We stopped only once at a small cluster of buildings, which included a general store, on my request to relieve myself. A deputy accompanied me to a rear privy but would not allow me to close the door. It was 5:15 p.m. when we arrived at the Laramie County Jail in Cheyenne. There, I was rudely received and cussed at by a deputy and placed in East Row among a group of about a dozen inmates. I was taken out less than five minutes later, and placed in solitary confinement upstairs in a vacant woman's quarter. The windows were screened off with metal grills and plastic strips with about one inch of space between them. Toward the top, up to a foot separated them. This allowed for a restricted view of the sky. The room contained a bed and a commode in the far north corner; a basin and a pitcher of water but no towel; and a bureau from which the mirror had been removed. The entry was a metal grill with a foot-square opening eighteen inches from the floor for passage of food and other items. I made requests for shaving articles, pencil, a pad, and reading materials, but all were denied.

"The only thing we can let you have are cigarettes," I was told.

The hours were long and boring. The indictment stated:

The Grand Jurors for the United States of America, selected, empaneled, sworn and charged in the District Court of the United States for the District

102

of Wyoming, at the May Term of said Court in the year 1944, on their oaths and affirmations respectively do present:

It then charged that I had "unlawfully, willfully, and knowingly combined, conspired, confederated, and agreed together" with leaders of the Fair Play Committee and "divers other persons . . . to evade the requirements of the Selective Training and Service Act of 1940 and the rules, regulations and directions made pursuant thereto and to counsel, aid and abet . . . other citizens of the United States of Japanese descent who had registered . . . to evade service in the land or naval forces of the United States."

On the fifth day, I was standing by the window and caught a glimpse of five Nisei being escorted into the jail. I reasoned that these must be the leaders of the Fair Play Committee. That assessment was confirmed when, the next afternoon, a jailer slipped me a cigarette and a couple of bars of candy.

"The boys downstairs asked whether you were here," he said. "They sent these up for you."

Caryl came up to see me on the ninth day and I was taken out to the office anteroom for the conference. I was informed that Sidney Jacobs had been retained and that the Studebaker was sold for $600, which I thought was a trifle low, to make the down payment.

Mr. Jacobs came to see me on the fifteenth day, on Friday, August 3. He was very brief and seemed to be in a huge rush to get back to Denver. He stated that he had retained L. C. Sampson, a secretary at the Wyoming Bar Association, as a stand-in attorney at $50.00 per day. He stated he had agreed with Caryl to take my case for $1,000 and promised to work hard on it. My opinion was not asked. He emphasized that the important thing was for me to get out on bail to help him with the case. He sloughed off my complaints of solitary confinement.

"Take it up with Mr. Sampson when he comes to see you Monday," he said.

I couldn't believe it. His somewhat cavalier attitude shocked me. Here I had been in solitary confinement for fifteen days. I had gone along with Sidney Jacobs, a civil lawyer, because of my conviction that the government did not have a case against me. The Fair Play Committee had hired Abraham Lincoln Wirin, an ACLU attorney in Los Angeles who also doubled as attorney for the JACL. Caryl had rejected an offer for inclusion from the Fair Play Committee in order to maintain independence.

Mr. Sampson was outraged to hear of the treatment accorded me when he arrived Monday morning. He immediately lodged a complaint with the sheriff. This prompted a deputy sheriff to provide a used safety razor, a small mirror, and other shaving paraphernalia. The sheriff's excuse was that I was being held in solitary to protect me from the other Japanese prisoners. I was transferred to the East Row with leaders of the Fair Play Committee the next afternoon, nineteen days after being in solitary. The reading and writing materials were furnished by Mr. Sampson himself. I was greeted with enthusiasm by the five FPC leaders and taken in tow by Paul Nakadate. I wanted to interview Kiyoshi Okamoto, the leader, who had a cell at the other end.

I found that Okamoto was not as young as were his compatriots. He was in his fifties. He wore eyeglasses, was dark-complexioned, small, thin, and favored graying whiskers. Okamoto had been lying down on his bunk but got up at my approach.

"I was the first to demand rectification of this injustice?" were his opening words.

I was shocked. I had been led to believe by Paul Nakadate that Okamoto didn't care about glory and here was a prime example of a man fishing for credit.

"No, I don't believe that's true," I replied.

"There are others who pre-dated you. I was one!"

That didn't set well with Okamoto. He seemed to have bristled at being contradicted. Without a word, Okamoto curled up in his bunk and clammed up, signifying that the interview was over. He was to continue this stance even after our transfer to the Albany County Jail in Laramie.

Caryl initiated a Defense Fund among Larimer Street merchants in Denver and through letters to contacts in my files. These efforts proved futile as merchants avoided her on the streets by jaywalking to the opposite side upon her approach. One merchant tossed her an envelope containing five dollars and showed her the door with a request not to return. An issei launderer of long standing and, previously, a staunch supporter asked her to take her business elsewhere. One young solicitor was gang-beaten in an alley and another was warned by a JACL leader not to make his rounds in the agricultural area because of the possibility of bodily harm. Responses to letter solicitations were negative and the Defense Fund collapsed.

Three major factors seemed to have resulted in turning the Japanese community against the Defense Fund. The first was the visit by the national JACL president, Saburo Kido, to the office of the Rocky Shimpo *and the rumor that he spread about my having done irreparable harm to the U.S. Japanese by testifying before the Tolan Committee in San Francisco. The second was the charge that I had drawn excessive public attention to the Japanese community of Denver, which preferred to bury its head in the sand until the war had blown over. The third reason was an article written in Japanese in the* Colorado Times, *which urged issei not to contribute to "a draft dodger."*

The Revitalization of a Robust Nikkei Tradition

Sampson succeeded in lowering my bail from $5,000 to $1,500. When I appeared before the U.S. Commissioner in Cheyenne, he said to me: "I've read your case. If I were determining your case, I'd throw it out of court." Sampson came often to consult and once when we were in the outer office, we heard people up on the roof and noticed a canister-type object lowered by a pole near the window. "They're eavesdropping," Mr. Sampson said. It was conducted at regular intervals.

Caryl's next trip to Cheyenne was August 11, the twenty-third day of my arrest. She reported that Rex, our Doberman Pinscher show dog, had been sold due to her inability to take care of him. She was selling anything of value to raise bond money and attorney's fees. We did not have a great deal of money because I went broke the year before while running the free placement bureau. With the Defense Fund's demise, Caryl had obtained a second job with Safeway Bakery in north Denver to raise the bond fee.

I was visited by Sampson three mornings per week and told not to send letters out through the usual channel, as they were being opened and read. We were allowed one letter per week but all my letters were smuggled out by Sampson or Caryl.

On Caryl's second trip I told her about the mediocre food and the lack of reading materials and urged her to write to the director of the Bureau of Prisons, a Mr. Bennett.. An inspector was dispatched on this first complaint and I noticed the inspector go into the sheriff's office and depart without visiting the cell blocks. Mr. Bennett wrote Caryl the reason for prohibiting reading materials was because the inmates insisted on burning newspapers to heat their coffee. I told Caryl this was a farce as we were never allowed to make coffee in the cells. I also told her to write Mr. Bennett of his inspector's faulty inspection. In the meantime, a deputy warned us that, if we continued to complain, we would be placed on "bread and water."

Jacobs was insistent that I be bonded out to prepare the case. None of the bonding companies in Denver, however, would touch a draft case.

Four of us—Okamoto, two draft resisters, and myself—were transferred on September 13 to the Albany County Jail in Laramie. We had the northernmost half of the floor, overlooking the treetops of Wyoming's interminable evergreen forest. There was plenty of room to stretch our legs and a long table for mess topped with magazines and newspapers. In addition, a local Issei restaurant operator graciously provided Japanese cuisine to appease our appetites. However our confinement there lasted only ten days and then, on September 23, we were bonded out by Frank Cooper of the Arizona Bail Bond Agency of Phoenix.

I returned to Denver in the company of Cooper. We visited the United States Fidelity and Guaranty office and were rudely met by its manager. He made his antipathy obvious to any draft cases involving Japanese.

A Matter of Conscience

He virtually tossed us out of his office. We next went to the Colorado Council of Churches to see Reverend Garman. It surprised me to see a hundred nisei girls, sitting at typewriters. The minister was out, but the nisei girl in charge repeatedly urged us to leave to avoid physical violence. It was shocking that a minister of the cloth would entertain such an attitude. Cooper chose to leave.

Immediately after my release on bond, I had met briefly with my attorney, Sidney Jacobs, in his office. He requested that I not bother him for two weeks so that he might clear his desk of pending cases. In the meantime I was to write a summary for him. The summary was written.

On Friday evening, October 20, my attorneys viewed the letters seized from me by the Office of Alien Property Custodian at the United States Attorney's office. I had to sign some papers on the desk of the prosecutor, Carl Sackett.

"Jimmie made a mistake," Sackett said. "He needs someone to look after him so he doesn't get into trouble."

I didn't pay any attention to what he said since he was the prosecutor. But I believe Sackett's words made a strong impression upon Caryl, to whom he was speaking, for later developments seemed to bear that fact out. After looking over the seized letters, we headed for Mr. Sampson's office. We were just approaching an intersection and I was remarking about a phase of the case.

"You've been keeping things from me," Jacobs angrily accused. He was furious and his face was red with rage.

"No, I haven't," I declared. "It was in the summary I made for you."

"In the editorials you wrote, you could have been clearer," he retorted.

"What do you mean?" I asked.

"You could have condemned draft resisting," he said.

I couldn't believe what I was hearing. He was acting like a prosecutor.

"You knew there was no alternative except to violate the law," he continued with visible anger in his face and tone.

"That's not true," I responded.

"What other way is there?" he demanded.

"Petition for a declaratory judgment," I replied.

"That won't work?" he said.

"It would work," interjected Mr. Sampson, who had listened in silence. "I found an authority on it. It's an obscure Oklahoma law. It's among the laws that I looked up."

Mr. Jacobs settled down after Mr. Sampson's statement. I welcomed this support for I was aware that my attorney was berating me. When we arrived at Mr. Sampson's office, his desk and the secretary's desk were covered with open law books. Mr. Jacobs went to the main desk and stood reading standing up.

> "Looks like I've got the night cut out for me," he remarked.
> "The office is yours," Mr. Sampson said. "Just turn off the light and lock the door when you leave."

Then turning to me, he said, "Let's leave Mr. Jacobs in his study. I'm going home to bed." We parted at the intersection, he going east and I straight south to the Windsor Hotel.

The next afternoon Paul Nakadate stopped by and stated that Jacobs had wanted to know if I were a member of the Fair Play Committee. Paul said that of course Jacobs prefaced his question with: "I believe Jimmie is telling the truth to me but I wanted to know in my own mind." I just thought to myself that if he really believed me he wouldn't have asked the question in the first place.

The trial got underway the next morning at ten o'clock. Mr. Sampson sat beside me throughout. On the third day, Mr. Jacobs remarked: "Why is Sampson hanging around? He isn't being paid to." I gave no answer but I think Mr. Sampson stood by me for moral support. He pointed out the weaknesses and the strong points in the testimonies. The seven Fair Play Committee leaders were tried first. Then, it was my turn. The prosecutor was John Picketts, Assistant U.S. Attorney. Picketts attempted to tie me into the FPC conspiracy by using implications in the editorials in the Rocky Shimpo. *Also the seized letters. Our defense was solidly built on the First Amendment principle of Freedom of the Press.*

During a short recess in the hallway, I caught the eyes of the jury foreman and he winked and smiled. I considered that a good omen. Between sessions, Vern Lichliter, a reporter for the Wyoming Eagle *newspaper, attached himself to me. He was not only very friendly, but expressed his opinion of my innocence. On the morning of November 1, 1944, a federal district court jury returned a verdict of "not guilty." It convicted the seven leaders of the Fair Play Committee. Agent Lawrence of the FBI stepped out of the judge's chambers for a smoke and seeing me at the end of the hall rushed all the way to congratulate me on my acquittal. He was the agent who had interrogated me on a number of occasions but surprised me by not testifying against me. It was Agent Lawrence who informed me the FBI was withdrawing all charges of inappropriate editorial conduct. I was grateful for Agent Lawrence's reaction upon my acquittal. I left Cheyenne immediately.*

A Matter of Conscience

CONCLUSION

Upon his post-trial return from Cheyenne to Denver, where he would reside until his 1994 death, Jimmie Omura found himself estranged from his racial-ethnic community. That his type of outspoken resistance to the government was out of favor with the Nikkei had become painfully clear to Omura during his time in jail when the drive for his defense fund was foiled. Branded a pariah, he was harassed by other Japanese Americans to the point where his employment opportunities dried up and his marriage ended in divorce. Switching from journalism to landscape gardening, Omura remarried, raised a family, and turned his back on other Japanese Americans and their concerns.

Then, in September 1981, Omura ended his long exile from Japanese American life and affairs by "coming home" to the high school within his native Seattle, Washington (where he had graduated in 1933), in order to testify at the Seattle hearings of the Commission on Wartime Relocation and Internment of Civilians. "Discovered" there by youthful Asian American dissidents and redress activists, Omura was drawn back by them into the social, political, and intellectual currents of Nikkei community life. Spearheaded by the Chinese American playwright Frank Chin, and abetted by two creative Sansei personalities, the poet Lawson Inada and the television journalist Frank Abe, these activists were primarily responsible during the 1980s for the participation of Omura, along with onetime members and leaders of the Heart Mountain Fair Play Committee, in academic and community forums that spotlighted their correlated wartime resistance experiences.

During the summer 1984 staging in Los Angeles of the East-West Players'Asian American History Project, two college-age Sansei sought out Omura for advice. These Sansei had attended a session, moderated by Chin and including Omura as a presenter, on "resistance in the camps." Clearly, the two Sansei felt ashamed because the Nikkei community had ostensibly accepted their World War II plight without putting up a firm protest. Seeing Omura as a palpable role model for having stood up for justice (and paid a steep price for doing so), they solicited his advice on how young Japanese Americans should cope with their heritage and culture.

A month after this encounter, Omura wrote to one of the Sansei students to enlarge on what he had said to him at the Los Angeles event. He first advised him to honor inherited ancestral traditions, such as the code of the Samurai, the doctrine of Bushido, and the spirit of Yamato. Having made this conventional bow to Japanese lineage, Omura then directed his Sansei correspondent's attention to the historical legacy of dissent within the Japanese American community. "If it seems the Nisei generation–your parents–pass on to you a tarnished heritage," noted Omura, "know that there were islands

108

of resistance and protests to oppression and tyranny." Omura then continued his inspirational message by adducing the example of the Heart Mountain Fair Play Committee resisters: "[Know further] that these brave and resolute young men who, too, were Nisei faced the wrath of an oppressive government in the historic tradition of free men to repression. In some tomorrow, future scholars and historians will pay them honor. Even now the seeds are stirring."[80]

The seeds were certainly stirring within Omura. So much so that already he had begun to write a memoir for future publication that would revolve around what he plainly regarded as the most significant action of resistance by Japanese Americans during World War II and perhaps in all of Nikkei history: the Heart Mountain draft resistance movement.

Although unfamiliar with Roger Gottlieb's concept of resistance glossed in this study's opening section, Omura's treatment in his memoir of what he called "The Resistance" suggests that these two men operated on the same wave length. Indeed, it can be argued that Omura's narrative account of the Heart Mountain draft resistance movement effectively affirms the following points in Gottlieb's historically grounded theoretical formulation. First, the Fair Play Committee was engaged in a moral evaluation of a specific set of power relations within a definable social conflict. Second, the FPC based its resistance to the draft on the conviction that the government was assaulting the legitimating norms of civil and human rights at the heart of a constitutional democracy like the United States. Third, the FPC responded to a particular relation of oppression in World War II-era America, wherein Japanese Americans were controlled, devalued, and abased by their government, while at the same time being urged to fight and perhaps die in the name of loyal Americanism. Fourth, the leaders and members of the FPC were motivated in their anti-draft actions to prevent, restrict, or terminate the U.S. government's exercise of unwarranted power over them. Fifth, those in the FPC intended to resist oppression and placed themselves in jeopardy by so doing. Sixth, those in the FPC were cognizant of what in both their individual and group identity was at risk through governmental oppression and how these dual identities were being assailed. Seventh, the FPC's resistance was especially notable because its agents more fully understood the political-legal-moral actions involved than did participants in the comparatively unorganized draft movements at camps other than Heart Mountain or in largely spontaneous, episodic, and situational demonstrations and riots occurring at any of the WRA camps, including Heart Mountain.

Moreover, Omura's memoir treatment of the Heart Mountain draft resistance movement clarifies that he regarded the actions of the Japanese American Citizens League's leadership at the Wyoming camp (and well beyond its boundaries) to have amounted to a species of what Gottlieb labeled as "self-deceptive non-resistance" or "unconscious complicity." Put another way, Omura assessed the JACL's performance as being of a piece with the actions of the Judenrat in wartime Poland as described by Gottlieb–that in denouncing the FPC membership as "draft dodgers" and urging Nisei to report for their selective service physicals and thereafter to fight and even die to "prove" their loyalty to America, the leaders of the JACL were not telling the truth about their intentions. Rather than seeking the collective safety and well being of their racial-ethnic group, the JACL leadership was actually looking out for their narrow self-interest and institutional advancement. In the process, they were treating the U.S. Constitution as a "scrap of paper" instead of a "sacred document." For them, good public relations evidently were more important than good law and government.

Finally, the interpretation Omura advanced in his memoir of the Heart Mountain draft resistance movement resonated with Gottlieb's notion of "unconscious resistance." During the dark days of World War II and for more than three decades thereafter it had been very difficult for Omura to appreciate how the FPC's defiance of the expressed urgings of the U.S. government, the WRA, and the JACL for Japanese Americans to cooperate with being drafted from behind barbed wire would ever catalyze widespread community resistance against the agents of their wartime oppression. But that such a development, however delayed, was indeed occurring became increasingly obvious to Omura and many others, inside and outside of the Japanese American community, during the redress movement of the 1980s. Drawing upon the legacy of those FPCers who, under the circumstances of their abridged Americanism, had declared in 1944 that "hell no, we won't go" until our rights are restored and our citizenship status clarified, the Nikkei community as a whole, which during the war had been threatened with cultural extinction, rose up to demand a government apology as well as reparations and to resoundingly declare that "we would rather fight than quit." Thus, was the Japanese American tradition of resistance honored in the practice rather than in the breach.

Notes

1. Lane Ryo Hirabayashi, "Re-reading the Archives: The Intersection of Ethnography, Biography, & Autobiography in the Historiography of Japanese Americans during World War II," in Mike Mackey, ed., *Remembering Heart Mountain: Essays on Japanese American Internment in Wyoming* (Powell, Wy: Western History Publications, 1998), 208, n. 26.

2. See Roger S. Gottlieb, "The Concept of Resistance: Jewish Resistance during the Holocaust," *Social Theory and Practice 9* (Spring 1983): 31-49. Unless otherwise specifically noted, the basis for the theoretical portion of this essay derives from Gottlieb's

article. I have shaped it to fit the similar but different circumstances of the Japanese American Internment experience. Although only specific quotations from the Gottlieb piece will be referenced here, my indebtedness to the author extends to its entirety.

3. Ibid, 41.

4. Ibid, 42.

5. Ibid, 34.

6. Ibid, 41.

7. Ibid, 34.

8. Ibid, 44.

9. Ibid, 44-45.

10. Ibid, 47.

11. Okihiro's published resistance writings were launched with his seminal "Japanese Resistance in America's Concentration Camps: A Reevaluation," *Amerasia Journal* 2 (Fall 1973): 20-34; they continued through a couple of other stellar journal articles: "Tule Lake under Martial Law: A Study of Japanese Resistance," *Journal of Ethnic Studies* 5 (Fall 1977): 71-86, and "Religion and Resistance in America's Concentration Camps," *Phylon* 45 (September 1985): 220-33, plus a trio of books: (with Timothy J. Lukes) *Japanese Legacy: Farming and Community Life in California's Santa Clara Valley* (Cupertino, CA: California History Center, 1985); *Cane Fires: The Anti-Japanese Movement in Hawaii, 1865-1945* (Philadelphia: Temple University Press, 1991); and *Whispered Silences: Japanese Americans and World War II* (Seattle: University of Washington Press, 1995). However, the basis for the examples of Japanese American resistance used here is Okihiro's introductory essay, "The Japanese in America," in Brian Niiya, ed., *Encyclopedia of Japanese American History: An A-Z Reference from 1868 to the Present* (Los Angeles: Japanese American National Museum, 2001), 1-23. Again, as with the above citations relating to the article by Roger Gottlieb on the concept of resistance, while only specific quoted passages from Okihiro's essay will be cited, my debt encompasses the author's full work.

12. Okihiro, "The Japanese in America," 2.

13. Ibid, 4-5.

14. Donald H. Estes, "Abe, Tokunosuke," entry in Niiya, ed., *Encyclopedia of Japanese American History*, 108.

15. Coverage of these epic events is beyond the scope of this assignment. For summarized treatment of each of them, along with suggestions for further reading, see the

following pertinent entries in Niiya, ed., *Encyclopedia of Japanese American History*: Glen Kitayama, "Yasui v. United States," 422-24; Glen Kitayama, "Hirabayashi v. United States," 194-95; Glen Kitayama, "Korematsu v. United States," 251-52; Glen Kitayama, "Endo, Ex Parte," 159-60; "Assembly Centers" and "Santa Anita Camouflage Net Project," 125, 360-61; "Poston Strike," 338; "Manzanar Incident," 267-68; and "Tule Lake 'Segregation Center,'" 395-97.

16. Okihiro began compiling the contributions for this anthology in the late 1970s and during the 1980s offered it several times, without success, for publication consideration to commercial and university presses. In the late 1980s-early 1990s, the present author joined editorial forces with Okihiro to revise and resubmit the manuscript for renewed consideration as a book, but this effort never reached fruition.

17. Bob Kumamoto, "The Search for Spies: American Counterintelligence and the Japanese American Community, 1931-1942," *Amerasia Journal* 6 (Fall 1979): 45-75.

18. Gary Okihiro, unpaginated introduction to "Resistance in America's Concentration Camps," as discussed in fn. 16 above.

19. Ibid. For an extended treatment of the essay referenced here, see the study from which it derived: David A. Hacker, "A Culture Resisted, A Culture Revived: The Loyalty Crisis of 1943 at the Manzanar War Relocation Center" (M.A. thesis, California State University, Fullerton, 1980).

20. See Arthur A. Hansen and David A. Hacker, "The Manzanar Riot: An Ethnic Perspective," *Amerasia Journal* 2 (Fall 1974): 112-57; and Okihiro, "Religion and Resistance in America's Concentration Camps."

21. See Richard Nishimoto, *Inside an American Concentration Camp: Japanese American Resistance at Poston, Arizona*, ed. Lane Ryo Hirabayashi (Tucson: University of Arizona Press, 1995).

22. Ibid, 164.

23. Ibid, 165.

24. T. A. Larson, *Wyoming's War Years 1941-1945* (Stanford, CA: Stanford University Press, 1954), particularly Chapter 12, "Heart Mountain," 297-321.

25. See, most notably, Roger Daniels, *Concentration Camps USA: Japanese Americans and World War II* (New York: Holt, Rinehart and Winston: 1971), especially Chapter 6, "A Question of Loyalty," 104-29.

26. Douglas W. Nelson, *Heart Mountain: The History of an American Concentration Camp* (Madison: State Historical Society of Wisconsin, 1976).

27. Mike Mackey, *Heart Mountain: Life in Wyoming's Concentration Camp* (Powell, WY:

The Revitalization of a Robust Nikkei Tradition

Western History Publications, 2000), and Mackey, ed., *Remembering Heart Mountain*. See also, in ibid, Mackey's essay "The Heart Mountain Relocation Center: Economic Opportunities in Wyoming," 51-59, and the same author's 1998 overview essay entitled "A Brief History of the Heart Mountain Relocation Center and the Japanese American Experience," Heart Mountain Digital Preservation Project, John Taggert Hinckley Library, Northwest College, Powell, Wyoming, available on a CD-ROM or on the project's website at http://chem..nwc.cc.wy.us/HMDP/Homepage.htm.

28. Louis Fiset, "The Heart Mountain Hospital Strike of June 24, 1943," in Mackey, ed., *Remembering Heart Mountain*, 101-18.

29. See Frank Chin, "Come All Ye Asian American Writers of the Real and the Fake," in Jeffrey Paul Chan et al., *The Big Aiiieeeee! An Anthology of Chinese American and Japanese American Literature* (New York: Meridian, 1991), 1-92, especially, 52-82.

30. William Minoru Hohri, ed., *Resistance: Challenging America's Wartime Internment of Japanese-Americans* (Los Angeles, The Epistolarian, 2001). This stunning volume includes first-person accounts by a leader of the Heart Mountain Fair Play Committee (Frank Seishi Emi) and three draft resisters associated with that Heart Mountain camp organization (Mits Koshiyama, Yosh Kuromiya, and Takashi Hoshizaki).

31. Eric L. Muller, *Free to Die for Their Country: The Story of the Japanese American Draft Resisters in World War II* (Chicago: University of Chicago Press, 2001).

32. Gwenn M. Jensen, "Illuminating the Shadows: Post-Traumatic Flashbacks from Heart Mountain and Other Camps," in Mackey, ed., *Remembering Heart Mountain*, 228.

33. Susan L. Smith, "Caregiving in Camp: Japanese American Women and Community Health in World War II," in Mike Mackey, ed., *Guilt by Association: Essays on Japanese Settlement, Internment, and Relocation in the Rocky Mountain West* (Powell, WY: Western History Publications, 2001), 187-201.

34. Frank T. Inouye, "Immediate Origins of the Heart Mountain Draft Resistance Movement," in Mackey, ed., *Remembering Heart Mountain*, 121-39, and the same author's unpublished memoir, "Odyssey of a Nisei: A Voyage of Self-Discovery," Department of Special Collections, Library, University of Cincinnati. Thanks are extended to Professor Roger Daniels for alerting me to the existence of this manuscript and arranging to have it copied and made available to me.

35. Aasel Hansen, "My Two Years at Heart Mountain: The Difficult Role of an Applied Anthropologist," in Roger Daniels, Sandra C. Taylor, and Harry H. L. Kitano, eds., *Japanese Americans: From Relocation to Redress* (Salt Lake City: University of Utah Press, 1986), 33-37.

36. Rita Takahashi Cates, "Comparative Administration and Management of Five War Relocation Authority Camps: America's Incarceration of Persons of Japanese Descent during World War II" (Ph.D. diss., University of Pittsburgh, 1980), passim.

37. See, in particular, Bill Hosokawa, "The Sentinel Story," in Mackey, ed., *Remembering Heart Mountain*, 63-73.

38. Lauren Kessler, "Fettered Freedoms: The Journalism of World War II Internment Camps," *Journalism History* 15 (Summer/Autumn 1988): 70-79, passim.

39. Estelle Peck Ishigo, *Lone Heart Mountain* (Los Angeles: Anderson, Ritchie & Simon, 1972).

40. See Masumi Hayashi's Internet website, csuohio.edu, for her American Concentration Camps series of photographs, especially those relating to the Heart Mountain camp ("Blue Room," 1995; "Hospital," 1995; and "Root Cellar," 1996).

41. See Mamoru Inouye and Grace Schaub, *The Heart Mountain Story: Photographs by Hansel Mieth and Otto Hagel of the World War II Internment of Japanese Americans* (Los Gatos, CA: Privately printed, 1997). See also, Mamoru Inouye, "Heart Mountain High School, 1942-1945," in Mackey, *Remembering Heart Mountain*, 75-100.

42. See Steven Okazaki, producer and director, *Days of Waiting* (1988), a documentary film about Heart Mountain artist Estelle Peck Ishigo, one of the few Caucasian internees in the War Relocation Center camps. Two years earlier, in 1986, KTWO News in Wyoming aired a documentary film on Heart Mountain titled *Winter in My Soul*.

43. Emiko Omori, producer and director, *Rabbit in the Moon* (1999), a documentary film about resistance activity in relation to the Japanese American Internment, including extensive footage devoted to such activity in relationship to the Heart Mountain camp.

44. See Frank Abe, producer and director, *Conscience and the Constitution* (2000), a documentary film about the Heart Mountain Fair Play Committee and the draft resistance movement at the Heart Mountain camp.

45. Gretchen Ehrlich, *Heart Mountain* (New York: Viking, 1988).

46. John Tateishi, ed., *And Justice For All: An Oral History of the Japanese American Detention Camps* (New York: Random House, 1984).

47. Susan McKay, "Young Women's Everyday Resistance: Heart Mountain, Wyoming," in Mackey, ed., *Guilt by Association*, 203-16.

48. Eric Bittner, "'Loyalty . . . is a Covenant': Japanese-American Internees and the Selective Service Act," *Prologue* 23 (Fall 1991): 248-334; and Eric Bittner, "Records at the National Archives-Rocky Mountain Region Relating to the Japanese American Internment Experience," in Mackey, ed., *Remembering Heart Mountain*, 209-14.

49. Frank Emi, "Resistance: The Heart Mountain Fair Play Committee's Fight for

Justice," *Amerasia Journal* 17 (1991): 47-51; and Frank Seishi Emi, "Draft Resistance at the Heart Mountain Concentration Camp and the Fair Play Committee," in *Frontiers of Asian American Studies: Writing, Research, and Commentary*, ed. Gail M. Nomura et al. (Pullman: Washington State University Press, 1989), 41-69.

50. James Omura, "Japanese American Journalism during World War II," in Nomura et al., *Frontiers of Asian American Studies*, 71-80.

51. Velma Kessel, "Remembering the Heart Mountain Hospital," in Mackey, ed., *Remembering Heart Mountain*, 187-92.

52. Peter K. Simpson, "Recollections of Heart Mountain," in ibid, 179-85.

53. As quoted in Cates, "Comparative Administration and Management of Five War Relocation Authority Camps," 190.

54. Inouye, "Immediate Origins of the Heart Mountain Draft Resistance Movement," 123.

55. Daniels, *Concentration Camps USA*, 118.

56. See Mike Mackey, "Media Influence on Local Attitudes Toward the Heart Mountain Relocation Center," in Mackey, ed., *Guilt by Association*, 239-52, particularly 248. See also, Jensen, "Illuminating the Shadows," for evidence that corroborates Mackey's assessment of greater community opposition in Cody than Powell to the Heart Mountain population.

57. On the *Denver Post's* anti-Japanese and generally racist editorial policies during World War II, see Kumiko Takahara's unpublished manuscript, "The *Denver Post's* Story of the Japanese American Internment in Colorado." Professor Takahara is a faculty member in the Department of East Asian Languages and Civilizations at the University of Colorado at Boulder. A portion of her book-length manuscript has been published as "Japanese American Women: Guilty by Race and Gender," in Mackey, ed., *Guilt by Association*, 219-38.

58. As quoted in Cates, "Comparative Administration and Management of Five War Relocation Authority Camps," 199.

59. See ibid, 203, and Daniels, *Concentration Camps USA*, 118.

60 As cited in Cates, "Comparative Administration and Management of Five War Relocation Authority Camps," 206.

61. As quoted in Inouye, "Immediate Origins of the Heart Mountain Draft Resistance Movement," 122. I have relied very heavily upon Inouye's article for resistance developments at the Heart Mountain camp through 1943, as the many subsequent references to this fine study manifestly testify.

62. Fiset, "The Heart Mountain Hospital Strike of June 24, 1943."

63. Inouye, "Immediate Origins of the Heart Mountain Draft Resistance Movement," 123.

64. Ibid.

65. Ibid.

66. McKay, "Young Women's Everyday Resistance: Heart Mountain, Wyoming," as cited in fn. 47 above.

67. Ibid, 208.

68. Cates, "Comparative Administration and Management of Five War Relocation Authority Camps," 485.

69. As quoted in Inouye, "Immediate Origins of the Heart Mountain Draft Resistance Movement," 125.

70. Ibid.

71. Ibid.

72. Ibid, 26.

73. As quoted in ibid.

74. Ibid, 126-27.

75. Ibid, 127.

76. Ibid.

77. Ibid, 127-28.

78. The narrative that follows about James Omura and his wartime activities is adapted from an earlier piece of mine; see Arthur A. Hansen, "The 1944 Nisei Draft at Heart Mountain, Wyoming: Its Relationship to the Historical Representation of the World War II Japanese American Evacuation," *Organization of American Historians Magazine of History* 10 (Summer 1996): 48-60, especially 49-50.

79. Tentatively titled "Nisei Naysayer: The Memoir of Dissident Japanese American Journalist Jimmie Omura, this manuscript is being prepared for publication with the support of a California Civil Liberties Public Education Program grant. The section quoted here has been slightly edited, with Omura's notes deleted, to accommodate space requirements and to facilitate readability. The author thanks Mary Kimoto

Tomita and Steve Yoda for their splendid and very generous editorial assistance on the Omura memoir. Yoda's fine 1999 senior thesis at Stanford University, "The Unquiet American: A Portrait of the Life of James M. Omura, American Champion of Civil Rights," represents the first comprehensive biographical study of the controversial Nisei journalist.

80. See the 1984-1987 correspondence between Warren Sata and James Omura in the James M. Omura Papers, especially Omura's letter to Sata, dated 28 September 1984, and Sata's letter to Omura, dated 18 December 1984. The James Omura Papers are currently in the possession of this author, but are scheduled for deposit at the Special Collections Department of the Green Library at Stanford University after the publication of Omura's memoir. The author thanks the many dedicated students enrolled in the five archives classes at the San Jose State University School of Library and Information Science who, under the supervision of Professor Debra Gold Hansen, did preliminary organization of the Omura Papers in 1997-1999. Special appreciation is extended to one of these students, Rebecca Manley, for subsequently organizing the Omura Papers as a comprehensive collection, replete with a finding aid, through funding support provided by a California Civil Liberties Public Education Program grant.

PART III

THE LEGAL ASPECTS OF RESISTANCE

Draft Resistance and the Selective Service Act of 1940

by William Hohri

NISEI DRAFT RESISTANCE: HOW WE REMEMBER

The historical blur of draft resistance may be explained in part by its unpopularity during the Second World War and the overwhelming desire by most of the Nisei internees to present themselves as loyal Americans to a hostile, suspicious public. We should also note, that while the individual constitutional test cases of Minoru Yasui, Gordon Hirabayashi, Fred Korematsu, and Mitsuye Endo have been thoroughly studied, little attention has been directed to the 315 draft resisters[1] and their constitutional and legal challenges to internment.[2] Simply put, while most of us may agree that the internment was unjust, most of us also believe that Selective Service is the law and must be obeyed, and that the courts must prosecute those who willfully violate its regulations.

Another aspect of the explanation may be the ignorance of most Americans, including the internees, of the legal and military machinations that led to the construction and management of the ten prison camps for housing the entire West Coast population of U.S. citizens and permanent resident aliens of Japanese ancestry, and the use of its inmates for promoting the nation's military objectives. The Second World War has been dubbed "The Good War."[3] We had been unmistakably attacked at Pearl Harbor by the Japanese Imperial Navy. We were on the side of the angels; our enemies were demonic. Our primary enemy was even a race apart, one that was colored, one that we believed, under the sway of cultural prejudice and Social Darwinism,[4] was pagan, devious, and not fully human.[5] By the end of 1944, a Gallup Poll indicated that 13 per cent of Americans believed that all Japanese should be exterminated.[6]

Most of the surviving internees, to this day, continue to describe their exclusion and detention as "the Evacuation," unaware that this euphemism was crafted, along with "relocation," "evacuee," "War Relocation Center," and "War Relocation Authority," to mask reality.[7] They remain unaware of our government's need to obscure its egregious violations of their basic constitutional rights as it ignored habeas corpus and due process, when it forcibly excluded and detained them.

We also assume that the WRA camps were defined by civilian authority. We shall soon learn that the authority for detention came from the War

121

Department, its doctrine of military necessity, and its power to designate the camps as military areas under its jurisdiction. One of the important roles of the War Relocation Authority was to provide the cosmetic effect of civilian control.

The draft resisters too, were unaware of these machinations. Nevertheless, they took the historic step of challenging the constitutionality of their detention and challenging the basic assumptions about our government and its wartime program of mass exclusion and detention. They did not resist because they were experts in constitutional law, and had discovered unshakable legal or constitutional principles that would ensure their vindication. They acted rather from their sure belief that their exclusion and detention were wrong and in violation of their fundamental right to freedom. They believed the war was a war between totalitarianism and democracy. They believed they too, were fighting in defense of their democratic freedoms. They resisted in order to challenge in court the constitutionality of their detention.

LEGAL IMPLICATIONS

Despite their lack of legal knowledge, the draft resisters touched upon two important legal questions about their resistance and almost succeeded in exposing them. The first question: Were the inmates of the camps being detained by the government? If true, the second question follows: Were the male inmates subject to conscription under the regulations of Selective Service? If the answer is affirmative to the first, then the answer to the second is negative.

We begin with the second question. The 1940 Selective Service Regulations, Section XIV, par. 246, states:

> 246. **Insane asylums, jails, penitentiaries, reformatories**. Any inmate of an asylum, jail, penitentiary, reformatory, or similar institution, who is subject to registration, shall be registered **on the day of his discharge**. The superintendent or warden shall complete the registration card, issue the registration certificate, explain to the registrant his obligations under the selective service law, and mail the registration card to the Governor of the registrant's home State with a receipt to be executed and returned to him.[8] [emphasis in original]

If the camps were included in the category of "asylum, jail, penitentiary, reformatory, or similar institution," then its inmates were not to be registered for Selective Service until the day they were discharged. Though the Fair Play Committee was asking for more than their freedom as fulfillment of their conditions for complying with Selective Service, these regulations are consistent with the Committee's assertion "that the present program of draft- ing us from this concentration camp is unjust."

Now we address the first question. Do the regulations apply? Were the camps similar to other detention facilities? This question is answered in Public Proclamation No. WD 1, issued by the War Department on August 20, 1942. After invoking the authority and terms of presidential executive order 9066 and determining the existence of military necessity, the order states:

> Now, therefore, I, Henry L. Stimson, Secretary of War, by virtue of the authority vested in me by the President of the United States, and my powers and prerogatives as Secretary of War, do here- by declare that: . . . (a) Pursuant to the determination of military necessity hereinbefore set out, all the territory with the established boundaries of Heart Mountain Relocation Project, approximately twelve miles northeast of Cody, Wyoming . . . are hereby established as Military Areas and are designated as War Relocation Project Areas.

I have omitted the descriptions of the three other campsites in Colorado and Arkansas. The Western Defense Command issued Public Proclamation No. 8 on June 27, 1942, which applied the same conditions to the six camps within its jurisdiction in California, Idaho, Utah, and Arizona. WD-1 continues with:

> (b) All persons of Japanese ancestry and all members of their families, both alien and nonalien, who now or shall hereafter be or reside, pursuant to orders and instructions of the Secretary of War or pursuant to the orders *or* instructions of the Commanding General, Western Defense Command and Fourth Army, or otherwise, within the bounds of any of said War Relocation Project Areas are required to remain within the bounds of said War Relocation Project Areas at all times unless specifically authorized to leave as set forth in para- graph (c) hereof.

Notice the order's explicit identification of "all persons of Japanese ancestry." Executive order 9066 used the fig leaf of "any person" to avoid constitution- al challenge.

SUPPOSITIONS

These two documents are to be found in the Federal Register for September 1940 (Selective Service Regulations) and for August 1942 (WD 1). Let us suppose that the attorneys representing the resisters had retrieved these documents as part of their legal preparations. The Selective Service

Regulations would have been required reading in order to determine the liability of their clients when they failed to report for their pre-induction physical examinations.

Let us further suppose their curiosity was evoked by Section XIV, paragraph 246: Could the Heart Mountain camp fall under the category of an institution similar to a jail or penitentiary? They would first have to penetrate the fog of euphemisms. They might reexamine Executive Order 9066 and ponder this key wording on the delegation of authority:

> . . . to prescribe military areas in such places and of such extent as he [Secretary of War] or the appropriate Military Commander may determine, from which any or all persons may be excluded, and with respect to which, the right of any person to enter, remain in, or leave shall be subject to whatever restrictions the Secretary of War or the appropriate Military Commander may impose in his discretion.

This appears to be authority to exclude, as was implemented in the western States. But as the precedent of prescribing the entire State of California to be a military area demonstrates,[9] this authority is broad and capricious as far as the term "military areas" is concerned. Moreover, the three verbs restricting a person's movement are not entirely consistent with exclusion: "to enter," "remain in," or "leave." While "entering" and "remaining" apply to exclusion, leaving sounds suspiciously like detention. Is this exclusion order also an order to detain?

They might then ask, under what specific order were these inmates being detained? What was the legal basis of their detention? When did inmates first arrive at Heart Mountain? August 12, 1942. Why not examine the Federal Register for August 1942? They would have to be thorough. The common understanding was that the camps fell under the jurisdiction of either the War Relocation Authority (civilian authority) or the Western Defense Command (military authority). An order from the War Department would be a surprise.

Had they persisted and reflected, they might have realized that Wyoming was beyond the Western Defense Command's jurisdiction. The WDC covered the states of Washington, Oregon, California, Idaho, Montana, Utah, Nevada, and Arizona. If they were thorough, they would find WD 1 on the pages for August 20, 1942. They would find the language of detention unmistakably clear and authoritative, signed by no less an authority than the Secretary of War, Henry L. Stimson.

First, they would find the capricious and invidious use of "military areas" so that the camp sites "are hereby established as Military Areas and are

Draft Resistance and the Selective Service Act of 1940

designated as War Relocation Project Areas." The camps, run by the civilian War Relocation Authority, clearly serve no visible military purpose—except for detaining Japanese-Americans.

Then they would find both the verbs "to leave" and "to remain" did indeed provide the power to detain: "All persons of Japanese ancestry . . . are required to remain within the bounds of said War Relocation Project Areas at all times unless specifically authorized to leave . . . ."[10] If one is required to remain within a place and must receive authorization to leave, one is being detained.

The inmates were being detained in a manner comparable to people in a jail or penitentiary; the Heart Mountain War Relocation Center was a similar institution. Therefore, its male inmates were not to be registered for Selective Service until the day they were discharged. If they were not to be registered for the draft, if they had been improperly registered for Selective Service, they could hardly be liable for violating its rules.

If we make the major supposition that the courts would rule accordingly, the government would be faced with two choices, both difficult: either cease conscripting Japanese-Americans from the camps, or close the camps and release their inmates, and then conscript the eligible males. The potential number of males eligible for Selective Service was about 9,200.[11] This is roughly enough to man one-half of the infantry division that the War Department estimated could be raised from the entire Japanese-American population in the U.S. and territories. Given the prospect the Allies faced in mounting a major military campaign in Europe, one-half an infantry division could represent true military necessity.

On the other hand, what would be the risk of closing the camps? The other military necessity for the West Coast, such as it was, had ceased to exist in April 1943, by the War Department's own assessment. Assistant Secretary of War John McCloy informed Colonel Bendetsen: ". . . there no longer existed any military necessity for the continued exclusion of all Japanese from the evacuation zone."[12] From the standpoint of military necessity, closing the camps would be the choice to make. But this, too, posed complications. According to Chief of Staff George C. Marshall in his memorandum of May 13, 1944 to Assistant Secretary of War John J. McCloy: "There are strong political reasons why the Japanese should not be returned to the West Coast before next November."[13] Next November was, of course, the presidential election. The challenge raised by the draft resisters was not quixotic; it could have changed the course of history with respect to the exclusion and detention of Japanese-Americans. At the very least, their resistance has revealed how our government flagrantly violated its own laws and our Constitution, and its officials violated their own oaths of office.

A Matter of Conscience

Notes

1. The Evacuated People: A Quantitative Description, U.S. Dept. of Interior, p. 128, Table 50.

2. Notable exceptions through the 1970s are: Roger Daniels, Concentration Camps USA: Japanese Americans and World War II. New York: Holt, Rinehart and Winston, 1970; and Frank F. Chuman, The Bamboo People (Del Mar, California: Publisher's Inc., 1976).

3. For an ironic treatment of this term, see Studs Terkel's "The Good War": An Oral History of World War Two (New York: Pantheon Books, 1984).

4. For a particularly illuminating insight into the role of Social Darwinism, see Christopher Thorne, Allies of a Kind: The United States, Britain, and the War Against Japan, 1941-1945 (New York: Oxford University Press, 1978), note 28, 1678. A quote from this appears in Hohri, Repairing America, 22.

5. John Dower, War Without Mercy: Race and Power In the Pacific War (New York) Pantheon Books, 1986).

6. Thorne, Allies of a Kind, 657.

7. George Yoshinaga, a popular Nisei columnist for The Rafu Shimpo and former internee, insists on naming the camps "relocation centers."

8. Federal Register, p. 3790, September 25, 1940.

9. This occurred on June 2, 1942 under Public Proclamation No. 6. Dorothy S. Thomas and Richard Nishimoto, The Spoilage: Japanese-American Evacuation and Resettlement During World War II, 12.

10. Ibid.

11. There were two estimates in November 1942: 9,200 by Calvert Dedrick, Chief Economist, Western Defense Command, memo to John J. McCloy & Col. Karl R. Bendetsen, 11/17/42; and 7,351 by Col. M. W. Pettigrew, Chief, Far Eastern Group, War Department, memo to J. J. McCloy, 11/21/42. I defer to Dedrick inasmuch as he was also serving as a statistician for the U.S. Census Bureau at the same time. Both documents from National Archives, Record Group 407.

12. National Archives Record Group 338; Memo from Bendetsen to DeWitt 5/3/43.

13. Hohri, Repairing America, 169.

The Nisei Draft Resisters and the Constitution

by Eric L. Muller

INTRODUCTION

Rarely does a cliché resolve a close constitutional case. But it was ultimately a cliché that resolved the case of the sixty-three Nisei draft resisters from the Heart Mountain Relocation Center. On appeal of their draft evasion convictions to the United States Court of Appeals for the Tenth Circuit, counsel for the resisters asked, rhetorically, whether the United States government could "subject its people to a loss of civil rights and property without due process of law and at the same time require compliance with the draft act?"[1] The Tenth Circuit's answer to this question was simple: "Two wrongs never make a right."[2]

As constitutional rulings go, this was a disappointment. The Heart Mountain draft resisters had presented the court with a claim of moral outrage. By uprooting them from their homes and placing them in concentration camps, the government had stripped them of all of the benefits of their U.S. citizenship. Now it was demanding that they shoulder citizenship's greatest burden by laying down their lives on a battlefield. Yet the resisters' situation did not pique the court's interest. Other than the cliché, the Tenth Circuit said precious little. "One may not," it explained, "refuse to heed a lawful call of his government merely because in another way it may have injured him."[3]

The resisters themselves saw their case as presenting far more difficult questions of constitutional law than the court so off-handedly addressed. From the start of their anti-draft activities at Heart Mountain, Kiyoshi Okamoto and the other leaders of the Fair Play Committee (FPC) understood draft resistance as a vehicle for challenging the constitutionality of the government's entire program of evicting and incarcerating the West Coast's Nisei population.[4] No less an authority than the Attorney General of the United States, Francis Biddle, saw their case in that same way. In an inter-office memorandum that Biddle wrote to one of his top assistants in the fall of 1944, he expressed his concern that the draft resisters' defense to the charge of violating the Selective Training and Service Act of 1940 would "involve the constitutionality of the whole program" of wartime incarceration.[5] And today, some fifty-six years later, the surviving resisters depict themselves,[6] and are depicted by many others,[7] as defenders of constitutional principle.

Missing from all of the writing about the resisters is a clear statement

127

of the constitutional principle that was at stake. In this essay, as in my other writing on the resisters,[8] I try to fill that gap. The task is, however, more of a struggle than I expected it would be. The moral bankruptcy of the government's position is so clear that I expected the Constitution to condemn it. Yet the law in 1944 did not clearly condemn the government's efforts to draft the young men it had incarcerated on suspicion of disloyalty. Neither did the law clearly permit it. The question was, and indeed still is, surprisingly open— much too open, and much too difficult, to be decided by a simple cliché.

DRAFT RESISTANCE: THE LEGAL BACKGROUND

The Nisei resisters' challenge to the lawfulness of drafting them out of the wartime camps brought before the courts two legal regimes within the federal system. One was the system that the federal government created in 1940 for conscripting men into the armed forces. The other was the system that the federal government created in 1942 for removing the Nikkei of the West Coast from their homes and holding them in so-called "assembly centers" and "relocation centers." The former system was a creature of statute and regulation; the latter system was born of an executive order.

A. The Selective Training and Service Act of 1940

In September of 1940, with war raging in Europe and Asia, Congress passed the Selective Training and Service Act (the "Act").[9] The Act, which created the nation's first peacetime program of conscription into the armed forces, made a remarkably broad class of people liable for training and service: "every male citizen of the United States, and every other male person residing in the United States, who is between the ages of eighteen and forty-five at the time fixed for his registration."[10] This was a rather long-winded way of saying "every male between 18 and 45," since every such male was either a "citizen" or "[an]other male person." The Act recognized only two exceptions to this broad liability. First, it allowed resident aliens who were citizens of neutral countries to opt out of liability for selective service, so long as they simultaneously gave up any chance later to be naturalized as a U.S. citizen.[11] And second, the Act disallowed the induction of any enemy alien unless he were declared "acceptable to the land or naval forces."[12] The Act allowed for the classification[13] and medical examination[14] of registrants, and authorized the president to proscribe rules and regulations to implement the Act[15] and to create a Selective Service System for overseeing the operation of the program.[16]

The Selective Service System did, in fact, promulgate regulations that established a system of classifying registrants. The regulations created a multi-tiered ladder of classifications, each marked by a letter and a roman numeral. Category "I-A" signified that the registrant was fit for military service. After the Japanese attack on Pearl Harbor, all Nisei registrants were placed in Category "IV-C," which initially signified that the registrant was a "nondeclarant alien,"[17] but later was amended to signify that the registrant belonged to the class of "registrants not acceptable for training and service because of nationality or ancestry, neutral aliens requesting relief from training and service, aliens not acceptable to the armed forces or to the Director of Selective Service, and aliens who have departed and are not residing in the United States."[18] The Nisei, who were all American citizens, were naturally quite offended by their placement in a classification for aliens. However, the government fixed this problem in 1943, reclassifying the Nisei into the I-A category before drafting them.

From the perspective of the Nisei resisters, the key provisions of the Selective Training and Service Act of 1940 were in Section 11, its enforcement section.[19] Section 11 authorized imprisonment of up to five years and a fine of up to $10,000 for any person who, among other things,

- "in any manner . . . knowingly fail[ed] or neglect[ed] to perform any duty required of him under the Act, or rules or regulations made pursuant to this Act,"
- "knowingly counsel[led], aid[ed], or abet[ted] another to evade . . . any of the requirements of this Act, or of said rules or regulations," or
- "conspired to do [any of these things]."

It was under the first of these three provisions that Wyoming's federal prosecutor charged the sixty-three Heart Mountain resisters.[20] In the spring of 1944, each received an order from his local selective service board, issued under the authority of paragraph 336 of the regulations of the Selective Service System,[21] to report for a pre-induction physical examination. When he refused, the local draft board, again acting under authority of selective service regulations,[22] referred his case to the United States Attorney for prosecution. The U.S. Attorney, in turn, sought and obtained an indictment from a federal grand jury in which the young man's refusal to show up for the pre-induction physical was pleaded as a knowing failure to perform a duty required of him under the Selective Training and Service Act of 1940 and its implementing regulations.

The Nisei resisters from Heart Mountain did not, of course, dispute the power of the federal government to raise an army and a navy through conscription. They contended instead that the government could not constitutionally draft them without first "clarifying" their status as U.S. citizens and restoring to them all of the rights it had taken from them. It was not enough, they contended, for the government merely to reclassify them from the IV-C to the I-A selective service classification and send them a new draft card. They wanted a real restoration of rights before complying with the draft, not just a paperwork ploy.

B. Executive Order 9066 and its Progeny

The claim for a restoration of civil rights was central to the draft resistance movement at Heart Mountain. This was neither a pacifist nor a pro-Japanese resistance. It was quite self-consciously a civil rights movement: "Restore our rights," the FPC announced, "and we will gladly serve." What, then, was the deprivation of civil rights that the members of the FPC were hoping a court would remedy in the context of their prosecution for resisting the draft?

The legal source, although not the precise focus of the resisters' constitutional claims, was Executive Order 9066, promulgated by President Franklin D. Roosevelt on February 19, 1942. This rather vaguely worded order authorized General John DeWitt, the commanding officer of the Pacific Defense Command, to prescribe military zones "from which any or all persons may be excluded." Within a month, Congress passed legislation making it a federal misdemeanor for any person to "enter, leave, or remain in any military area or military zone" in which the military had forbidden citizens or aliens to reside.

With the President's authorization, General DeWitt quickly turned to the tasks of creating military zones within the Pacific Defense Command, ordering first the curfew, and then the out-and-out removal of all people of Japanese descent from those zones. By spring's end, one hundred ten thousand people of Japanese ancestry were behind barbed wire in so-called "assembly centers," most of which were racetracks and fairgrounds that had been quickly and sloppily converted to camps for mass confinement. Then, by late summer of 1942, all of these uprooted people were on their way to indefinite incarceration in the ten so-called "relocation centers" that the newly created War Relocation Authority (WRA) had scattered across some of the most hostile and uninviting landscape of the U.S. interior.

From a constitutional standpoint, two features of the government's program of eviction and incarceration stood out. First, the government implemented the entire program without offering any of the affected Nikkei even the most rudimentary of procedural protections. Nobody was ever charged with any offense. Nobody got a hearing, nobody was offered the services of an attorney, nobody had a right to appeal the government's decision. It was simply a warehousing of people *en masse*, undertaken entirely outside the normal processes of law.

The Nisei Draft Resisters and the Constitution

Second, the government chose the people it wished to warehouse on the basis of their Japanese ethnicity. There was no mass incarceration of people of German or Italian ancestry—aliens or citizens. To be sure, the government advanced claims of military necessity for removing all people of Japanese ancestry from their West Coast homes. Even at the time, these claims stretched credulity, and later they were discovered to be trumped up. But whatever support the government may have had for its military concerns, the line it chose to draw was starkly ethnic.

This ethnic line drawing became the focus of the constitutional test cases that several courageous Japanese Americans took to the United States Supreme Court in 1943 and 1944. The first two of these—criminal prosecutions of Gordon Hirabayashi and Minoru Yasui for breaking the curfew that General DeWitt had imposed on the Nikkei of the West Coast—reached the Supreme Court in 1943. In contending that General DeWitt's curfew order violated their rights under the Due Process Clause of the Fifth Amendment, Hirabayashi and Yasui both emphasized the flagrantly disparate treatment of Americans of Japanese ancestry, on the one hand, and those of German and Italian ancestry, on the other. To modern eyes, this ethnicity-based line drawing appears to run squarely up against the constitutional guarantee that no person shall be denied "the equal protection of the laws." The trouble for Hirabayashi and Yasui, however, was that this guarantee of equal protection appears in the Constitution's Fourteenth Amendment, which by its terms prevents only *states* from denying the equal protection of the laws. Surprising as it may seem, the federal government in 1944 was under no obligation—at least as a matter of the Constitution's textual commands—to guarantee anyone the equal protection of its laws. The law would later change to require the federal government to honor the text of the Equal Protection Clause, but in 1944 that change was still ten years off.[23]

With no equal protection guarantee to enforce, the Supreme Court, in the *Hirabayashi* and *Yasui* cases, asked only whether General DeWitt's order had a "rational basis"—the least rigorous form of judicial review that the law recognized. Applying this minimal standard, the Court held unanimously that the curfew order had a rational basis in the government's concerns about possible Fifth Column activity by people of Japanese ancestry, and was therefore not unconstitutional.[24] Justice Murphy filed a concurring opinion in which he openly worried that the government's actions pushed to "the very brink of constitutional power."[25]

A year later, the Supreme Court decided Fred Korematsu's constitutional challenge to his prosecution for refusing to report for removal to, and incarceration in, the Tanforan Assembly Center. While Korematsu's attorneys tried to persuade the Court to decide the constitutionality of both Korematsu's eviction and incarceration, the Court instead chose to address only the lawfulness of the eviction, and to leave the question of incarceration for another day. This time by a five-to-four vote, the Supreme Court rejected Korematsu's constitutional attack.[26] Again crediting the government's claim of military necessity, the Court rejected the argument that the government had excluded the Nikkei because of racial prejudice. The Court did take the occasion to make some new law in the case, announcing for the first time that it would apply "the most rigid scrutiny" to laws that draw lines on the basis of race. However, this change in the law did not help Fred Korematsu, because the Court found that General DeWitt's exclusion order survived this most rigorous review. Justice Murphy, this time in dissent, asserted that the exclusion order had taken the government "over 'the very brink of constitutional power' and . . . into the ugly abyss of racism."[27]

That same day, the Supreme Court brought the incarceration of loyal Japanese Americans to an end, but not on the basis of anything in the Constitution. In *Ex parte Endo*,[28] the Court granted a petition for a writ of habeas corpus filed by Mitsuye Endo, a concededly loyal Nisei who had spent the summer of 1942 in the Tanforan Assembly Center and who was, by the time the Supreme Court decided her case, under confinement in the Topaz Relocation Center in Utah. The Court held that nothing in Executive Order 9066 or the legislation Congress passed to implement it had conferred on the War Relocation Authority the power to detain concededly loyal Japanese Americans. Executive Order 9066 authorized only the "exclusion" of people from military zones, not their continued imprisonment. Thus, Mitsuye Endo was entitled to her liberty—not because the War Relocation Authority violated anything in the Constitution by holding her, but because the WRA simply strayed beyond the power that the president and Congress had given it.

Notably, the Court never returned to the question it left for another day in *Korematsu*—namely, whether the incarceration of Japanese Americans in concentration camps violated the Constitution. Once the Court decided *Endo* as it did, and the WRA was forced to open the gates of the relocation centers, the Court had no reason to take up the constitutional question it had avoided. But this is where the Nisei draft resisters came into the picture. In refusing to appear for their pre-induction physical examinations, they were asserting that *all* facets of the program of exclusion and incarceration had violated their constitutional rights. (Hence Attorney General Biddle's above-mentioned worry that the draft resisters' defense to the charge of violating the Selective Training and Service Act of 1940 would "involve the constitutionality of the whole program."[29]) For the resisters, this was the ultimate showdown—the moment of constitutional truth that the Supreme Court wished to avoid.

As a matter of constitutional law, were the resisters right?[30]

The Nisei Draft Resisters and the Constitution

THE DRAFT, THE NISEI, AND THE CONSTITUTION

Fred Korematsu, Gordon Hirabayashi, and Min Yasui—their Supreme Court losses notwithstanding—all had an advantage in court that the Nisei draft resisters lacked. Each of these three men was challenging the constitutionality of one of General DeWitt's orders *as a defense to a criminal charge for violating that very order*. Min Yasui, for example, was prosecuted for violating General DeWitt's curfew order, and offered the unconstitutionality of that very order as his defense to the charge. The Heart Mountain draft resisters, on the other hand, attempted to mount a challenge to the constitutionality of their eviction and incarceration in the context of a prosecution for refusing to appear for a pre-induction physical examination.

This was a significant distinction, one that takes no special legal acumen to see. Indeed, this was what the Tenth Circuit seized upon in its decision on appeal in the *Fujii* case, when it so tersely stated that two wrongs never make a right. What the court meant was that the government's refusal to honor the civil rights of the Nisei did not give the Nisei *carte blanche* to violate other laws. And surely, in a great number of cases that we might imagine, this principle was right. An easy case would be the criminal prosecution of a Nisei for stealing goods from the camp canteen. That shoplifting prosecution would not be a proper place for the accused Nisei to seek a declaration that his exclusion from the West Coast and incarceration at Heart Mountain were unconstitutional. The connection between the shoplifting charge and the deprivation of the Nisei's rights would simply be too tenuous.

For the Tenth Circuit in the *Fujii* case, the charge of resisting the draft was just like the hypothetical shoplifting charge. "One may not," it explained, "refuse to heed a lawful call of his government merely because in another way it may have injured him." Here, however, is where the Tenth Circuit's resort to cliché was mistaken. For there was a rather obvious connection between what the government had done to the Nisei since 1942 and what it was demanding of them in 1944. The government had stripped the Nisei of nearly every benefit of U.S. citizenship, and then demanded that they make citizenship's greatest sacrifice. It took little imagination to see why a person confined in a concentration camp on account of nothing but his ethnic background might hesitate before answering the government's call to arms. This is not to say that the resisters' legal claim was self-evidently correct; indeed, as will soon become clear, it was not self-evidently correct. But neither was it as easy as the Tenth Circuit made it in *Fujii*. The Heart Mountain resisters presented novel questions of law that deserved thoughtful treatment.

Had the Tenth Circuit devoted more attention to the legal issues in *Fujii*, it would have been compelled to reflect deeply on issues of both government power and individual liberty. The seemingly unitary question of whether the government violated the Constitution by drafting the interned Nisei actually broke down into two distinct constitutional questions. First, did the government have the power to draft them? Second, if it did have such power, did the government nonetheless violate their constitutional rights by drafting them? To a layperson, these questions might look redundant, but they are not. The government created by the Constitution was a doubly limited invention: it was given only certain enumerated and circumscribed powers, and it was also subjected to certain specific prohibitions. The first, second, and third articles of the Constitution conferred on the government its powers, and (for the most part) the Bill of Rights announced what it was prohibited from doing. Because of this structure of double limitation, many seemingly unitary constitutional questions break in two. Think, for example, about a federal statute imposing a nickel-per-copy sales tax on newspapers. This statute might violate the Constitution in two distinct ways. First, it might be the case that the federal government simply lacks the power to impose a sales tax at all. Second, even if the government has the power to impose a sales tax, a court might nonetheless conclude that imposing such a tax on *newspapers* violates the freedom of the press that the First Amendment protects from federal government infringement.

The first constitutional question that the Nisei resisters' cases posed was thus a question of government power: Did the federal government have the raw power to conscript young American citizens whom it had incarcerated on suspicion of disloyalty? There was little law on this question in 1944— indeed, there is little still today—but the answer to the question is most likely that the government had such power. Article I, Section 8 of the Constitution confers on the Congress the powers "[t]o raise and support Armies, . . . [t]o provide and maintain a Navy[, and t]o make Rules for the Government and Regulation of the land and naval Forces." These powers provided the constitutional basis for passage of the Selective Training and Service Act of 1940. As noted earlier, that statute made broad classes of male citizens and aliens liable for registration and for induction into the military. Notably, even *enemy aliens* were liable for training and service so long as they were deemed acceptable by the armed forces.

This provision of the 1940 Act pushed federal conscription power to its outer limits. To be sure, the military had long drafted aliens into the American military in wartime; aliens were drafted by the Union during the Civil War and by the federal government during the Spanish-American War and World War I.[31] In these earlier wars, however, Congress extended the draft only to aliens who had declared their intention to seek naturalization as U.S. citizens. The assertion of power to draft *enemy* aliens in the 1940 Selective Training Act was new. That it was a new assertion of power, however, did not make it illegal. As a federal appellate court held during the Korean Conflict,

The Nisei Draft Resisters and the Constitution

"[t]he question of whether or not aliens should be conscripted is a question of policy—a political question which is for the executive and legislative branches of the Government to solve."[32] It is not a question for the courts.

If the federal government had the raw power under Article I of the Constitution to draft even enemy aliens into the armed forces, then it surely had the lesser power to draft American citizens, such as the incarcerated Nisei, whose loyalty it doubted. This is not to say that the government was wise, considerate, or fair in drafting Nisei from behind barbed wire. It is simply to say that, as a matter of constitutional law, the government had the raw power to do so, and that the wisdom of doing so entailed a political, not a judicial, calculus.

The second constitutional question posed by the Nisei resisters' defiance of the draft was, by contrast, very much one for judges to resolve. Even if the government had the raw power to draft the incarcerated Nisei, did the decision to do so violate their individual rights? To answer this question carefully, the Tenth Circuit in the *Fujii* case would have had to do some hard thinking about the meaning of the due process guarantee in the Fifth Amendment to the Constitution.

Even today, this is tricky terrain. Modern due process law has two distinct strands, one of them somewhat redundantly called "procedural due process" and the other somewhat oxymoronically called "substantive due process." Procedural due process is the law that determines what sorts of procedural protections the government must offer a person before it does something to them. If, for example, the government wishes to send a person to jail for marrying his second cousin, the Due Process Clause will demand that the government first announce that marrying one's second cousin is a crime, that it provide him with a trial before a neutral arbiter, that it prove his guilt beyond a reasonable doubt, and so on. That is not all that the Due Process Clause does, however. The Due Process Clause also functions as a guarantee of certain *substantive* freedoms from all governmental interference, no matter how much process the government offers. In the above example, it may be that the government simply may not, as a matter of due process, criminalize marriage with a second cousin, even if it undertakes to prove the defendant's guilt beyond not just a reasonable doubt, but *any* doubt, and even if it offers to pay for Alan Dershowitz's services as defense attorney.

Throughout the twentieth-century, the substantive meaning of the Due Process Clause was—and today it remains—the U.S. Supreme Court's most bitterly contested constitutional battleground. Ground zero is the word "liberty" in the clause's assurance that no person shall be deprived of "life, liberty, or property without due process of law." To what does the word "liberty" refer? It is a shorthand for certain fundamental freedoms, but which ones? This is the question that has brought us many of the constitutional controversies we know best today. Does a woman have a constitutionally protected "liberty" to terminate a pregnancy? Does an old, ill person have a constitutionally protected "liberty" to end his own life with a doctor's assistance? Do two men or two women, or, for that matter, two second cousins, have a constitutionally protected "liberty" to marry? And, most importantly, with little but the word "liberty" to go on, how is an unelected and politically unaccountable federal judge to know which freedoms are fundamental and which are not?

In 1944, the Supreme Court had not yet reached these vexing questions, but was deeply mired in a related, and equally contentious, debate about the meaning of the word "liberty" in the Due Process Clause. On one side of the debate were justices who maintained that, in criminal cases, the Due Process Clause authorized judges to do nothing more, and nothing less, than insure that criminal defendants received the specific criminal process guarantees in the Bill of Rights—the rights to counsel and to a jury trial in the Sixth Amendment, the right not to incriminate themselves and not to be subjected to double jeopardy in the Fifth Amendment, and so on. On the other side of the debate were justices who maintained that the Court's responsibility was to guarantee that criminal prosecutions met vaguely defined standards of "fundamental" fairness—standards that were neither coextensive with, nor exhausted by, the specific guarantees of the Bill of Rights. Today we know that it is the latter position that prevailed, but in 1944 the question was still open.

Also nascent at that time was a test that judges could use under the Due Process Clause to gauge the fundamental fairness of government conduct in a criminal prosecution. That test called upon the judge applying it to determine whether the challenged government conduct was so outrageous as to be "shocking to the conscience." It was not until 1952, eight years after the trials of the Nisei draft resisters, that the Supreme Court firmly established this "shocks the conscience" test as a valid measure of due process in criminal cases. They did so in a case in which law enforcement agents forcibly pumped a suspect's stomach in search of illegal drugs. Pumping a suspect's stomach against his will and then offering the extracted drugs in evidence against him at a criminal trial, held the Court, was "conduct that shocks the conscience . . . , bound to offend even hardened sensibilities."[33] Dissenting justices lampooned this "shocks the conscience" test as no test at all, but merely a self-created license for judges to impose their own preferences and sensibilities in the name of applying the Constitution.

Had a judge in 1944 wished to take the constitutional claims of the Nisei draft resisters seriously, he would have been obliged to step into this newly developing, and highly contentious, area of law. The question was simple to state, but difficult to resolve: Was it "shocking to the conscience" to

The Nisei Draft Resisters and the Constitution

incarcerate American citizens on mass suspicion of disloyalty, strip from them of the benefits of their citizenship, and then demand that they make citizenship's greatest sacrifice? One judge held that it was. Judge Louis E. Goodman of the United States District Court for the Northern District of California, hearing the case of twenty-six draft resisters from the Tule Lake Segregation Center in California, dismissed the charges against them on due process grounds. "It is shocking to the conscience," he wrote, "that an American citizen be confined on the ground of disloyalty, and then, while so under duress and restraint, be compelled to serve in the armed forces, or be prosecuted for not yielding to such compulsion."[34] The trouble with Judge Goodman's opinion, however, is that this is where it ended. Judge Goodman cited no precedent and, indeed, made no argument to support his claim that the prosecution of the Tule Lake resisters shocked his conscience. He just asserted it.

T. Blake Kennedy, the judge who heard the trial of the Heart Mountain draft resisters in federal district court in Wyoming, saw things quite differently. He made quick work of the resisters' claim that they were owed a clarification of their rights as citizens before being drafted, and added his "personal" observation that the Nisei resisters "made a serious mistake in arriving at their conclusions which brought about [their] criminal prosecutions. If they are truly loyal American citizens," Judge Kennedy stated, "they should . . . embrace the opportunity to discharge the duties of citizens by offering themselves in the cause of our National defense."[35] Plainly, Judge Kennedy's conscience was not shocked by the government's treatment of the Nisei. And, as we have seen, neither were the consciences of the three judges of the U.S. Court of Appeals for the Tenth Circuit who affirmed Judge Kennedy's ruling on appeal in the *Fujii* case. For them, the case was so easy that it could be resolved with a cliché.

Somewhere between the *Fujii* court's terse rejection of the Heart Mountain resisters' claims and Judge Goodman's legally unsatisfying order dismissing the charges against the Tule Lake resisters was a careful judicial opinion that no judge in 1944 wrote. It would not have been an easy opinion to draft, because due process doctrine, as it then stood, offered little guidance. For exactly that reason, though, it would have been a pathbreaking opinion. Perhaps Judge Goodman hoped that the government would appeal his order to the U.S. Court of Appeals for the Ninth Circuit, and that that court, with the benefits of deliberation and time that appellate judges enjoy, would produce such an opinion. Perhaps he even hoped that the case would make it all the way to the U.S. Supreme Court, where the justices might put flesh onto the bones of his innovative use of the Due Process Clause. As it happened, the government never appealed Judge Goodman's order, and the High Court declined to hear the case of the Heart Mountain draft resisters. Such an opportunity was thereby lost, as was the chance to develop a constitutional doctrine that would clearly and soundly condemn a government decision to take nearly everything from a group of citizens on account of their race and then force them to risk the one thing they had left—their lives.

CONCLUSION

The constitutional question that the Nisei resisters presented was both open and difficult in 1944, and it remains so today. It had great moral power, but its legal basis was surprisingly undeveloped. It pressed judges to the limits of their power to interpret and enforce the Constitution. It is disappointing that nearly all of the judges hearing the cases of the Nisei resisters refused to explore those limits. And it is disturbing that Judge Goodman, the one judge who was willing to explore those limits, was unable to justify his decision in a satisfying way.

That the legal question was open, difficult, and contentious does not mean the Nisei resisters were wrong to press it. When Rosa Parks refused to give up her seat in the front of a Montgomery bus, insisting she had a right to sit there, that legal question was also open, difficult, and contentious. Constitutional law does not change when people meekly accept their government's conduct without questioning it. Only when brave litigants, lawyers, and judges are willing to press on the limits of the law do those limits shift. That is what the Nisei draft resisters did, and for their efforts they deserved far more than a cliché.

Notes

1. Brief of Appellant, *Shigeru Fujii v. United States*, No. 2973, United States Court of Appeals for the Tenth Circuit, Samuel D. Menin Collection, Archives/Special Collections, Auraria Library, Denver, Colo.

2. *Fujii v United States*, 148 F2d 298, 299 (10th Cir 1945).

3. Ibid.

4. Okamoto presented this position in characteristically incendiary form in a circular that the FPC distributed at Heart Mountain on March 4, 1944: "We would gladly sacrifice our lives to protect and uphold the principles and ideas of our country as set forth in the Constitution, for on its inviolability depends the freedom, liberty, justice, and protection of all people including Japanese-Americans and all other minority groups. But have we been given such freedom, such liberty, such justice, such protection? NO!! Without any hearings, without due process of law as guaranteed by the Constitution and Bill of Rights, without any charges filed against us, without any evidence of wrongdoing on our part, one hundred and ten thousand innocent people

were kicked out of their homes, literally uprooted from where they have lived for the greater part of their life, and herded like dangerous criminals into concentration camps with barb [sic] wire fence and military police guarding it, AND THEN, WITHOUT RECTIFICATION OF THE INJUSTICES COMMITTED AGAINST US NOR WITHOUT [sic] RESTORATION OF OUR RIGHTS AS GUARANTEED BY THE CONSTITUTION, WE ARE ORDERED TO JOIN THE ARMY THRU DISRIMINATORY PROCEDURES INTOA SEGREGATED COMBAT UNIT!" Fair Play Committee, Third Bulletin of the Fair Play Committee, 4 March 1944, attached to stipulation dated 23 October 1944, *United States v. Kiyoshi Okamoto et al.*, United States Court of Appeals for the Tenth Circuit, National Archives Branch Depository, Denver, Colo., RG 276, Transcripts of Records on Appeal, 1929-54, Box 386.

5. Francis Biddle to Herbert Wechsler, 14 October 1944, National Archives, RG 60, Class 146-28, Box 66, File 146-28-282, Section 8.

6. See Frank Emi, "Protest and Resistance: An American Tradition," 51, and Yosh Kuromiya, "The Fourth Option," 77, this volume.

7. See Frank Abe, *Conscience and the Constitution.* (Seattle: Frank Abe and Independent Television Service, 2000).

8. See Eric L. Muller, *Free to Die for their Country: The Story of the Japanese American Draft Resisters of World War II* (Chicago: University of Chicago Press, 2001).

9. See *Selective Training and Service Act of 1940, U.S. Code*, vol. 50 App., secs. 301 et seq. (1944).

10. Ibid, sec. 303.

11. See ibid.

12. Ibid.

13. See *Selective Training and Service Act*, sec. 304(a).

14. See ibid., sec. 304a.

15. See ibid., sec. 310(a)(1).

16. See ibid., sec. 310(a)(2).

17. See 32 CFR sec. 603.359 (1940). A "nondeclarant alien" was an alien who had filed no declaration of intention to become a U.S. citizen.

18. 32 CFR sec. 622.43 (1944).

19. See *Selective Training and Service Act*, sec 311.

20. And it was under the second and third, in combination, that the U.S. Attorney for the District of Wyoming later indicted the leadership of the Fair Play Committee and Denver newspaperman Jimmie Omura, on a theory that they had conspired to counsel young men at Heart Mountain to evade the draft.

21. See 32 CFR sec. 603.336 (1940).

22. See 32 CFR sec. 603.391 (1940) .

23. This change came about in the case of *Bolling v. Sharpe*, 347 US 497 (1954), a companion case to the landmark case of *Brown v. Board of Education*, 347 US 483 (1954). In *Bolling*, the Supreme Court decided that the District of Columbia could not run racially segregated schools without violating the Constitution. Because the Fourteenth Amendment's Equal Protection Clause did not apply to the District of Columbia (which is a federal city ultimately administered under congressional authority), the Court had to interpret the Fifth Amendment's Due Process Clause to include a guarantee of equal protection of the laws.

24. *United States v. Hirabayashi*, 320 US 81, 101 (1943).

25. Ibid., 110 (Murphy concurring).

26. *Korematsu v. United States*, 323 US 214 (1944).

27. Ibid., 233 (Murphy concurring).

28. 323 US 283 (1944).

29. Francis Biddle to Herbert Wechsler, 14 October 1944, National Archives, RG 60, Class 146- 28, Box 66, File 146-28-282, Section 8.

30. In his contribution to this volume, William Hohri maintains that the government's decision to draft the incarcerated Nisei was illegal in light of a regulation of the Selective Service System that delayed until discharge the obligation of any "inmate of an asylum, jail, penitentiary, reformatory, or similar institution" to register for the draft. See 32 CFR ß 602.246 (1942); William Hohri; William Hohri, "Draft Resistance and the Selective Service Act," 121, this volume. Hohri contends Hohri contends that because a WRA-administered relocation center was an institution similar to those listed in the regulation, the law blocked the drafting of those in the WRA camps until the date of their discharge.

    Hohri's argument is creative, and it is surprising that none of the attorneys representing the Nisei resisters from any of the camps made use of it. At least at a general level, the regulation appears to express a preference to suspend operation of the draft as to incarcerated people.

    However, on close examination, the regulation does not sustain Hohri's position. While I agree that a camp such as the Heart Mountain Relocation Center is analogous to an "asylum, jail, penitentiary [or] reformatory," the regulation's specific terms suspend only the registration of inmates until their date of discharge, not the further operation of the Selective Training and Service Act. In other words, the regulation says nothing whatsoever about the liability for induction of inmates who registered under the Act before their incarceration.

As to those registrants, the selective service regulations did require compliance with the draft laws even while incarcerated. See 32 C.F.R. sec. 642.32 (1943) ("[n]o man is relieved from complying with the selective service law during the time he is in custody, confinement, or imprisonment. He shall perform the duties and shall be accorded the rights and privileges of all registrants. . . .").

Far more importantly, this regulation on which Hohri relies does not sustain the resisters' objection to the draft as a *constitutional* objection. Even if the regulation had suspended all draft obligations of "inmates" until the day of their discharge, rather than just their obligation to register for the draft, the Selective Service System would have violated nothing more than *its own regulations* by drafting internees out of concentration camps. When an agency contravenes its own regulations, it violates the law, but it does not violate the Constitution.

31. See, e.g., Gerald L. Neuman, *"We Are the People": Alien Suffrage in German and American Perspective*, 13 Mich J Intl L 258, 305 (1992); William W. Fitzhugh, Jr. & Charles C. Hyde, *The Drafting of Neutral Aliens by the United States*, 36 Am J Intl L 369 (1942); Charles E. Roh, Jr. & Frank K. Upham, *The Status of Aliens Under United States Draft Laws*, 13 Harv Intl L J 501 (1972).

32. *United States v Rumsa*, 212 F.2d 927, 936 (7th Cir 1954).

33. *Rochin v California*, 342 US 165, 172 (1952).

34. *United States v Kuwabara*, 56 F Supp 716, 719 (ND Cal 1944).

35. *United States v Fujii*, 55 F Supp 928, 932 (D Wyo 1944).

PART IV

THE PSYCHOLOGICAL ASPECT OF INTERNMENT AND RESISTANCE

Psychological Effects of Internment

by Amy Iwasaki Mass

THE PREWAR EXPERIENCE

In order to understand the response of Japanese Americans to the U.S. government's policy of mass incarceration during World War II, it is important to know the pre-war experience and mindset of the first group of Japanese immigrants who came the U.S. between 1868 and 1924. This first generation of immigrants, the Issei, were mostly young, single men who came from farming backgrounds and saw themselves as sojourners—temporary residents who were going abroad to make their fortunes, help their families who were experiencing economic hardships at home, and who looked forward to returning to their homelands as wealthy men.[1]

Exclusion, intense resentment, and race discrimination were the predominant responses of American society to Japanese immigrants. Because of strong anti-Chinese racism during the latter decades of the 1800's, Japanese immigrants also suffered the legacy of the "yellow peril"— fear on the part of Caucasian society that Asians would invade their country and take over the domination established by the white man. It was believed that Japanese were too alien to be able to become part of American society. Discrimination by the majority society forced Japanese to develop their own communities, institutions, and services. Because they were restricted to their own social circles, Issei parents were able to effectively transmit traditional Japanese cultural values and behavioral guidelines to their children.

One primary concept in socializing Japanese children was that of *Yamato damashi*, or the Japanese spirit. According to the principle of *Yamato damashi*, Japanese people were required to live up to the heritage of an emperor, who according to the Shinto religion, descended from the gods. The government was a paternalistic institution that ruled in the name of the emperor. Japanese were expected to show unqualified allegiance to their leader, and were taught to be strong, righteous, and responsible in their personal, civic, and national pursuits. The values of obligation and respect for authority, persistence and tenacity in pursuing goals, perseverance and forbearance in the face of hardship or pain, were guiding precepts which shaped Japanese behavior. Another significant source of instruction for proper behavior were the Confucian principles of group cohesion over individual achievement; harmony over the expression of conflict or difference; emotional equanimity and self restraint over assertion and self expression; respect for parents and authority figures; and prescribed roles based on age and gender.

In the socially isolated Japanese community in America, children were raised with a strong sense of family obligation, sensitivity to the attitudes of others, and an awareness that their behavior—whether of honor or shame—would reflect not only on themselves, but on their parents, families, and the Japanese community. Parental disapproval, being laughed at or shamed, and the collectivistic mentality of community opinion were powerful instruments of social control. Even today in Japanese society fitting into the group and being conventional—i.e. not "sticking out"—is considered correct behavior. For example, when we compare the Japanese proverb, "The nail that sticks up gets pounded down," with the American saying, "The wheel that squeaks the loudest is the one that gets the grease," we see a clear contrast in what is seen as desirable behavior in the two cultures.

The Nisei, the children of the immigrants, were taught to do well in school. Education is held in high esteem in Confucian societies. Children were encouraged to be diligent in their studies, to respect authority, and to do their very best. In school, Nisei students pledged allegiance to the American flag, and learned about the American values of democracy and freedom. In the public school system, Nisei were exposed to the customs and mores of American life. They wanted to be fully American, but they had also internalized their parents' values and felt pressure at home to honor their parents' ways. In spite of their efforts to behave as good Americans, they were not fully accepted by the majority society. One of the ways Nisei mobilized themselves to be accepted into American society was through the Japanese American Citizen's League (JACL). The aim of JACL was to educate the larger society about the achievements of Japanese Americans. They emphasized patriotism as the key to acceptance and worked to demonstrate their loyalty and worthiness as real Americans.

WARTIME EXPERIENCE

World War II had a tremendous impact on the character of the Nisei.[2] They were stunned—along with the rest of the country—with the news of the attack on Pearl Harbor. The ensuing weeks and months became a period of intense fear, confusion, and anxiety for the Japanese living in America. With President Franklin Delano Roosevelt's Executive Order to remove all people of Japanese ancestry on the West Coast to assembly centers and then to permanent camps, the Nisei's dreams of being accepted in American society were shattered.

The evacuation of 110,000 people in the Japanese community was rapid, smooth, and efficient, primarily because of the cooperativeness of the

Psychological Effects of Internment

Japanese population.[3] Gaman, which means emotional self-restraint and endurance—the Japanese way to handle hardship—was the main psychological defense used to survive this period. Feelings of fear, rage, and helplessness were repressed, and a cooperative, obedient, quiet American facade was used to cope with an overtly hostile, dangerous, racist America.[4]

A number of factors and sources of influence explain the cooperative response. A major element was the helplessness and lack of power Japanese had experienced for years in America. Both Issei and Nisei were fully aware of the reality and power of American institutions that kept them outside the decision making process of American democracy. Protest and resistance were not viable options at the height of anti-Japanese hysteria. Also, Japanese Americans were told that they were being put away for their own safety to protect them from the hostile prejudice of Americans caught up in war hysteria. They were told this was a patriotic sacrifice necessary for national security. By believing these rationalizations, Japanese Americans felt virtuous that they were helping the war effort and proving their loyalty and allegiance to the American government. There was some comfort in believing the contrived explanations. As people who had been raised to respect and trust authority, Japanese Americans could lull themselves into feeling safe in the care of a benevolent and protective Uncle Sam.[5] The JACL method of proving patriotism as a way to gain acceptance was a natural response for a people who had been taught that good works would be recognized and rewarded by parents, teachers, and other respected leaders in the community.

In reality, the government that they trusted, the country they loved and pledged allegiance to, had betrayed them and had turned against them. Their deep, raw feelings of rage, fear, and helplessness were turned inward and buried. Experiencing and recognizing betrayal by a trusted source leads to a deep depression, a sense of shame, a feeling of being an inferior or bad person. It was too painful for most Japanese Americans to acknowledge that the U.S. government was in fact acting against them. It was easier to believe the racist based rationalizations of the   government in order to defend themselves against the truth. Their psychological coping mechanisms can be compared to those of abused children who love their parents and keep trying to "act right" so their parents will not hurt them.[6] Victims of spousal abuse also think in this way. The idea is to try to find the right formula for proper behavior. The hope is to influence those with power to approve of them and to accept them. The sense of being dishonored was so painful, most victims of the camp experience did not allow themselves to acknowledge their feelings. For the Japanese, self-esteem is highly dependent on how others see them. To admit that they were hated, as if they were the enemy, was so painfully unacceptable to them, that they did not speak of the harsh reality of rejection and the degrading experience of being excluded by the country they tried so hard to be a part of.

A Matter of Conscience

POSTWAR EXPERIENCE

Lessons from the incarceration were profound and far reaching. If those affected were excluded from America because of being Japanese, they felt they needed to be as American as possible (i.e.: non-Japanese). After their release from the camps, they tried to be quiet and hardworking, drawing as little attention to being Japanese as possible. There was an emphasis on surface qualities such as a pleasant, non-offensive manner, neat grooming and appearance, a well-kept house and yard, new cars, and well behaved children who performed successfully in school. By the mid 1960's, the success story of Japanese Americans was being lauded in widely distributed publications such as the *New York Times* and *Newsweek* magazine.[7] Japanese Americans were referred to as a model minority, an example of how well other minorities could succeed if they tried hard enough. The accommodationist approach seemed to be working for Japanese Americans.

The problem with acceptance by accommodation is that it exacts a high price. It comes at the expense of the individual's sense of true self-acceptance and self-worth.[8] It becomes necessary for that individual to hide and deny problems and difficulties that can discredit the acceptable facade. For many years, there was no public or private discussion about the ugly experience of the camps. Unfortunately, there were negative consequences for using repression and denial as a way to cope. Alcoholism, marital conflict, psychosomatic disorders, gangs, and youth drug abuse were problems in the Japanese American community that the general public did not see. *When You're Smiling*, a recent documentary by Sansei film maker Janice Tanaka, chronicles the widespread and destructive impact of drug overdoses in the Japanese American community in Los Angeles during the early 1970's.[9]

The silence of many internees about the camps was disturbed in the days of the civil rights movement when Sansei (third-generation Japanese Americans) began asking their parents about their wartime experiences. As part of the ethnic awareness movement, Sansei sought to find pride in the Japanese roots their parents had painfully tried to put aside. This questioning within the context of the civil rights movement helped Japanese Americans to consider redress—a way to rectify the wrongs committed against them during World War II. In 1981 and 1982 the Commission on Wartime Relocation and Internment of Civilians held hearings to take the testimony of more than 750 persons in several major cities throughout the country. The outpouring of stories was an immensely cathartic experience for Japanese Americans who had suppressed their experiences for thirty years. The mass of evidence collected led the Commission to conclude that the incarceration was the product of "race prejudice, war hysteria and failure of political leadership."[10] It recommended a payment of $20,000 to all living internees, and a government apology. With the combined efforts of grass roots organizations in the Japanese American community, Washington lobbyists, and Japanese American legislators in the House and Senate, the Civil Liberties Act of 1989 was passed and signed into law. Japanese Americans were finally vindicated of the suspicion and distrust that led to their incarceration during World War II.

DIFFERENCES BETWEEN RESISTERS, VOLUNTEERS, AND DRAFTEES

The resisters of conscience from Heart Mountain, Wyoming, were fully aware of the flagrant wrong-doings of the U.S. government fifty-seven years ago in 1944. For them, the government order to be inducted into the U.S. Army was the final affront in a series of insults and attacks on their lawful rights as American citizens. It was bad enough that Japanese Americans were uprooted from their homes and communities to be imprisoned behind barbed wire in remote desserts and wilderness areas, but the Nisei were also being ordered to fight and possibly die for a country, for a government, that had taken away their freedom, had doubted their loyalty and honor, and imprisoned them and their families. The resisters believed that drafting Nisei from concentration camps without restoring their civil rights was morally and legally wrong. They chose to stand up for the American way by refusing to be inducted and by fighting for their principles in court.

The volunteers and draftees represented a totally different viewpoint of what it meant to be an American. They identified with the powerful current of patriotism that was pervasive during World War II, and they believed fighting for America was what a loyal American should do. Participation in the armed forces was a course the JACL zealously advocated. They wanted to prove patriotism by unconditional devotion to the government. Issei parents had taught their children always to respect authority, and the Japanese tradition of a collective mentality—putting forth a united front—did not allow for individual decision making or dissension. Those who disagreed with the JACL response were accused of being disloyal, traitorous, cowardly, and obstructionist, and tremendous pressure was applied to bring dissenters into the fold.

From today's vantage point, after our country has been through powerful changes with the Vietnam War protests and the civil rights movement, it is hard for people who did not live through the Second World War, to picture how unacceptable resistance was. In 1944, when American patriotism was synonymous with serving in the armed services, the decision and actions of the resisters were truly courageous and bold. Speaking one's conscience, as an individual, was heresy for Japanese Americans raised in a community where fitting into the majority mold was the standard for proper and desirable behavior. Given the upbringing and mentality of Japanese Americans, the men who chose to resist orders to be inducted into the U.S. Army were uncommon in their independent thinking and their willingness to stand up for their principles.

One of the most destructive consequences of this chapter in Japanese American history is the bitterness and rancor that still remains in different parts of the Japanese community. The resisters and their families paid a big price for their stand. They have been verbally and physically assaulted by people who were adamantly against their efforts; they were ostracized by many in their community; and their ideas and actions have been ignored and discounted in the telling of Japanese American history for the past fifty years. As recently as last year, some members of the JACL withdrew their membership from the organization in protest to that entity's resolution to apologize to the resisters for the way the organization treated them in 1944.

The U.S. government's treatment of Japanese Americans during World War II made this a painful, confusing, and desperate period for all. People made decisions based on a multitude of reasons. Draft resisters included intelligent, principled men who were educated and aware enough to understand the true meaning of the United States Constitution. Also among them were men who were primarily acting out of anger and despair against an unjust government. They also included young men who followed their parents' direction—parents who were pro-Japan, or who did not want their sons to serve in the Pacific Theater of Operations where they might be killing their own relatives. The volunteers and draftees were comprised of men who loved America and sincerely believed their military service was a way to show loyalty and honor. They also included men who volunteered as a way to get out of camp or who did not want to risk the experience and record of imprisonment in a federal penitentiary.

During the time of incarceration, Japanese Americans did not know how the war would turn out, who the victors would be, and what their future would be when it all ended. Everyone struggled to make difficult personal decisions, and all of them were victims. Unfortunately, too much of their anger and blame have been directed toward fellow Japanese Americans instead of toward the real culprits, the powerful political and military leaders who caused their suffering and pain.

FUTURE PROJECTIONS

Today, in the year 2001, Americans continue to express a negative public reaction toward Japanese Americans whenever Asians pose an economic threat or are accused of wrongdoing, as in the Wen Ho Lee case, and the downing of an American aircraft in China. In America, the number of

Psychological Effects of Internment

hate crimes against Asians has risen since the 1980's. An audit of violence against Asian Americans in 1999 documents an increasing number of incidents ranging from threats, harassment, and vandalism to homicide and bodily harm.[11] In the past twenty years, coalitions of Asian American community and professional groups have actively responded to such events with protest and public education. Members of the Japanese American community have taken the lead and played significant roles in many of these responses. Most recently, the JACL took proactive measures to combat potential negative public reactions against Japanese Americans before the release of the movie, *Pearl Harbor*. They have come a long way from the quiet, accommodating stance of earlier Japanese Americans. The response of Japanese Americans in the twenty-first century will reflect a people who are clearly confident about their rights as American citizens and their responsibility to protest and resist any form of bigotry and injustice. In retrospect one can see that the action of the resisters of conscience in 1944 was truly informed and visionary.

Notes

1.Amy Iwasaki Mass, "Japanese Americans," in *The Asian American Encyclopedia*, ed. Franklin Ng (New York: Marshall Cavendish), 735-45.

2.Amy Iwasaki Mass, "Asians as Individuals: The Japanese Community," *Social Casework* 57, No. 3 (March 1976): 160-64.

3.Harry H. L. Kitano, *Japanese Americans: The Evolution of a Subculture* (Englewood Cliffs, NJ: Prentice Hall, 1969) 33.

4.Amy Iwasaki Mass, "Socio-Psychological Effects of the Concentration Camp Experience on Japanese Americans," *Bridge* 6, No. 4 (Winter 1978-9): 61-63.

5.Ibid., 62.

6.Ibid., 63.

7.Amy Rachiki, *An Asian American Reader* (Los Angeles: Continental Graphics, 1971), 1.

8.Mass, "Socio-Psychological Effects," 63.

9.Janice Tanaka, *When You're Smiling*, 60 minutes, Visual Communications, Los Angeles, 1999.

10.*Personal Justice Denied* (Washington D.C.: Commission on Wartime Relocation and Internment of Civilians, 1982), 18.

11.Ross M. Nakanishi, "Anti-Asian Violence," *The NAPALC Review* (Spring 1995), 2.

The Battle Between the Nisei Veterans and the Resisters of Conscience

by George Tsukuda

PURPOSE OF MY STUDY

In this research project, I will focus on the prolonged and oftentimes acrimonious dispute between two groups: Nisei veterans and the resisters of conscience. Rather than analyzing the pros and cons of each position, or otherwise taking sides in the matter, I will instead examine what role, if any, the matter of temperament, family culture, and or peer group influence or pressure may have played relative to the diverging decisions each group made regarding the matter of the draft while Japanese Americans were incarcerated during World War II. Whereas the Nisei veterans made the decision to enlist in the army or comply with the draft, the resisters of conscience responded to the same question with a conditional yes. Members of the latter group insisted, among other things, that the United States government, who had incarcerated persons of Japanese descent without due process, restore their rights as citizens as a condition of their enlisting.

The variables examined were selected based on current psychological theory. Theory informs us, among other things, that temperament and family culture may play significant roles in shaping and/or defining a person's life over the course of the entire life span. Additionally, peer group influence and/or pressure has been acknowledged as playing a role during the period of adolescence, and perhaps into the young adult years. The men whom I interviewed were between the ages of eighteen and twenty four at the time they made their respective decisions.

RATIONALE OR NEED FOR THE STUDY

Both sides have given their rationale for the decisions they made. To paraphrase their positions, the Nisei veterans I interviewed have stated that "It was war and therefore a simple matter of loyalty," whereas the resisters of conscience have stated relative to the stance they took that "It was a matter of principle." Why should they serve a country that had suspended or severed their rights as citizens, unless those rights were first restored? Although their respective positions have been framed as being diametrically opposed, ie. those who were loyal vs those who were disloyal, or those who accom-

153

A Matter of Conscience

modated vs those who resisted, when one clears chaff from the wheat, and from a phenomenological perspective, they simply viewed matters from two different perspectives. Accordingly, what both groups shared in common, although it is unstated yet implicit, is that they based their decisions on what they deemed to be of utmost importance or relevance to them at that time.

The crucial question then becomes one of how best to evaluate the efficacy of their decisions. One can use a moralistic yardstick by which to judge them, ie. right vs. wrong, good vs. bad, positive vs. negative etc. This has often been the case in the present conflict. Either suggested or implied is the notion that their actions were reflections of the nobility of their character or moral fiber and that of the other represented a lack thereof.

Another choice we have is using a humanistic perspective. Rather than making judgments about their respective decisions, we make an effort to understand the motivational underpinnings of their behavior. In other words, what factors in their personal histories, such as the family they grew up within, may have inclined or predisposed them to act as they did. From this model we may discover that the actions that the disputants took on the matter of the draft were largely predictable and understandable given the type of family culture they grew up within.

As implied, what has been most troublesome in the current debate has been the moralistic overtone accompanying it. Each side has staked out an ideological position. This is not problematic in itself. What has been bothersome has been their tendency to stick to them in such a rigid and steadfast fashion. I should add that from the evidence I have gleaned from reading the Japanese American dailies, that the Nisei veterans have been more prone towards taking such a stance than the resisters of conscience. One might call this arthritic thinking, where an issue is viewed in black and white terms with no shades of gray involved.

To illustrate what I have said, let us look briefly at the abortion debate and the position of some members of the Christian right. Their stance has been "abortion is murder," period, no question mark. In effect they have issued a moral imperative, a commandment from on high, if you will. In so doing they are claiming to have sole and exclusive possession of the truth. In their eyes it then becomes a matter of right vs. wrong, or the good guys vs. the bad guys. Furthermore, there is no room for discussion or debate. One is then left with defending one's position and/or attacking the position of the other.

The conflict in question has been suffused with a similar energetic. The participants have been enwrapped in a conflict model and an attack and defend mode. Relative to the listening audience, the intent then is not to capture our imagination and thus promote a spirit of inquiry, but rather to hold us hostage to an ideological position.

Battle Between the Nisei Veterans and the Resisters

The very real danger, as in the abortion debate, is to simplify a matter that was quite controversial and infinitely complex. Also, overlaying the subject with a moralistic overtone is to render virtually meaningless and irrelevant the human dimension. It has also tended to stifle attempts to more fully comprehend and deeply understand why in individuals under consideration may have acted as they did.

OBJECTIVE OF THE STUDY

In working with people in a professional capacity, I have often discovered that there is an internal validity and integrity to people's actions. This has not only allowed me to comprehend their behavior, but also evoked my empathic response from within, one that has been more conducive to working with the person and fostering the spirit of reconciliation of any differences we may have had. Hopefully, the present inquiry will serve a similar purpose for the disputants involved or members of the reading audience, rather than generating the infighting, divisiveness, and factionalism that seems to invariably result from a moralistic perspective.

CENTRAL HYPOTHESES

The different manner in which the Nisei veterans and the resisters of conscience responded to the matter of the draft, the former by complying and the latter by rebelling, resulted from the diverging manner in which they had been reared. It is being hypothesized that the Nisei veterans in this study had been reared to be more Japanese than American; thus, coming from a conformist based culture, they reacted by complying with the government's dictates. Conversely, the resisters of conscience had been reared or allowed to be more American than Japanese. They therefore reacted to the matter of the draft as one might have expected the average white American to if they had been placed under similar circumstances, that is by rebelling.

A secondary and related hypothesis suggests that the differences in temperament or innate predisposition (which is being defined for the purposes of this study to mean a heightened sensitivity to unfairness and or injustice) can be said to account for the differential nature of the responses that cannot be accounted for by differences in family culture. In this regard, one would expect to see the emergence or display of temperament as a factor in the decision making process—more so amongst the resisters of conscience than the Nisei veterans. In a conformist based culture, such as Japanese culture, the expression of temperament would likely be more diluted or muted than in American culture, which tends to encourage a greater degree of freedom of expression. From my experience in working with child abuse, an extreme sensitivity to matters of unfairness or injustice can also have its origins in a child growing up within an extremely chaotic and abusive family structure. If the foregoing hypotheses are valid, one should then see significant differences between the two Japanese American groups in matters related to the family culture within which they grew up and or in the factor of temperament playing a predominant role involving matters of unfairness and/or injustice.

Additionally, and presuming the concept of identity to be crucial in shaping and defining one's life, then one would also expect to see some significant differences between the two groups relative to how they responded to Japan's attack on Pearl Harbor and/or the mass hysteria that ensued shortly thereafter, and likewise significant differences in the manner in which the two groups reacted to the process of being evacuated and incarcerated. In this regard, it is being suggested that the Nisei veterans were more likely to react to the aforesaid events based on their identity as Japanese more than their identity as American, and conversely the resisters of conscience to react more so on the basis of their identity as Americans than as Japanese. More specifically, one should see more evidence of fear or trauma reported by the Nisei veterans than the resisters of conscience related to the foregoing events, if one assumes that the former group had a greater degree of identification with that which was Japanese than did the resisters of conscience. It was that which was Japanese which was regarded as an anathema before World War II, and that which was Japanese which was viewed as un-American and antithetical to that which was American shortly after Japan's attack on Pearl Harbor.

THE BASIS FOR THE GENERATION OF THE HYPOTHESES

Strongly informing my analysis of the data, and likewise the generation of the hypotheses I developed to explain the differential nature of the decisions that both groups made with respect to the draft, was the construct of identity. It was initially formulated by Erik Erikson, a psychological theorist and psychoanalyst.

Contrary to popular opinion, it was not the question of loyalty or disloyalty per se that was being addressed in the loyalty oath, which included the question of the draft. In the context of the times, the matter of loyalty or disloyalty was deemed to be a byproduct of one's ethnicity or racial identity. Thus, the question that was central to the design and administration of the loyalty questionnaire was the question of identity, ie. "Are you American or are you Japanese?"

In the jingoistic climate of the times, the equation utilized by the military arm of the Roosevelt administration in designing and administering the questionnaire was as follows: White equals American equals loyal. Non-white equals foreign equals disloyal. The U.S. military used the gauge of whether or not Japanese American men fully affirmed the questionnaire as the principal indicator of whether they were or could be American and therefore potentially or actually loyal, or whether they were Japanese and therefore inherently disloyal. Of course this was a fallacious indicator. If one wished to be or were a spy, then he would have answered "yes" without any reservations, in order to avoid suspicion or detection. This paper proposes that what the so called loyalty oath symbolized, represented, and gave expression to, in extreme and concretized form, was the culturally schizophrenic nature of American thinking towards Japanese Americans. In this regard, Japanese Americans received the very powerful message that they could not be both American and Japanese, as the two were antithetical to one another.

It is my contention that the above state of affairs arose from the military arm of the Roosevelt administration playing on and exacerbating the unresolved racist and xenophobic fears of the American public shortly after Japan's attack on Pearl Harbor. By fusing and wedding those of Japanese ancestry on the West Coast with the people and country of Japan, what they had created in the white imagination was the fiction of an enemy within who were replicas of, and counterparts to, the enemy without in Japan. Thus Japanese Americans in particular came to be perceived as Japanese more so than American, and solely on the basis of their ancestral lineage. Thus it was that the question of who they really were, or their identity that came to take on such great significance in the design and administration of the loyalty oath.

Thus, relative to the loyalty oath, what Japanese Americans were forced to choose between was that which was American, and that which was Japanese. On an explicit level, it was on the level of country, however, implicitly and more importantly, it was on the level of identity. In this study it is being hypothesized that the Nisei veterans reacted to the questionnaire, and more specifically the matter of the draft contained therein, as Japanese, by complying, but did so, in a rather contradictory and paradoxical fashion, in order to demonstrate or prove that they were American and therefore loyal. On the other hand, the resisters of conscience reacted like Americans, by rebelling against the authoritarian dictates of the U.S. government, but in doing so were suspected or accused of being Japanese, and therefore disloyal. Further amplifying the drama, and increasing the stakes involved, were the rumors and threats of imprisonment in a maximum security facility for an indefinite period of time and/or deportation en masse, if those of Japanese descent failed to fully affirm the terms and conditions of the questionnaire.

In effect, the overt expectation/demand that the U.S. military had placed on those of Japanese ancestry, on the level of country, was that they give their unquestioned and undivided loyalty to the U.S. government while simultaneously forswearing their allegiance to the country of Japan. Even on this level, the questionnaire was an inherently contradictory one. The Nisei were implicitly being forced to admit to the notion of guilt by association as a means of affirming their ability to be potentially or actually loyal, and likewise to affirm their loyalty to a country that had betrayed them in the most fundamental manner.

However, the aspect of the questionnaire that was most disturbing and potentially divisive for the Nisei, on an internal and psychological, familial and community level, was the unstated yet implicit expectation/demand that the U.S. government had placed on them, which involved the question of identity. Essentially, they were being coerced into choosing between that which was American and that which was Japanese, with the potentially calamitous consequences of their decisions hanging over them like the veritable sword of Damocles. This would force the Nisei into a position of having to affirm one side or aspect of who they were, while simultaneously and in equal measure, having to deny or betray another significant side or aspect of who they were. Accordingly, and in significant respects, they would be damned if they did comply, and damned if they didn't.

What many, if not most, Nisei feared by not fully complying was being left both country-less and identity-less. The other scenario was that if they failed to comply and were allowed to remain in the United States, they faced the probability of being regarded as and treated as virtual lepers for decades to come, and thereby be prohibited from meaningful participation in mainstream American life, much like those who were blackballed in consequence of being associated with the Communist party during the phenomenon of McCarthyism that permeated American politics during the early part of the 1950's.

THE EVOLUTION OF THE "JAPANESE PROBLEM"
AND THE EVOLUTION OF THE
JAPANESE AMERICAN RESPONSE TO IT:

To more fully comprehend why the loyalty questionnaire was designed and administered in the manner that it was, and likewise the predominant Japanese American response to it, it would be useful to provide a psycho-historical perspective on the matter. I shall trace its origins back to the pre-war era of American race politics, through Japan's attack on Pearl Harbor and the U.S. military propaganda campaign against persons of Japanese descent on the West Coast and finally the process of those of Japanese ancestry being evacuated and incarcerated. From a psycho-historical perspective, what is being suggested is that there was an order, coherence, and meaning to the events that transpired and likewise to the Japanese American response to them.

PRE-WAR PERIOD

Essentially the roots of white America's reaction towards persons of Japanese ancestry go back to how persons of color in the United States have generally been regarded and treated. Psycho-historically it has been through the lens of white Americans' unresolved racist and xenophobic fears, which have existed in latent or manifest form, depending largely on the perceived threat that they have been deemed to represent in the white imagination at any point in time.

In its mildest form, persons of color have been regarded as curiosity pieces, and at times as exotic. Under these circumstances, the latent distrust and hostility only become manifest when the numbers of persons of color have reached a critical mass in a particular area, or the person or persons of color are perceived as hostile and/or engage in acts, even non-violent ones, that seem to threaten the status quo, including the maintenance of a WASP national identity and white cultural hegemony.

The underlying distrust and hostility, which are byproducts of their unresolved fears, can quickly become transmuted into an attitude of paranoia towards a particular ethnic group, especially during times of crisis or wartime, in relation to a foreign power or country whose people share the same ethnic background. In this regard, a recent case in point has been many white Americans' view of Arab Americans since the terrorist assault on the World Trade Center buildings in New York. In one poll taken shortly thereafter, over thirty percent of Americans, likely including non-whites also, felt that Arab Americans should be rounded up for national security purposes.

To reiterate, the formulation that has given rise to the paranoia most recently and in the case of Japanese Americans during World War II, was "white equals American equals loyal" and conversely "non-white equals foreign equals disloyal." Implicit in the foregoing is the notion of innocence or guilt by association and based on one's ethnicity. Whereas white Americans are, by and large, adjudged to be innocent until proven guilty, the opposite has been the case for persons of color, with the additional burden, given the attitude of paranoia towards them, that they demonstrate or prove their innocence beyond a reasonable doubt. The matter of racial profiling that has been receiving national attention, especially towards blacks and Hispanics, is a good case in point in regard to the phenomenon of racism even during times of peace. However, during wartime the same dynamic can be magnified at least tenfold, especially under a climate of mass hysteria and the paranoia it evokes, and with concerns about national security seeming to be at stake.

Under the circumstances just described, the matter of one's ethnicity, presumed identity as white or non-white, and one's loyalty or disloyalty tended to be commingled. Persons of color are likely automatically to be branded as foreign, therefore un-American rather than American, relative to their identity, and therefore perceived as being potentially or actually disloyal.

Psycho-historically, and for their part, targets of aggression or oppression, have oftentimes, and in varying degrees, tended to internalize the aggressor's definition of the problem and react by placing the onus for the problem onto themselves. In other words, the target of aggression is blamed for being the source of the problem, and he or she, or the entire group being targeted, internalizes the blame, either consciously and/or unconsciously. In so doing, it perpetuates the status quo. This vicious circle is oftentimes perpetuated by the ability of the aggressor to threaten retaliation or actually retaliate if the target of aggression attempts to hold the aggressor accountable, as it represents an implicit threat to the established order. Bruno Bettelheim, a former Jewish psychiatrist first noted this dynamic among his fellow prisoners of war who were in Nazi concentration camps. What he observed was some of his fellow prisoners of war, over time, increasingly taking on the same attitude towards their fellow prisoners as that of the Nazi guards. This is also not an uncommon phenomenon to observe among women who have been raped or molested and children who have been severely abused.

THE NISEI DURING THE PRE-WAR YEARS

The Nisei had grown up thinking that they were like all other Americans with whom they had gone to school and played as youngsters. However, as they began to come of age, they were confronted with increasing barriers to their fuller participation in mainstream American life. In this regard, they came to the haunting realization that it was on the basis of their ancestral lineage alone that they were being treated differently than their white peers.

Unlike persons of color who grew up in the post civil rights era of American politics, the Nisei, like other persons of color back then, responded to the dilemma confronting them by feeling disappointment, frustration and resignation, rather than the emotions of deep resentment and anger which were more likely to serve as fuel for a sense of outrage directed at the established order.

Also, given the proclivity in some Asian cultures to nurture a collective sense of self vs. a more individualized sense of self, such as traditional

Japanese and Chinese cultures (Smith College Studies in Social Work, 69 (3) the onus of responsibility is placed on the individual rather than the family, or larger social structure.

Consequently, the Nisei were inclined to place the burden of responsibility for the problems they were confronted with onto themselves. Over time, and like other groups who have been the targets of oppression, including women, the disabled etc., they began to internalize the aggressor's perception of them. In the case of the Nisei, they began increasingly to perceive and identify themselves as being Japanese. However, associated with that which was Japanese was also the perception that the latter was both different from, and inferior to, that which was American.

In conjunction with this perceptual shift, they began to idealize that which was white and American and wished that they could be regarded and treated in like fashion. Simultaneously they began to experience some feelings of shame and guilt, and additionally feelings of insecurity, inadequacy and inferiority, relative to their ancestral lineage.

With the exception of those who had resigned themselves to the status quo and their fate as second class citizens, others felt that if they redoubled their efforts and persevered, like their Issei parents had done, that perhaps they, and/or their kind, would be able to overcome the barriers they were being confronted with.

JAPAN'S SURPRISE ATTACK ON PEARL HARBOR
AND THE MILITARY PROPAGANDA CAMPAIGN WHICH FUSED
AND WED THOSE OF JAPANESE ANCESTRY
ON THE WEST COAST WITH JAPAN

Most Americans were shocked by the news they heard over their radios on the morning of December 7, 1941 when it was broadcast that Japan had bombed Pearl Harbor. Shortly thereafter, President Franklin Delano Roosevelt declared war on Japan.

First of all, it was not a surprise attack as has been reported. According to many sources (Charles Beard, Robert Stinnett, Husband Kimmel et al) the Roosevelt administration knew at least three to six hours in advance of the impending attack. The most significant question therefore is why the Pearl Harbor command was not notified in advance. This latter matter has been rife with speculation, ranging from it being a deliberate maneuver on the part of President Roosevelt, to negligence on the part of his staff, and/or technical difficulties they encountered in relaying the information to the Pearl Harbor command. The most recent and authoritative account on this matter was written by Robert Stinnett in his book, *Day of Deceit*.

A Matter of Conscience

Regardless, following this incident and again contrary to popular opinion, there was no mass hysteria or public outcry to do something about the Japanese problem on the West Coast. In a speech he gave at Santa Clara University on February 19, 1998, Professor Peter Irons provided some additional confirmation of this position, which I had arrived at, based on the many interviews I conducted with Japanese Americans who had been incarcerated during World War II. Also, the press reports at that time provide additional confirmation. The incident did evoke in many American's their unresolved racist and xenophobic fears and did result in some sporadic acts of violence being directed at persons of Japanese lineage on the West Coast, but it had yet to reach epidemic proportions.

Thus, Japan's attack on Pearl Harbor may have been a necessary cause but was not sufficient unto itself to have generated the hysterical atmosphere that eventuated in a delegation from the West Coast calling on President Roosevelt to do something about the "Japanese problem."

The timing and order of events indicates that it was the military propaganda campaign instituted by various members of the U.S. military in or around February of 1942 that played a decisive role in manufacturing a crisis. According to Professor Irons, they had the influence and authority to do so. In separate statements released to the press, and/or recommendations made to Secretary of War Henry Stimson, General John DeWitt, who was the head of the Western Defense Command at the time, Col. Karl Bendetsen, who was his chief assistant, and U.S. Attorney General Francis Biddle, among others made inflammatory statements regarding the threat that those of Japanese ancestry who resided on the West Coast represented to America. In essence, what they propagated was what Peter Irons called "The genetic theory of disloyalty." In the case of those of Japanese descent, one could not discern the loyal from the disloyal because it was an inherited racial characteristic. The net effect of this propaganda was to fuse and wed those of Japanese lineage on the West Coast with Japan and its emperor. In consequence, virtually overnight those of Japanese ancestry on the West Coast came to be perceived as the enemy within, who were the counterparts to the enemy without in Japan.

It is my contention that it was the creation of the fiction of an enemy within that generated the mass hysteria and the vociferous outcry to do something about the "Japanese problem" on the West Coast. It was various members of the U.S. military, along with a collusive American press, by playing on and exacerbating the underlying racist and xenophobic fears of the American public, that jerked the public out of its deeply entrenched isolationist mode, and accordingly, generated the mass hysteria that culminated in President Roosevelt signing Executive Order 9066.

The growing hysteria and the basis for it is illustrated and summarized by a column written from San Francisco by the then eminent columnist Walter Lippman. In it he essentially summarized the points made by the members of the military referred to above.

> . . . the Pacific Coast is in imminent danger of a combined attack from within and from without. . . . It is [true] . . . that since the outbreak of the Japanese war there has been no important sabotage on the Pacific Coast. From what we know about the fifth-column in Europe, this is not, as some have liked to think, a sign that there is nothing to be feared. It is a sign that the blow is well organized and that it is held back until it can be struck with maximum effect. . . . I am sure I understand fully and appreciate thoroughly the unwillingness of Washington to adopt a policy of mass evacuation and internment [sic] of all those who are technically enemy aliens. But I submit that Washington is not defining the problem on the Pacific Coast correctly. . . .The Pacific Coast is officially a combat zone . . . some part of it may at any moment be a battlefield. No one's constitutional rights include the right to reside and do business on a battlefield who has no good reason for being there.

A day after this column appeared, a congressional delegation from the West Coast addressed a letter to President Roosevelt recommending the immediate evacuation of all persons of Japanese ancestry from the west coast states of Alaska, Washington, Oregon and California. Immediately thereafter, and at the height of the hysteria, the President signed Executive Order 9066.

Although Professor Irons and others seem easily to dismiss or forgive the role that President Roosevelt may have played in the evacuation and incarceration of those of Japanese descent by suggesting that he was preoccupied with other matters at the time, or was really acquiescing to the public opinion of the day, I have some serious reservations about it.

For one, President Roosevelt was not only the President, but also Commander in Chief of the Armed Services. Likewise, and over three terms in office he was the one who was responsible, directly or indirectly, for placing the aforementioned men in positions of influence and authority. Also, in the U.S. military, strict adherence to the chain of command is required, and if one fails in this, he can quickly be fired or demoted. To the best of my knowledge, these men were not reprimanded by the president, nor did the president do anything to turn the tide of public opinion. This then begs the question of whether Roosevelt was in fact acquiescing to public opinion at that time, or did in fact have a hand in orchestrating it towards his own ends, those being to have the American public strongly behind him in his conduct of the war. In this manner, he could more easily neutralize the opposition within Congress towards America's involvement in the war effort.

In consequence of the mass hysteria generated by the military arm of the Roosevelt administration, via the creation of an enemy within, no longer were the Nisei just perceived as an anathema, but that which was Japanese which they were accused of being, came to be perceived as the enemy of, and antithetical to, that which was American, thus practically synonymous with being un-American. Thus it was that the question of identity came to the forefront of the psyche of the Nisei.

Amidst the supercharged climate of mass hysteria that had been generated by linking those of Japanese ancestry on the West Coast with the people and country of Japan, the Nisei became increasingly confused, doubtful and conflicted about who they were. Were they American as they had once thought, or were they truly Japanese, as they were accused of being?

Within the context of the substantial identity vacuum that had been created by the U.S. government, the Nisei became ever more vulnerable to internalizing the aggressor's definition of the problem (in this case the aggressor is the U.S. government and the American public). They started to think that perhaps they were more Japanese than they previously had thought, and perhaps were not as American as they had believed. Worse yet, perhaps they were not even American at all, but rather full-blooded Japanese. This ever increasing identification with that which was Japanese only served to magnify their pre-existing feelings of shame and guilt, and the associated affects of insecurity, inadequacy and inferiority.

Giving voice to some of the foregoing was a Nisei female who was attending the University of California at Berkeley at the time. She vividly recalled the sense of identity confusion she experienced at that time, stating she no longer knew who she was, and was terribly confused and frightened about whether she was American or Japanese.

THE EVACUATION AND INCARCERATION
OF THOSE OF JAPANESE ANCESTRY

Upon President Roosevelt signing Executive Order 9066, those of Japanese descent in the west coast states of Alaska, Washington, Oregon and Washington were forcibly removed to various inland detention facilities across the United States

In conjunction with their mass removal and detention, they were given dual and inherently contradictory reasons for that removal. On the one hand, they were told that it was based on military necessity given that they were deemed to be enemy aliens. On the other hand, they were unofficially informed that their removal had been for their own protection against the acts of violence that had been directed at them after Japan bombed Pearl Harbor.

Battle Between the Nisei Veterans and the Resisters

For the Nisei, their evacuation and incarceration had exacerbated their childhood fears of ostracism and provided them with further confirmation that they were Japanese, or too Japanese, and thereafter concluded that they had not been American enough. With the threats and rumors afloat of deportation en masse increasing in intensity and frequency, it further revivified their fears of exclusion, not only from participation in life in mainstream America, but from America itself.

For the Nisei, unlike the Kibei (who were also American born but reared and educated in Japan, with many returning to America in their teens and early twenties) and Issei (first generation Japanese in America) Japan was a foreign country. Thus, they faced the possibility of being left without a country or identity.

In consequence, they experienced an increasing compulsion to somehow demonstrate or prove that they were American, all American, and not Japanese, either in whole or in part. Giving voice to these concerns, and likewise some of the bases for them, was a Nisei who was coming of age at that time. He stated:

> "When an American general says you're a Jap (referring to a comment made by General Dewitt that a Jap was a Jap, whether American or foreign born) you are inclined to believe him. I was beginning to wonder if we were Americans you know. We didn't even know if we were citizens. I mean when they talked to you like that . . . I thought at the time we were going to be deported, that had crossed my mind a lot. So, I say to myself, 'I'm going to have to do something to prove that I was [sic] American.'"

It was within the foregoing framework and this contextual shift in the psyche of the Nisei that the Japanese American Citizens League (JACL) made a request of the U.S. government that Japanese Americans be reclassified from 4-F to 1-A, thereby affording them an opportunity to enlist in the military and serve their country in a time of great need.

During the course of events being discussed, Mike Masaoka was the executive secretary of the Nisei lead JACL. He has been variously credited, or damned, for having originated and or proposed the idea to the U.S. military that Americans of Japanese ancestry be allowed to serve their country.

A historical perspective and also the dynamics of group psychology would suggest that what he had done was to evoke a sympathetic chord within the collective psyche of many, if not most, Nisei at the time. In fact, when we research the matter, it becomes quite apparent that the motivational underpinnings for the Nisei's overwhelming support for his proposal had existed within the hearts and minds of the Nisei prior to him giving voice to it. Through his proposal and implicit call to action, he had evoked within the Nisei what had theretofore only existed as a vague but nevertheless pregnant possibility. It was the historical circumstances the Nisei found themselves in and their unique interpretation of the events that had transpired, that had provided the impetus and urgency for such an idea to emerge.

In fact, there was almost an historical inevitability that the solution being proposed would take the precise form that it did. As the Nisei viewed it at that historic moment, it was the perfect solution to the dilemma they found themselves in. As it was, they were increasingly becoming mortified by the possibility that mass deportation would become an eventuality unless they could somehow demonstrate, or prove beyond a reasonable doubt, that they could be or were loyal Americans. If they failed to do so, it was likely that their worst nightmares would unfold.

The Design and Administration of the Loyalty Questionnaire

In regard to the JACL's request for the U.S. government to allow Japanese Americans to be conscripted, the members of the military were of two minds. There were those who were adamantly opposed to it on the grounds that persons of Japanese lineage could not be trusted, period, no question mark. On the other hand, there were those among them who believed in the principles of fair play and felt that American's of Japanese descent should be afforded an opportunity to enlist (Ref. Eric Muller's book *Free to Die for Their Country*).

What emerged from their ambivalent feelings and conflicting opinions about Americans of Japanese ancestry was what might be called a compromise formation. Yes, Japanese Americans would be allowed to enlist provided that they answered questions number 27 and 28, in particular, in the affirmative. The questionnaire came to be known as the loyalty oath. Although it may consciously have been intended to be a simple litmus test of loyalty, for Japanese Americans, it was anything but.

Question number 27 asked Japanese Americans if they were willing to serve in the armed forces of the United States on combat duty wherever ordered. Question number 28 asked them to swear their unqualified allegiance to the United States of America and to faithfully defend the United States from any or all attack by foreign or domestic forces, and forswear any form of allegiance or obedience to the Japanese emperor, or to any other foreign government, power or organization.

Implicit in question number 28 was the presumption of guilt by association in that it asked Japanese Americans to forswear their loyalty to the emperor of Japan. This served to underscore the point that what was central to, and lay at the heart of the questionnaire, was not the matter of loyalty or disloyalty per se, but the question of identity. What Uncle Sam really wanted to know was whether Americans of Japanese descent were, or could be

American, and therefore potentially or actually loyal, or whether they were Japanese and therefore inherently disloyal. The manner in which they attempted to discern the loyal from the disloyal has already been discussed so will not be repeated here.

The distorted nature of white American thinking about Japanese Americans at that time was actually no different from the operational philosophy that the German secret police employed during World War II, under Hitler. It was "if you are not for me then you must be against me." Accordingly, one must be either a friend or foe, a patriot or the enemy, and in the present case, American or Japanese. Furthermore, there was no room for discussion or dissent. In fact those who dissented were automatically suspect.

Lest one think that this type of paranoid thinking was an anomaly and reflected a perversion in American thinking at the time, one need only look at President Bush's reaction to the assault on the World Trade Center wherein he declared that if a country was not for the United States in our search and destroy mission in relation to Osama Bin Laden and the Al Qaeda organization, then it would automatically be presumed that they were against us. Likewise, critics of the administration policy were, early on, perceived as being un-American or even communists by many American's.

Although some resisters of conscience initially answered yes to both questions, those who did, later changed their minds. At the time they were told to report for their physicals the actuality of what they had affirmed hit home. Although the alteration in their response may be open to question, it is my considered opinion that they had initially viewed the questionnaire, including the question of the draft, in a rather philosophical manner and/or as a philosophical exercise. However, when confronted with the implications of what they had agreed to earlier, it was then that their indignity and outrage at the U.S. government's inhumane and unfair treatment of them and members of their family struck home.

THE RESEARCH STUDY

For purposes of my study, I decided to limit it to ten men from each group, given the constraints of time, money and considerations regarding the availability of research subjects. I intentionally chose to interview those amongst the Nisei veterans who had been the most adamantly opposed to the JACL issuing an apology to the resisters of conscience, and likewise those resisters of conscience who had been the most vocal in the press in defending the position they took on the question of the draft during World War II. In choosing such a select and polarized sample, I hoped to be better able to filter out and illuminate the potentially relevant variables that might help to account for the differential nature of the decisions the two groups had made regarding the question of the draft.

For the purposes of this study, I conducted semi-structure interviews varying in length from one to two hours in duration per interview. I asked them questions about their lives over three periods of time, that is, before camp, during camp, and after camp.

Regarding the pre-war period, I asked them to describe the kind of community they had grown up within, answer questions about their parents and relationship with their parents, friendship patterns and behavioral patterns, with the point of the latter being to elucidate the variable of temperament. I also asked them questions about whether or not they had been aware of, or been exposed to, incidents of prejudice or discrimination.

With reference to Japan's attack on Pearl Harbor I asked them how they had received the news and what their reaction to it had been, and likewise that of their parents and other family members and/or friends. I also asked them if they had heard about or personally knew of any Issei who had been interrogated or rounded up by the FBI at that time, and if so, what their reaction to it was. I also inquired about any backlash or support they themselves or any member of their family had been the recipient of. There were also some general questions about the extent to which their lives had been disrupted by Japan's attack on Pearl Harbor and its aftermath.

I then proceeded to ask them questions about the curfew that had been instituted after Pearl Harbor and how it may have affected them or members of their family. I then made inquiries about the process of evacuation and their incarceration, and their reactions to those events. Additionally I asked them questions about what camp life was like for them and what type of reaction they had to being in camp.

Lastly, I asked the interviewees about the draft, the loyalty questionnaire, and why they answered it in the manner that they did. I also questioned the subjects regarding their thoughts and feelings about the decisions of members of the opposing group at that time and later. In regard to the question of the draft, I asked them specifically about what role, if any, their parents or peers may have played in the decision making process.

I concluded by asking them some questions about the post camp period and more specifically, of the Nisei veterans, the basis for their opposition to the JACL having issued an apology to the resisters of conscience. I also asked the resisters how they felt about the JACL having issued an apology and what it meant to them, if anything.

ANALYSIS OF THE FINDINGS

In analyzing the family culture that the Nisei veterans and the resisters of conscience grew up within, the differences between the two groups were quite marked. The Nisei veterans in this study had been reared in the context of the traditional Japanese family structure, wherein the man was the boss and the women was a relatively subservient figure. Although in most instances this was the pattern, in three of the ten cases the roles were reversed. Nevertheless, the principal feature of these households was that the head of the household was an authoritarian figure, and one whose dictates the children in the household were expected fully to comply with, usually with no questions asked.

In citing a typical example, one Nisei veteran whom I interviewed described his father as a stern man and his mother as being subservient to him. In one instance when it was the mother who headed the household, she was described as being very strict.

In contrast, the households that the resisters of conscience reported growing up within were relatively more democratic or egalitarian in nature, thus either encouraging or allowing behaviors that were more independent or assertive in nature or otherwise promoting the spirit of inquiry. In some of these households it was the Issei mother who seemed to model these behaviors for her children by freely expressing her views on various matters to her spouse, and without the spouse retaliating in consequence.

Within the resisters of conscience group, three of the ten men I interviewed grew up in households that were rather atypical, but which seemed to allow, encourage, or otherwise facilitate the emergence of the predominant role that temperament would come to play in their lives. Generally, the matter of temperament arose within the context of households wherein the father was reported to be inconsistent and or extremely abusive towards his wife and or children. These behaviors seemed to sensitize these men as youngsters to matters of unfairness and injustice, and or otherwise compelled them to act more assertively and or independently.

The foregoing findings are generally consistent with the hypothesis that the Nisei veterans in this study were reared to be more Japanese than American, and conversely, that the resisters of conscience were raised or allowed to be more American than Japanese.

Secondarily, the findings seem to support the role that the matter of temperament may have played in regard to some of the resisters of conscience and their decision to rebel against Uncle Sam's dictates. No support was found, however, for the role that peer influence or pressure may have played in these men's decisions, to either enlist in the draft or to resist. The foregoing findings are consistent with the study hypotheses that the Nisei veterans were reared to be more Japanese than American and therefore felt compelled to comply with Uncle Sam's dictates. Conversely, the resisters of conscience, by way of their family culture and or temperament were reared or conditioned to be more American than Japanese. Their decisions in connection with the question of the draft can be viewed as expressions of independence and or rebellion against what they perceived or experienced as an act of unfairness or injustice on the part of the U.S. government.

There is evidence from the data I gathered from the interviews to suggest that the decisions these men made in regards to the draft were consistent with how they had previously reacted to Japan's attack on Pearl Harbor and or the military propaganda campaign that followed, and likewise their reaction to being evacuated and incarcerated. In other words, the Nisei veterans reacted to the aforesaid events more as Japanese than American, and conversely, the resisters reacted to the same events more as Americans than Japanese.

When the Nisei veterans were asked by this researcher what their reaction was to Japan's attack on Pearl Harbor they reported being shocked, and in varying degrees devastated. Likewise, they were more inclined than the resisters of conscience to fear some form of repercussion and or retaliation as a result. As one Nisei veteran remarked, " That's terrible, we had our apprehension. I was devastated, I had no country now."

In contrast to the above, when I asked the same question of the resisters of conscience, they reported being surprised like other Americans but did not believe that the attack would have any repercussions upon them as they were American citizens. However, some of them recalled being concerned about their Issei parents due to the latter's status as resident aliens.

In brief, the Nisei veterans were much more inclined to personalize Japan's attack on Pearl Harbor, whereas the resisters of conscience, with one exception, did not. In the latter case, this man had lost his father before World War II began, and perhaps because of it, did not have the availability or support of both of his parents during this time of crisis.

A plausible explanation for the Nisei veterans reacting as they did was that they were more inclined than were the resisters of conscience to view themselves as being Japanese, and thus concerned about being identified with the enemy. This may have resulted from the manner of their upbringing and or because of their upbringing generally more inclined to internalize white American's perception of them as being Japanese, and therefore somehow culpable.

Relative to the two groups, reactions to being evacuated and incarcerated, there were some similarities as well as some significant differences reported. In terms of similarities, both groups responded with the attitude of *shikataganai* or "it could not be helped," which was quite typical for those of Japanese descent at the time, be they American citizens or not.

However, in conjunction with the attitude of *shikataganai*, the Nisei veterans were also much more likely than the resisters to support the rationale given them by the U.S. government for their evacuation and incarceration. In contrast, the resisters of conscience whom I interviewed stated that although they could not do anything about being evacuated and incarcerated, they were resentful and angry about it. As one resister stated, "I felt restricted and felt that we were getting a raw deal."

DISCUSSION OF FINDINGS

Although the central hypotheses were strongly supported by the evidence gathered from the interviews, the small sample size I utilized for this research project suggests the possibility that it may not have been a representative sample. In other words, interviews with an additional group of men of the same persuasion may not have yielded the same results. Along similar lines, and whenever possible, I also chose to interview the most outspoken members of each group and or the ones of them who were the most willing or able to be interviewed, which may have skewed the results.

On the other hand, the central hypotheses are also supported by the data I gathered regarding the differential nature of the two groups' reactions to Japan's attack on Pearl Harbor, and similarly their reaction to being evacuated and incarcerated. In overall terms, and within the sample size selected, there was a strong consistency and uniformity in their responses to the aforesaid events and their reaction to the question of the draft. This seems to underscore the general validity of the findings and also the explanatory power of the concept of identity in explaining the differential nature of their attitudes and behaviors, even, or especially, under conditions of great stress or trauma.

Caution should be exercised in rendering these findings to be conclusive. For one, it was a retrospective analysis, thus the process of selectively remembering and or forgetting may likely have played a role in what these men recalled and reported to me. Additionally, these findings do not establish cause between one variable, but rather strongly suggest an association between them. In other words, there may be other plausible explanations for the association between the variables being examined in this research project.

Also, the findings cannot be extended to include the Nisei veterans who were ambivalent or neutral about, or in support of, the Japanese American Citizens League's decision to apologize to the resisters of conscience for the name calling the organization engaged in, relative to them, during World War II. It raises the question of what factor or factors may have accounted for the differences in attitude amongst the Nisei veterans on this matter. In reviewing the data I gathered for this research project, one possible explanation suggests itself in five of the ten cases of the Nisei veterans I interviewed. In these cases, their fathers actively encouraged them to fight in

A Matter of Conscience

behalf of the United States, thus indirectly supporting the U.S. government's position on the matter and possibly reinforcing the idea that it was a matter of duty and honor. Thus, to not comply or obey would then be viewed as an act of betrayal, not only of the U.S. government but also their fathers whom they had been reared to obey. It would then stand to reason why these men would have viewed the resisters of conscience decision as cowardly and/or involved in an act of betrayal. However, it does not offer an explanation in the other five cases where such a linkage could not be found.

For purposes of further elucidating the differences between the Nisei veterans who have been and remain staunchly opposed to the JACL having given an apology to the resisters of conscience, and those Nisei veterans who were ambivalent about or supportive of the JACL's decision, it would be useful for a researcher to interview some of the men in these latter categories. From my viewpoint, a prime reason for doing same would be to discern if there were any significant differences in family culture or other factors that might help to account for the differences in attitude between these various groups.

One final matter that I would like to touch upon relative to the findings and implications for further research is the matter of the role of the U.S. government in this entire affair. Although it was not the principal focus of this research project, the U.S. government did in fact play a significant role in shaping and defining both the nature of the problem that the Nisei were forced to address, and the nature of the response given. Thus, it was not a disinterested or unbiased party.

In forcing the Nisei to choose between that which was American and that which was Japanese it was implicitly, and on a more unconscious than conscious level, engaging in the tactic of divide and conquer, albeit psychospiritually rather than militarily. It did so by playing on and exacerbating differences in temperament and or family culture between the two groups. In this regard I would like to suggest that the underlying intent of the questionnaire, although it was not a conscious one, was to somehow quell or otherwise neutralize and or destroy the "Japanese problem," not only from without and militarily relative to Japan, but simultaneously from within, and internally and psychologically, relative to the perceived threat that those of Japanese ancestry posed in the white imagination.

I believe that the foregoing conclusion may have been what Emiko Omori, the award winning documentarian of *Rabbit in the Moon,* may have had in mind when she made the incisive comment that the loyalty questionnaire "sliced through the camps like a knife." Not only did it result in much infighting, divisiveness and factionalism within the Nisei as a group, it also resulted in an intense amount of conflict between many Nisei sons and their Issei fathers as well as conflicts between the Nisei and Kibei, many of whose

172

primary or increasing identification came to be with Japan, especially given their perspective of the U.S. government at that time. In this regard, the ongoing conflict between the Nisei veterans and the resisters of conscience can be viewed as being a symptom of the conflict that pervaded the entire Japanese/Japanese-American community at that time.

The dynamics that the U.S. government generated during World War II would also have an impact on many younger generations of Japanese Americans ie. the Sansei, Yonsei, Gosei etc. as reflected in these searing and deeply insightful comments made by a Sansei who was approximately twenty years of age at the time she made them. I quote,

> My mother told me when I was seven that she never wanted me to learn Japanese. She wanted me to be Americanized, all American. I cried and begged her at the time because my two friends in school were going to Japanese school on Saturdays and they had fun. I kept asking my mother, "Why won't you let me take Japanese?" She shook me in exasperation one day and said just one sentence, "so you won't be thrown into a concentration like I was." I realized in a child's way then and in an adult way now that her spirit had been crushed, as had the spirit of numerous Japanese Americans. They had succeeded in killing themselves to prove their loyalty to white America in order to save their children and to survive. From that moment thirteen years ago till now and through the rest of my life, I feel that a piece of me died with my people.

Bibliography

Erikson, Erik. (1980) *Identity and the Life Cycle.* New York, W.W. Norton.

Irons, Peter. February 19, 1998. Lecture I attended at Santa Clara University. A synopsis of his lecture appeared in the *Hokubei Mainichi* within a week, newspaper numbered 14464.

Kimmel, Husband E. (1955) *Admiral Kimmel's Story.* Henry Regnery Co., Chicago. Ppgs. 13-14.

Kitagawa, D. (1967) *Issei and Nisei: The Internment Years.* New York, The Seabury Press, pg. 221. Quotes were from an early study done by Edward K. Strong in 1929.

Lippman, Walter. (1942) *Salt Lake Tribune,* February 20, 1942. (The date mentioned may be wrong as this article is reported to have appeared before February 19, 1942, the day on which President Roosevelt signed Executive Order 9066).

Morgenstern, George. (1947) *Pearl Harbor: The Story of the Secret War.* The Devin-Adair

A Matter of Conscience

Co., N.Y. ppgs. 13-14.

Muller, Eric. (2001) *Free to Die for Their Country*. The University of Chicago Press, ppgs. 43- 51.

New York Times (November 29, 1999) Big brother is still haunting society in Germany's East. The actual quote was "If you do not work with us you are against us."
Omori, Emiko. (July 2, 1999) *Hokubei Mainichi*. Quote from a news article about her documentary, *Rabbit in the Moon*.

Sarnoff, I. (1952) "Identification with the Agressor: Some Personality Correlates of Anti- Semitism Among Jews." *Journal of Personality*, 20, 199-200.

Seko, Sachiko Wada. (1997) *Missing Stories: An Oral History of Ethnic and Minority Groups in Utah*. Eds. Kelen, Leslie G. & Stone, Eileen Hallet. University of Utah Press, Salt Lake City, ppgs. 356-357.

Shen Wu, J.Y. (1984) "Breaking Silence and Finding Voice: The Emergence of Meaning in Asian American Inner Dialogue and a Critique of Some Current Psychological Literature. (Doctoral dissertation, Harvard University, Cambridge, Ma., Dissertation Abstracts International, 45-06A, 1699.

Stinnett, Robert. (2000) *Day of Deceit: The Truth About FDR and Pearl Harbor*. Discussion of issue on ppgs 115-118, 203-208 & 223-233.

Tsukuda, George T. (1998) From field note interviews gathered in conjunction with unpublished doctoral dissertation titled, "The Long Term Effects of Internment on Pre-adolescent Japanese American Males."

Tsukuda, George T. (1999, June) Smith College Studies in Social Work Commentary on the paper by Ino and Glicken, "Treating Asian American clients in crisis: A collectivist approach." Ppgs 543-544.

Yoo, David K. (2000) *Growing Up Nisei: Generation, and Culture Among Japanese Americans of California, 1924-49*. Good general reference for what it was like for the Nisei who were coming of age before World War II. University of Illinois Press, Urbana.

AFTERWORD

Teaching the Camps

by Lawson Fusao Inada

INTRODUCTION

In keeping with the theme of this anthology, it felt in order for me to share what might be termed "instances of protest and resistance in the private sector," such as current remembrances by my mother:

1. "The fairgrounds were *not even ready* for us—that's why you had to stuff our mattresses with *straw*." (She was recovering from recent abdominal surgery, while my father, a dentist, was occupied with setting up medical facilities.)

2. "Everything was a dangerous mess, nails laying all over. When you stuck that nail into the outlet, you got shocked unconscious. That *wouldn't have happened at home*."

3. "When the train stopped in the middle of nowhere the soldiers told us to get out, stretch our legs, but don't try to run away. *Where could we go?* I wouldn't move. As cooped up as you were, I knew you would dash about outside and could get *shot*."

4. "When the train stopped someplace in Arkansas, a Black woman my age, holding a boy your age, came up to the closed window and whispered: 'What you-all doing on that train?' She had a scared look in her eyes. I just smiled. *What could I say?*"

As for myself, in Arkansas my *constitution* weakened, my *resistance* was shot, and my body *protested*—with dangerous fevers, and convulsions. But I was not the only *regular* in the infirmary; there were many kids—most survived, some became disabled.

SOCIAL STUDIES

My first two years of schooling were in camp—Arkansas and Colorado—and my teachers were thereby provided with a golden opportunity to instruct me and my classmates about an interesting, meaningful subject: American concentration camps. There we all were, including the teachers, actually engaged in a history-making situation, under "textbook" conditions, like a perfect "social-studies unit" waiting to be activated; moreover, in our midst were numerous qualified resource-persons (many with advanced degrees) ready to be called up to impart knowledge regarding aspects of removal and incarceration.

And how mutually instructive it would have been to have had classroom visits from the administrative and military sectors. They could have taken us on tours of our respective facilities—security, management, sewage treatment, and so on—and what a learning experience that could have been, about the actual workings of our society and community. There could have been hand shakes all around, maybe even snacks, and certainly hands-on activities with telephones and printing machines, demonstrations on rifle cleaning, and the use of fire hoses, and perhaps we might have even been given access to our individual files—as part of the day's reading lesson. (Consider the educational impact: "Boy, when I grow up, I want to work in the office." "Not me—I'm going to be a soldier in the guard tower.")

Then, from camp, our studies could have branched out to a related area— "uncamp" life. Field trips may not have been workable, but visitations from uncamp could have been feasible. And what a motivating factor that would have been, for both parties, as they readied for the exciting occasion. (In Arkansas, separate black and white school visitations would have been scheduled; also, somewhere in the mix would have been Latino and Chinese American kids from the region, and perhaps some American Indian children.)[1]

What fun! Presentations, displays, sing-alongs, games—even special food in the mess hall. These could have evolved into regular events, with parents in attendance, chatting, mingling. . . .

Alas, nothing of the kind happened. The educational opportunity was lost, as teachers *confined themselves* to the conventional curriculum, the generic "three R's," and the "fourth R"— "Relocation"—right under their very noses, got lost in the shuffle. . . . What a shame.[2]

FISHING

Now, one may very well ask: "What is the value of teaching the camps in this day and age?" Well, as any teacher knows, if students are presented with interesting material, they naturally get interested—and the camps are certainly as "interesting" as anything that happened on American soil in the twentieth-century.

So there surely must be something of value in there to teach—something that can make a difference, something that can be put to good use, something with staying power for the twenty-first century. And with an abundance of material available for all grade levels, with new materials appearing all the time to provide access in all forms of media, one may very well ask: "Why *aren't* you teaching the camps?"

For the positive, productive, constructive sense, teaching the camps is like opening a "can of worms"—ah, but then students can be taught to fish. . . .[3]

FULL COVERAGE

Now, as an English teacher, I have never "taught the camps" *per se*; rather, my job dictates that I teach literature and writing courses; my training in the 1950s and 60s never included anything having to do with the camps. But on the other hand, how could I *not* offer my students a once-in-a-lifetime opportunity? How could I deprive *them* of an experience that could literally change their lives, that could expand their vision of, not only the "war years," but life, humanity, the world?

So it was, then, that I began to share profound *literature* regarding the camp experiences— and literature, as with any of the arts, has a way of providing "full coverage" of life, for a single poem or story can serve as a "touchstone" and "lens" to greater understanding. And, regarded in the right light, each poem or story can also function as a "mirror"—to reflect upon current life.

INTERN NET

Even as a camps person, I tend not to invoke my "power of internee"; rather, I encourage students to undertake their own journey of exploration and discovery, for I certainly do not have "all the answers," and they come up with concepts, questions, and interpretations, that are new and news to me. And today's students can "surf" and "fish" the Internet in ways that are beyond me.

But what I do is lead them to the "shore"—of camp, that is—providing access to, and context for, the literary material we are about to partake of and venture into—and what an adventure it is.

All I do, on single sheet of paper, is provide, literally, some instructions and a map. . . .

SEVEN WORDS

On one side there's a copy of the actual "hand-out," the "instructions to all persons" document; on the other side there is a copy of the "Michi

A Matter of Conscience

Weglyn map" from *Years of Infamy*.[4]

That document is an undeniable classic, one of the truly enduring works of American history. It is "dated" but not "outdated," for it can still send chills through any reader. And as a work of writing alone, it is perfect—it has rhythm, clarity, perfect structure (building plot-like to the conclusion: "Go to the Civil Control Station. . . ."), and perfect diction. I would not change a word.

As such, it is worthy of word-by-word discussion. (Because of its dated nature and delineation of specific locales, students will gloss over the first half and "cut to the chase," and that part about "*pets*" always hits home, hard: "Then I won't go!") But the meat, the essence, is really in the first seven words—the "instructions" phrase that can be spoken in less than *five* seconds.

Why is the government giving "instructions"? What is this "how-to" for? How might it feel to receive this? And does "all" really mean *all*? The blind? The infirm? The mentally and physically disabled? The newly born? American military personnel? Students in college away from home? And what determines "Japanese"? Have borders of nations ever changed? How about if. . . ? Can there be mix-ups and complications? And is "ancestry" the same as "race" or "nationality"? How far back in "ancestry" are we talking about? Before there was a "Japan"? When my "ancestry" was domesticating sheep in "Caucasia"?

Still, what do those seven words add up to? Do the math. Go figure.

DECIPHER

Then there is the map. What's *wrong* with this picture? But use it as a treasure-map, and see what you can find, decipher. Or it looks like a little board-game doesn't it? Yes, "Topaz" sounds good; "Santa Fe," okay. And "Crystal City" must be a winner. "Heart Mountain"—"Big Sky" country! But a "Leupp," a "Gila," a "Poston"—on another map, it says "reservation." And who is this "cartographer"—this Michi Weglyn? What kind of name is that?[5]

THANKS TO CAMP

Moving right along, we are ready to venture into exotic-sounding Tule Lake, to partake of the not-so-exotic poetry written by inmates there; this poetry, by its place of origin and "ancestry" on American soil, is very much *American* poetry, and since it was composed by male and female elders in Japanese in this "segregation center," it is also *resistance* poetry of world-class caliber, suitable for study as *poetry*, period, anywhere in the world.[6]

Thus, I have shared this poetry, to large effect, with both literature *and* writing classes (along with public agencies and civic groups), for poetry is poetry, and the world cannot get enough of it. And since this is a micro-cosmic-poetry, my handout consists of poetry on one side, with the other side left blank, for readers to write poetry of their own—"American haiku," not necessarily adhering to traditional Japanese "rules" (which are rather loose, anyway, as I have learned), but which simply *approximate* the poems on the other side—in essence, "live" and "instant-ramen"-type poems, a guaranteed delight. Thanks to camp.

As the poetry teaches itself, so does John Okada's novel, *No-No Boy*,[7] a great American work in the American tradition of *protest* and *resistance*. It is self-contained, self-starting, and self-sustaining, and in a matter of pages, like magic, students begin referring to Ichiro, Emi, Kenji, and other "fictional characters," as *people* they actually know.

Teaching the camps reaches the heart. Do not just take my word for it though. The one word my students use: "*Unforgettable.*"

Notes

1.Our camp site was ideally located for the activation of what is now termed "multi cultural studies," for the delta region was a multi cultural crossroads. In addition to the considerable African American populace, Mexican laborers had been recruited for plantation work (and they introduced the *guitar* to the region), there were long-standing Jewish and Chinese American enclaves, and although the American Indians had been "relocated" to Oklahoma on the "Trail of Tears," surely some had managed to hide away in, or had managed to return to, their home vicinity.

Or, our camp population alone was representative of what is now referred to as "diversity." As stated in a 1942 *Harper's* magazine, there were "Koreans, Chinese, Mexicans, and Negroes swept into the camps by virtue of their being married to Japanese." (And it can be said that the Japanese themselves are a "diverse" lot, for the nation includes Okinawans and the Ainu people.) Thus, my playmates included a "Caucasian" girl, and American Indian boy (who told me one frozen-puddle morning: "Last night I looked up at the sky and saw the face of God"), and, in the sizable Japanese-Hawaiian sector, there was *everybody.*

2.Another educational opportunity was lost—by our surrounding communities. Which is to say, each camp could have readily become a "campus," serving the needs of regional, rural residents, Each camp was packed with agricultural, cultural, entrepreneurial, professional, spiritual, and technical expertise; each camp shone with achievement awards, certificates, credentials, degrees, diplomas, and licenses; therefore, each camp[us] could have offered at the very least, weekend courses and workshops on just about anything (from art to zoology), and any number of vocational training sessions. ("Free tuition. Plenty of parking available. Security guaranteed.") Everyone would have benefitted. If only. . . .

3.A very effective way of establishing "relatability" with the camps and time-period is to have students inquire about where they were—genetically—in 1942; this can

A Matter of Conscience

inspire them to go "fish" into family history (for the first time, perhaps), which may result in a "catch"—some direct connection to, or recollection of (including rumors), the widespread camps.

It is also very "catchy"—among all the issues—to have students look into the lives of their "peers" in camp—kids, teens, young adults—for, after all, young people are young people, with similar concerns anywhere. So how did the young cope in camp? How was school? Vacations? Churches? How about clothes, music, dances? Food? Sports? Were there graduation ceremonies, yearbooks? How about college? (Materials are available on all these aspects; moreover, current student findings would be valuable additions to the knowledge of this neglected area.)

Since practically *all* of the resisters were young adults, teens, at the time (while Martin Luther King Jr., born in 1929, was attending a segregated school in Georgia), it would be relevant to ask today's students: How would *you* react? What would *you* do? (Then, too, they could contact some resisters.)

One of the real "catches" of *Only What We Could Carry* (Berkeley: Heyday Books, 2000) was the fortuitous finding and publishing of the diary of Stanley Hayami—high school senior, eighteen, Heart Mountain. He reveals himself to be pretty much a teen being a teen, worrying about his grades, into sports, contemplating his future, Through his remarkable artwork and insightful writing, he comes alive as a gifted, well-rounded person—an all-American kid, actually who passed his physical . . . . (And was killed in combat in Italy.)

4.Michi Nishiura Weglyn, *Years of Infamy* (Seattle: University of Washington Press, 1996), 6. The "instructions" document—"Civilian Exclusion Order"—is available in just about any book dealing with the camps. Michi was a teen in camp; her path went on to included Broadway—and the Holocaust. As a follow-up to reading the document, I usually ask students to list the "ten things you would take to camp," and the "ten things you are sure to miss." At the very least this allows them to "prioritize" aspects of their life, engage their thinking/creative skills, and certainly results in their appreciation of freedom. (Which includes the rights to privacy and pizza! And, of course, decent schooling. . . .)

5.This "Michi map" ("michi"—"road," "way"), regarded the right way, has more to it than meets the eye, for a probe at each camp site reveals previous 'encampments"—layers of history, life—and the map then begins to resonate, resound, with a *soundtrack* that can be heard to this day.

6.The Tule Lake poetry included in *Only What We Could Carry* was taken from a major compilation of camp poetry: Violet Kazue de Cristoforo, trans. And ed., *May Sky: There Is Always Tomorrow* (Los Angeles: Sun & Moon Press, 1997). Students will find this book, and Violet, to be intriguing; to this day, she is a "resistant" person in keeping with her stay in Tule Lake.

Teaching haiku and the writing of haiku (or "American haiku") is similar to gifting students with a Polaroid camera, with which they can capture all the "Haiku moments" that come our way; for example, here is one that "tapped my shoulder" recently:

Teaching the Camps

As I drop the dime
Into the slot, FDR
Drops me into camp.

Then there is this conference sighting:

Those who shade their eyes
With there hands are actually
Saluting the sun.

(The haiku tradition is actually at the very foundation of modern *American* poetry; Pound, Eliot, Williams, Stevens, etc., were profoundly influenced by it, as was novelist Richard Wright.)

One of the truly great camp poems, though, was written by a kid in Amache Camp, directly into my autograph book. It is an enduring and endearing work, for it has to do with freedom, resistance, and the human spirit:

Dear Lawson,
    I meet you early,
    I meet you late,
    I meet you at
    Amache Gate.
        Always,
        Naomi

7.John Okada, *No-No Boy* (Seattle: University of Washington Press, 1976).

INDEX